Confessions
of an
X-Codependent

Confessions
of an
X-Codependent

Jami Salters

Confessions of an X-Codependent

Copyright © 2020, by Jami Salters. All rights reserved.

No part of this publication may be reproduced, stored in a retrieval system or transmitted in any way by any means, electronic, mechanical, photocopy, recording or otherwise without the prior permission of the author except as provided by USA copyright law.

Scripture quotation marked "NAS" are taken from the New American Standard Bible, Copyright 1960, 1962, 1968, 1971, 1972, 1973, 1975, 1977, 1995 by The Lockman Foundation. Used by permission. All rights reserved.

Cover design and interior artwork by Terrance McDow, *https://www.terrancemcdow.com/*
Editing by Pamela Scholtes, Helen Melcher, Melissa Collins, and Alexys Wolf
Interior layout by Aalishaa with Fiverr

Published by *The Fiery Sword Publications*
Published in the United States of America

ISBN: 978-1-952668-04-3
ISBN: 978-1-952668-05-0
ISBN: 978-1-952668-06-7

REL012070: Religion / Christian Living / Personal Growth
REL012120: Religion / Christian Living / Spiritual Growth
REL050000: Religion / Christian Ministry / Counseling & Recovery

Dedication

To my amazing children and grandchildren, present and future.

I pray each of you find your identity in Christ alone.

May you be as overcome with the love and grace of God as I am.

"A good person leaves an inheritance for their children's children." Proverbs 13:22

Table of Contents

Acknowledgments xi

Endorsements xiii

Foreword xvii

Introduction xix

Chapter One: Time Heals All Wounds? 1

Chapter Two: Sticks and Stones 7

Chapter Three: Sick and Tired of Being Sick and Tired 15

Chapter Four: Delivered but Still Very Broken 21

Chapter Five: Saved from Myself 29

Chapter Six: The Residue 37

Chapter Seven: Making Peace with My Past 43

Chapter Eight: O Lord, I'm Codependent! 51

Table of Contents

Chapter Nine: Addicted to Love 63

Chapter Ten: Hoarders Buried Alive 71

Chapter Eleven: New Negative Labels 79

Chapter Twelve: The Power of Friendships................................87

Chapter Thirteen: Men and Children 97

Chapter Fourteen: The Root of the Problem 107

Chapter Fifteen: Abused but Not Abandoned.........................117

Chapter Sixteen: Changing Our Reaction................................123

Chapter Seventeen: Bag Lady 131

Chapter Eighteen: The Parenting Bag......................................139

Chapter Nineteen: Baggage Check..145

Chapter Twenty: First Things First 153

Chapter Twenty-One: Unpacking and Forgiving....................161

Chapter Twenty-Two: Same Experiences,
                      Very Different Outcomes 167

Chapter Twenty-Three: I Would Change Everything............175

Chapter Twenty-Four: I Am Forgiven......................................185

Chapter Twenty-Five: The Heart of the Matter Is
                      a Matter of the Heart........................195

Chapter Twenty-Six: Anyway, Back To the Drama 205

Chapter Twenty-Seven: Which Ground Are You? 215

Chapter Twenty-Eight: The Fruit of God's Seed 223

Chapter Twenty-Nine: Who Told You That? 233

Chapter Thirty: Label's Lie vs. God's Truth 243

Chapter Thirty-One: A Sinful Woman 255

Chapter Thirty-Two: We Are All Sinners 267

Chapter Thirty-Three: Only God Can Judge Me? 275

Chapter Thirty-Four: Dealing with Adultery 285

Chapter Thirty-Five: Fit for the Master's Use 291

Chapter Thirty-Six: Reflection of God 301

Chapter Thirty-Seven: Diamond in the Rough 315

Chapter Thirty-Eight: Sinclair 323

Chapter Thirty-Nine: The Codeword 333

Chapter Forty: The First and Greatest 345

Chapter Forty-One: A Shift in Our Thinking 355

Chapter Forty-Two: Anchored in Truth 367

Chapter Forty-Three: Marriage on a Mission 379

Chapter Forty-Four: Life Lessons..387

Chapter Forty-Five: Sinclair's Closing Words........................399

    Afterword 425

    Author Bio..431

    Bibliography...433

Acknowledgments

I want to thank my amazing husband, Sinclair, for believing in me, encouraging me, and for having patience with me. Most of all, I thank him for loving me the way Christ loves the church. His leadership is supernatural and I happily submit to following him as he follows Christ.

Special thanks to Author, Minister, and Publisher Alexys V. Wolf of *The Fiery Sword Global Ministries* and *The Fiery Sword Publications*. She has been a godsend. This book is what it is because of who she is. Unselfishly, she gave of her time, energy, money, and many resources. I am honored to call her "friend" and I am eternally grateful for her and her ministry.

A special "Thank you" to all those who prayed for me, encouraged me, and financially supported me through this arduous journey. It was long but, because of all of you, it came to fruition!

Endorsements

I was immediately captivated by the author's willingness to be so transparent. It is apparent that Jami's reveal of self lets the reader know she has let go of a lot of her "junky stuff." I also appreciate how Jami takes her readers through her journey of self discovery and spiritual awakening. The beauty of her forgiveness is inspiring! The research is compelling and sound and Jami is good about stating her interpretations but encouraging the reader to "go see for themselves." This book is an autobiography, a testimony, and a workbook all in one. I enjoyed reading the "gem" Jami turned out to be. I will use it in my continued work with youths. ~ K.M. Stevens, Google Review

I feel that anyone, man or woman, can benefit from reading this very well written book. Jami is painfully honest about her journey through very difficult situations. There is obvious anointing in the pages of her autobiography. So much to learn from her experiences and hope to be gained from her current walk with Christ. I loved this book from cover to cover! ~ Tracy Pedigo, Google Review

This was an awesome inspiration! I am now sharing the copies I purchased with others. Thank you, Jami, for opening your life to us. ~ Google Review

I could not put down this book! Jami's story is amazing! And even more amazing is what God can do in our life when we let Him. This truly shows that God can turn any situation into a testimony if we surrender to Him. Thank you for sharing your story. ~ Mandi, Google Review

I could not put this book down. It is a great read for anyone who has been through trauma and dysfunctional relationships pointing the way to Jesus. ~ Carlotta Williams, South Carolina

This book is layered and definitely has something for everyone. I pulled from chapter four to express how I feel about this amazing woman and her testimony. I believe we can all identify with Jami in chapter 4 where she shares how she maintained an outward appearance that said everything is all good and life is great, when, in fact, it's all just a façade. I can appreciate her openness to share some of her most vulnerable moments in life and painful experiences because we overcome by the blood of the Lamb and the word of our testimony. Jami is a living witness of how steadfast our Father God is and that He will restore. She is an example that confession is good for the soul. It brings life! ~ A. Moore, Google Review

Confessions is a chronicle of Jami's life of upheaval. She is candid and expressive all throughout the book. Her candor is refreshing as you don't get much of that in more mainstream writing. It is this candor that allows the reader to recognize that the worst of times can lead to the best of lives when surrendered to God. It's an amazing read start to finish! ~ Pamela M. Scholtes, South Carolina

You won't want to put this book down. There isn't a boring moment in the book. Some of what she has been through may be disturbing and shocking to some readers, yet unfortunately familiar to many others. It's almost like you are sitting across the table from her as she tells of her experiences and then gives you the tools, along with scriptures to remind you of God's truth in His word. She demonstrates how to apply them in your life in order to set you free from the lies that might have held your mind and emotions captive leading to destructive decisions and behaviors. She asks you questions that challenge you to pause and ponder, with an invitation for the Lord to come in and heal your heart and mind. Not only is it written in a way that encourages the readers who are living destructive lifestyles but it also helps the families and friends of those in the bondage to understand the mindsets and reasons for their destructive patterns and behaviors that may include codependency and to give them hope through the times of suffering. May this book give you and your loved ones the hope and tools you need to see victory manifest in your lives. ~ Brenda Dukes, Founder/Instructor of Odyssey of the ARK, Kingdom of Heaven Conferences and Prophetic Training thru ART Workshops

Foreword

Confessions of an X-Codependent is the chronicles of a woman's journey of seeking and finding true freedom in Christ. Author Jami Salters takes her readers on an intricate voyage through the deepest, darkest recesses of abuse, abandonment, depression, shame, guilt, lies, bitterness, fear, rejection, and much more. Her goal in scribing this book was not merely to express her emotions about her tribulations, but rather to expose the lies of an invisible enemy who is always afoot; one who purposes to kill, steal, and destroy all of us. She desires to reveal the heart of God who saved her wholly and completely – not just from eternal hell. Holy Spirit became her guiding source into the liberty that can come only from God. By discovering her true identity founded in Christ, she became empowered so as to overcome the false identities the world encroached upon her from numerous outside sources. Currently, her directive in this life is the same as that of Jesus Christ, which is stated in Luke 4:18-19 and Isaiah 61:1: *to open blind eyes, bring good news to the poor, comfort the brokenhearted, and to proclaim liberty to captives and freedom to prisoners.*

    I had the honor of working with Jami on this fantastically vital book. What I knew instantly, and what I have found to be true over the last many years, is that Jami is an amazing, humble woman of God whose spirit and heart are pure through and through. She is a gentle, kindhearted woman whose only desire is to serve the Lord and aid others in their journey through life. Her story will lead people out of bondage and into the liberty of Christ. Her life is nothing short of a miracle. Jami is a rare gem in this world and what she offers is priceless to anyone attempting with futility to walk this earth while bound in the shackles of codependency.

Codependency is a vicious, insidious villain who, once it gets its claws in a person, refuses to willingly let go. One must first learn and accept that they are codependent. Secondly, they must recognize their situation isn't hopeless, regardless of how it may feel in the moment. In *Confessions of an X-Codependent*, Jami has well articulated the problem as well as the solution. In between the problem and solution, she takes her readers on a harrowing journey of sorrow and heartache all the way into relief and peace. Join Jami in her experiences so as to discover whether or not this may be you or someone you love. I implore you to take a serious and genuine look at yourself and your life. Ask the hard questions of, *"Is this me? Could this be me on some level?"* Knowledge is power and, once we gain knowledge and learn what to do with it, power is combined with authority. Everyone has authority over their own life whether or not one can realize it. We all have a choice. We all have the power to change our narrative. Christ is the answer and the narrative-changer. No one has to be what they've always been unless they so choose.

Alexys V. Wolf, Author and Minister
Founder of The Fiery Sword Global Ministries
and The Fiery Sword Publications

Introduction

We are learning that most people who are codependent have Complex Trauma. In other words, codependency is a symptom of Complex Trauma. In the past 10 years, a new field of study has opened up which has enabled us to better understand many problems with which people deal. This field of study is called Complex Trauma – or CPTSD. Unlike Simple Trauma, which is a one-time event, Complex Trauma describes what happens inside a person who continually lives in danger.

Complex Trauma can happen in three different environments:

1. **Abuse**: Living in a family where physical, verbal, emotional, or sexual abuse takes place, or receiving abuse at school at the hands of a bully.
2. **Abandonment**: This can result from being put into the foster care system, or possibly from being adopted or experiencing the divorce of parents. The child feels that no one has their back and that they are facing a scary world all by themselves, with very few tools or resources.
3. **Neglect**: Their physical needs were met, but their parents weren't there for them emotionally. When they tried to connect with their parents, they were unsuccessful. They also feel alone and abandoned.

As you can see, there is a spectrum of Complex Trauma that goes from severe danger to more subtle forms of danger. But the results are the same—the child lives in survival mode. If they are too little to fight or flight, they have no option but to freeze. Another way to say this is, in order to stay safe and to try and get needs met, the child must adapt their behaviour. The problem with Complex Trauma is that the adaptations are maladaptive systems. They kept the child safe, but they prevent that child from having healthy relationships and coping in adult life. The child grows up to be an adult who hurts themselves and others.

We are learning that Complex Trauma can result in physical and mental health problems, addiction, eating disorders, self-harm behaviours, criminal behaviour, and codependency. A missing piece in dealing with codependency has been the piece of Complex Trauma. Unless people deal with underlying trauma, their chances of growing out of codependent relational patterns is minimal.

For everyone who begins looking at their childhood trauma, it is important that the purpose is *not* to blame the parents. Rather, it is to understand how the wounds of childhood, regardless of how they were inflicted, impacted them. There are three things that influence a child:

1. how their parents treated them – parents wounding them
2. how the child perceived the events of their childhood
3. the decisions the child made in response to those wounds, which resulted in wounding self

The danger in facing the underlying trauma is it triggers the trauma and can re-traumatize the person if they don't have tools so as to resolve it. This could result in a *fight, flight,* or *freeze* response, which could hurt them and those they love. Our concern here is that reading this book could potentially stir memories of your trauma. I recommend that you do not read this book unless you have two things in your life:

1. Tools with which to ground yourself so as to deescalate your triggered emotions
2. A support person who understands trauma and who can help you process it so that you can productively resolve it

> Tim Fletcher
> Founder and President of
> "Finding Freedom Media" and RE:ACT
> www.findingfreedom.ca
> YouTube channel, "Finding Freedom Media"

Additionally, addiction specialist and Author Gabor Matè says that dealing with past trauma may be the key to breaking addiction. He says: "*Addiction is not a choice anybody makes, it's a response to emotional pain*" He also says "*Every person who has had trauma may not be an addict but every addict has had some type of trauma, so the question we should be asking is not why the addiction but why the pain.*"

CHAPTER ONE

Time Heals All Wounds?

> *"When a person tells you that you have hurt them, you don't get to decide that you didn't."* ~ Louis C.K.

As true as Louis C.K.'s statement is, what is more important is the answer to, *"What are we going to do with that hurt?"* The world says, *"Time heals all wounds."* This is a lie many of us have believed. Time does *not* heal all wounds, or any wounds, for that matter. Time is not a healer. True healing comes only from The Healer—Jesus. All other means are a temporary bandage which is sure to eventually fall at some point in our life. Naturally, we usually put on a mask for the outside world. This is the easier route rather than dealing with pain head-on. Some of us self-medicate with all types of substances. Some people become overly involved in work or the affairs of others. The list is broad.

"What's really happening on the inside?" is the question which needs to be addressed. Oftentimes, the inside tells a much different story than the outside. What's life like for *you* on the inside? Do you feel empty, unworthy, hopeless, depressed, or anything of the like? Do you feel as though you have a void as though you are dying inside?

Why do we take the natural route, the one which demands we put on a mask or self-medicate? It's because the recovery process is usually very painful as well as time-consuming. In this, we would rather ignore, mask, and/or suppress the pain. When we do this, we deceive ourselves into thinking, "*I'm okay.*" The truth is, we are *not* okay. It will only be a matter of time before the pain of our past or present begins to handicap our future. The road to recovery is often excruciatingly painful. We would much rather not deal with it altogether. It is easier to think it will magically go away. Unfortunately, recovery doesn't happen this way. We must become intentional about wanting healing. We must understand that recovery is a process and there is nothing magical about it. I spent years trying to mask, suppress, ignore, and self-medicate my internal pain. I felt like my life was one big failure. I kept going around and around in one gigantic circle. Have you ever felt like that?

A wise person once told me, "*You can't keep doing the same things expecting different results.*" I didn't fully understand its meaning and I didn't know *how* or *what* to change. I just knew I needed change. I tried changing the things of which I thought I was in control, but that only seemed to make things worse for me. People would continue to hurt me. In my mind, it was always someone else's fault. My focus was always on what someone else had done or said to me. I saw others as the blame for my pain, never holding myself accountable for my behavior and poor choices. I blamed everyone else for my life being so miserable. There was something in me causing a cycle of dysfunction. My behavior and my responses were deeply rooted in the lies of my past, though I didn't know it. I started on a journey of self-evaluation and it was not easy. I had to decide for myself that I not only wanted something different, but I had to go after it.

I must warn you that, any time we desire change, it will come at a great price. It will be up to us whether or not we will choose the road to recovery or continuously idle going around and around in circles. If you choose the road to recovery, as I did, remember, real and lasting change does not happen overnight. There is no such thing as an *easy fix*. During my recovery process, I had days where the pain seemed unbearable. Many times, I felt like giving up and going back. If you stay focused on the recovery process, press into the pain and trust in the process, greater will come. I am a witness to this truth. Despite the pain, we must press through.

I invite you to come along with me on a journey through my personal experiences all the way to recovery. My intention is to bring you hope and encouragement as you experience your own healing and freedom. As we know, there are always three sides to every story: our side, their side, and the truth which lies somewhere in between. What you are about to read is my side of the story. It is my perception of my life and my experiences. Right or wrong, these experiences became my truth. Unfortunately, many of my "truths" were based on lies. I'll explain as we go along. Some people who know me may disagree with what I am going to share. They may have a much different account of the things I have experienced and that's okay. Again, this is *my* perspective of my story.

The sole purpose for writing this book is to relate to others how God can take a messed-up life, much like mine, and turn it into a beautiful life. You too can begin to live in the truth— *God's* truth. My prayer for sharing my story is to give hope to the hopeless, freedom to the oppressed, and healing to the broken. No longer do we have to be held captive by our side of the story or their side of the story. We can begin to live in freedom as we allow God's truth to penetrate our hearts. Throughout this book, I will reference many Scriptures which have caused healing, transformation, and freedom to take root in my own personal life.

Disclaimer: at one point in my life, I used to think the Bible was just a book written by man. This is one of the many lies I grew up believing, so I understand if you may feel the same way. Trust me—I get it. All I ask is for you to be willing to open your heart. It is God's desire for you to know Him and His Word; simply give Him a chance. That being said, John 10:10 says that the thief's – Satan – purpose is to steal, kill, and destroy, but Jesus' objective is to give us life in all its fullness.

At the age of forty-two, the time of penning this book, I am currently living a life I never dreamed possible. It is the gospel of Jesus Christ which has saved me and set me free. It is only by God's grace, His love, and His forgiveness that my life has become complete. Through Christ, I have been healed! I have become whole and my identity has been restored. No longer do I live in the shame of my past. I went from living in despair, pain, abandonment, addiction, rejection, depression, loneliness, and more of the same, into living life to its fullest. I now live rooted in God's love for me. I know who I am as well as my purpose in life. I live resting in His presence where joy, kindness, goodness, and His faithfulness surround me, regardless of my surroundings.

As you take this journey with me, I want you to know, you will hear some of the same things over and over again. It is intentional as repetition is how we retain what we learn. Sometimes, most of the time, we need to hear things more than once before we actually get it. Trust the process. Time does not heal all wounds. Christ does.

Reflection Activity

Do you have wounds which need healing? Have you been unable to ascertain such healing? Don't expect time to heal it. What would you like God to heal in your life?

_____

_____

_____

_____

_____

_____

_____

CHAPTER TWO

Sticks and Stones

"The tongue has the power of life and death (Proverbs 18:21).*"*

As I felt my fiancé's hands grip tighter and tighter around my neck, all I could think about were his words being screamed at me. My fiancé, a man who claimed to love me, screamed loudly, *"You no-good whore! You are nothing but a stupid bitch. I hate you. This is why nobody wants you. You good-for-nothing bitch!"*

Over and over again, I heard him shout insults. I just wanted to make it stop. I just wanted the shouting to end. The physical pain I was feeling was nothing compared to the words being blasted at me. In that moment, I wanted life altogether to end. In my mind, it was all true: I *was* stupid, I *was* a whore, I *wasn't* good for anything. Because I believed every word to be true, I desperately wanted the shouting to stop. He was not the first person to tell me how worthless I was, nor was this his first time speaking such words of disdain. I hated who I was. Inside I was pleading with myself, *"How could you be so stupid? Look what you have done now."*

Internally, I was reasoning with myself that I only wanted someone to love me, someone to show me affection. I desired someone to tell me I was beautiful, someone to accept me and to believe in me. I just wanted someone to respect me; someone who wanted me for me and not what I could do for them. I tried my best, but it was never good enough. I told myself I wasn't worthy of love, much less respect. I was certain the fight was my fault; that I had caused the outburst of rage and I deserved what was happening. If only I had not done what I did.

Allow me to explain. I had only been home a few days after taking my daughter to the beach for her 16th birthday. It was a trip my fiancé didn't want to take with us. While at the beach, I met a man with whom I exchanged numbers and made plans to hang out. I didn't intentionally set out to meet someone, although this was my character in the past. My fiancé and I had been together a little over a year. Up until this point, I had been faithful. I didn't want to go back to who I used to be. As much as I desired to be faithful, I found myself in a very vulnerable position. I had gotten caught up in my emotions and allowed them to get the better of me.

My daughter and I and a few of our friends sat on the deck of a local restaurant enjoying the music and people-watching. That's when I saw him. He took a seat right behind us. I looked back trying not to stare as tears welled up in my eyes. I'm sure the alcohol consumption wasn't helping the situation. *"What's wrong with me?"* I asked myself. *"Girl, get it together,"* I told myself. My daughter looked at me and saw I was having an emotional moment. She started laughing at me asking, *"What's wrong with you?"*

"Don't make it obvious," I said, *"but turn around and look at the guy sitting behind us. He looks just like your dad."* Very obviously, she turns around and looked at him. She was just as in shock as I was. Now we were both staring! He really did look like her dad. From the unique style of clothes to the piercings in his ears, even his style of hair and beard looked like her father's clone.

He and I made eye contact—those eyes! I motioned for him to come over. He smiled and headed our way. Oh my, his smile. *"Focus, Jami,"* I told myself. I apologized for us blatantly staring at him and introduced myself and my daughter.

"This is my daughter, Jaz. At two-and-half years old, we lost her father to a cancerous brain tumor and you look just like him. I just wanted to apologize for being so rude," I explained to him. He gave us that big smile again and my heart melted. Even his smile reminded me of Jaz's dad. He expressed his condolences for our loss. With compassion in his eyes, he held out his hand and said, "Hi, my name is Joe." I almost choked. I felt tears swell up in my eyes again. A few of them fell before I could catch them; I tried to play it off. I smiled while fighting back more tears. Joe? I couldn't believe it. Then I said to him, "That was her dad's name. You're kidding, right?" He smiled as he pulled out his wallet and handed us his driver's license. His name really was Joe!

Now, let me set the stage. We were in Myrtle Beach, South Carolina during Memorial Day weekend, better known as "Black Bike Week." People attend from all over. This is not a weekend where you would want to plan a family trip to the beach, but it just so happened that Jaz's birthday fell on this weekend. A family member had allowed us the use of her condo for her birthday. Bike Week has a pretty horrible reputation involving disorder, drugs, alcohol, partying, and sex. In my younger years, this was where I would come to participate in all the aforementioned. This particular trip, contrarily, was much different. We weren't there for Bike Week but, as I said, it happened to fall on the same weekend as my daughter's birthday. Knowing the reputation of Bike Week and the type of people who attended and their motives for attending, giving one's real name was rare, even unheard. In the preceding years, when my crew and I would go there to participate in the partying, we never gave our real names; neither did the men we met. It had been ten plus years since I participated in Bike Week.

Needless to say, I was shocked when Joe offered his driver's license so as to prove his name really was the one he had given. I thought to myself, *"Surely this is not a coincidence. What if this was some kind of sign from God?"* My imagination began to run wild.

I was intoxicated. Not from the alcohol I had been drinking, but from his smile, his voice, the scent of his cologne, and even his very name. We all spent the rest of the evening hanging out together laughing and enjoying ourselves. I was emotional when the night ended and we went our separate ways. I didn't want to say goodbye. I wanted to stay there with him forever.

Over the duration of the weekend, we talked on the phone a few times and made plans to meet up, but I canceled. I knew I couldn't be around him, especially not alone. I came up with some lame excuse as to why I couldn't meet him. The truth was, I didn't trust myself and I was feeling guilty knowing my fiancé was at home. We sent a few text messages back and forth, but nothing more than that. Although we had plans to meet and I backed out, I didn't really get the impression he was that interested in me. If he had put forth any effort or pressed the issue about spending time with me, I would probably still be trying to chase that rabbit trail. God saved me from becoming a character in a real-life fatal attraction movie.

On the way home, I made sure to delete his number and the few text messages we had exchanged. I tried to put him out of my mind. Nevertheless, meeting him opened up a place in my heart I thought was healed. Oh, how I missed my Joe! I longed for his big smile and personality, thoughts of what our life would be like if God had not taken him home, and more. I definitely wouldn't be going through the ups and downs of my current relationship. In my messed-up mind, I believed that, if Joe was still alive, we would be living happily ever after. I was so emotional.

But, back to reality. When I arrived home, I wasn't welcomed with a warm smile. I wasn't welcomed with, "*I missed you.*" I wasn't welcomed with, "*How was your trip?*" I was greeted, however, with attitude and sarcasm. I felt guilty inside. *"Did he know? How could he?"* I wondered. Besides, this was his normal behavior toward me unless, of course, he wanted or needed something from me. The next few days home were very difficult. I tried to suppress all the emotions I was feeling ranging from guilt to sadness. I found myself sneaking around looking at old pictures of Joe and me, *my* Joe. I spent most of my time playing his favorite songs and recalling how silly he would act while lip syncing and dancing just to make me laugh. Oh, how I missed him! I simply couldn't get it together. *"Why? Why can't I get it together?"* I kept asking myself.

One night, while I was in the shower, my fiancé went through my phone. He found a text message between me and my girlfriend who accompanied us on the beach trip. She had sent me a message asking if I was going to meet Joe while at the beach. How could I be so stupid? I hadn't thought to erase my messages from her. I had forgotten she sent that. I knew better, I should have erased it as soon as she sent it. When I got out of the shower, he asked me, *"Who is Joe?"*

I couldn't think fast enough and I tried to lie. Why was I lying? Why couldn't I just tell the truth? It's not like we did anything. He immediately began accusing me of having sex with this guy. As I said before, this was the reputation of Bike Week and he didn't want me to go in the first place. I immediately became defensive and then I became angry because he went through my phone. I started reminding him of the things he had done to me. I started shouting at him about the way he treated me, *"Why do you care anyway? There are nights you don't even come home. Just leave me alone!"*

He was so full of anger and hatred against me. I could hear it in his voice and see it in his eyes. It was as if he had turned into someone else. As he came toward me, he shouted *"I knew you had been sleeping with someone else! I could feel it."* That's when his strong hands wrapped around my throat and his words of how awful I was spewed from his lips like venom. It felt like forever before his hands began to loosen. He shoved me to the closet floor. More shouts of how stupid I was and how I was nothing but a whore.

"This is why your husband didn't want your sorry ass," he screamed. For a moment, I was disappointed I was still alive. I lay on the closet floor replaying what just happened. If only I hadn't given

Joe my number. He didn't want me anyway, how could I be so stupid? *"You mess up everything,"* I told myself. I heard the front door slam. I was alone once again. Normally, when we would fight, I would run after him and tell him how sorry I was, even when it wasn't my fault. I would quickly attend to *his* emotions and *his* feelings while ignoring my own. If I could just make him okay, I would be okay. This time was different. I made my way to the front door, locked it, and fell to my knees. As I did, I felt something inside me break. Nothing in me wanted to run after him. I was tired. I was done.

I began to cry out to God asking, *"What is wrong with me that I continue to attract these kinds of men in my life?"* I raised my hands in complete surrender as I cried out for God to help me. Something in me knew only God had the answers for which I was so desperate. I was incredibly hurt. I began to feel all the weight of all the pain I had ever endured. I felt the weight of my mistakes, brokenness, guilt, shame, anger, and utter loneliness. Physically, my whole body hurt and it wasn't from the physical abuse I had just endured—this was deeper. It was bigger and stronger. I was broken. My life was in pieces. *"How did I get here? More importantly, how do I get out of here?"* I wondered.

I didn't know the answer to either of those questions but, I did know I was sick and tired of being sick and tired. I was tired of going around and around in a never-ending cycle of hurt, disappointment, and abuse. Those verbal "sticks and stones" were surely breaking my "bones." Inevitably, he did come back as we'll discuss in later chapters.

Reflection Activity

Ask yourself what "sticks and stones" have afflicted you so far in life. What imprint have those words made on your life?

_____
_____
_____
_____
_____
_____
_____
_____
_____
_____

CHAPTER THREE

Sick and Tired of Being Sick and Tired

"Oh I am very weary, though tears no longer flow; my eyes are tired of weeping, my heart is sick of woe."
~ Anne Bronte

Shortly after this incident, I was told of a woman in the Bible who had been bleeding for twelve long years. As I read her story, I began to gain strength—strength to do something different. I realized this woman was like me. She was sick and tired of being sick and tired. Much like me, she had tried everything. Finally, she was making one of the hardest decisions she would ever have to make. All the odds were stacked against her, but she made up in her mind that it didn't matter. She was determined to become healed and whole again.

Let's look at her story found in Luke 8:43-48:

> And a woman who had suffered bleeding for twelve years and had spent all her money on physicians, and could not be healed by anyone, came up behind Him and touched the fringe of His outer robe, and immediately

her bleeding stopped. Jesus said, "Who touched Me?" While they all were denying it, Peter and those who were with him said, "Master, the people are crowding and pushing against you." But Jesus said, "Someone did touch me, because I was aware that healing power had gone out of me." When the woman saw that she had not escaped notice, she came up trembling and fell down before Him. She declared in the presence of all the people the reason why she had touched Him, and how she had been immediately healed. He said to her, "Daughter, your faith, your personal trust and confidence in Me, has made you well. Go in peace."

I spent twelve-plus years "bleeding" all over the place. My life was toxic, just like this woman in the passage. I had not only spent all I had, but I had given all I had. I was utterly depleted. Like her, I heard about Jesus and how he had healed others. Surely He could heal me. For this woman, healing started with a thought followed by a decision and was completed by stepping out in faith—action. This woman thought to herself, *"If I could just touch the hem of His garment."* I too had made up my mind. I was desperate to get to Jesus, despite my circumstances. I was determined. I had to override the thoughts of fear which were, at that time, very real and intimidating. Regardless, as fearful as I was, I was sick and I was tired. I was desperate for God to heal me. This time, I wasn't seeking God to restore a broken relationship or a broken man; I needed God for myself. I needed Him to restore me. I needed Him to heal me of all my brokenness. This time was different. I needed this for me. I longed to be whole.

The woman in the text had to make some tough decisions. She had to do some things she had never done before. It was against the law for her to leave her house while bleeding, but she didn't let that stop her. By any means necessary, she was going after what she knew only Jesus could do for her. I had to make that same decision. *You* will have to decide for yourself. Will you stay stuck or will you press on despite it all?

"What did that look like in my life?" I wondered. I started seeking God like never before. I committed myself to staying off social media. Previously, I would find myself spending countless hours on Facebook. I didn't know it then, but it was causing me to mask and ignore my own issues. I was always getting involved with everyone else's mess as a way of escape. I recognized it as the distraction it was and stayed away. As for my phone, I began to cut it off or purposely leave it in another room so it wouldn't become a hindrance. I stopped calling people and telling them about the issues I was going through and the pain I felt. I stopped replaying the story in my head. I became consumed with wanting God more than I wanted the relationship with my fiancé.

I didn't watch TV unless it was preaching. I longed to know more about God. Joyce Meyer quickly became my favorite TV evangelist with her simple but powerful messages. She helped me learn how to stop the negative self-talk and grow in my relationship with Christ. The same thing with music: if it wasn't gospel, I wasn't listening. I was consuming myself with the things of God through any means possible. Whatever emotion I would feel, I found Scripture to help me overcome. For instance, if I was feeling lonely, I would find Scripture which told me God is always with me. For example, *"Don't be afraid, for I am with you. Don't be discouraged, for I am your God. I will strengthen you and help you. I will hold you up with my victorious right hand,"* reads Isaiah 41:10."

I would repeat this over and over again until my emotions caught up with truth. If I felt depressed, I would pull teachings or Scriptures on depression. One particular night, I searched YouTube for sermons on depression. I found a sermon entitled "Dealing with Depression" by T.D. Jakes. As I listened and watched this sermon, I literally felt the spirit of depression leave my body. The heaviness, the sadness, the darkness – it all began to lift as I listened to truth being told as it related to Scripture. I felt as if I could breathe again, as though I could actually take a deep breath without pain or heaviness in my chest.

About a year before the incident with my fiancé, he and I started attending church at *Life Living Ministry* in Columbia, South Carolina. We would attend occasionally but, after the choking incident, I became heavily involved in all church activities they offered there. He was only attending every once in a while. This made it extremely difficult, but we'll talk more about this later. This was where I found most of my strength so as to continue moving forward. On Tuesday nights at *Life Living Ministry,* they had what's called "self-identity ministry," aka "The Circle," facilitated by Billy Shiver. This was a place my fiancé and I would attend fairly regularly. Again, after the incident, attendance became a priority. It became my lifeline.

The circle is and was a place of true authenticity, a place where one can take off the mask and talk about real life issues. *"Keep it real"* is their motto. It is not a Bible study, but rather a place to just go and talk about everyday life issues, good and bad, on which most churches fail to even touch. Usually, we would have a specific topic which we would bounce off each other relating to our experiences or our take concerning that particular subject. If, on the other hand, someone had something personal they wanted to share, we would talk about that. People could share if they wanted or sit quietly and listen. For me, it was a place of safety, transparency, and, most importantly, a place where I felt no judgment and lots of opportunity for spiritual growth. This was definitely a place God used mightily so as to encourage and strengthen me.

I was committed to being there on Tuesday nights. It was my commitment to myself and it was life-saving for me. In order to stop being sick and tired all the time, I needed accountability. I needed to feel connected. I needed guidance and direction. I needed to hear other peoples' testimonies about overcoming the things I was currently going through. Too often, we hide behind our church clothes and never talk about real issues we face on a day-to-day basis. There, in the circle, I was able to get all I needed and so much more. For more information about *Life Living Ministries* please visit *www.lifeliving.org.*

Reflection Activity

Ask yourself how this makes you feel. Maybe jot down some emotions which are stirring in yourself regarding your own situation.

_____

_____

_____

_____

_____

_____

_____

_____

_____

CHAPTER FOUR

Delivered but Still Very Broken

"If the Son sets you free, you will be free indeed (John 8:36).*"*

Most of my life, I was what you would call a "functional alcoholic." What I mean by "functional" is that I took care of my adult responsibilities. I had a good job, nice car, house, etc. I always made sure the bills were paid on time. I maintained an outward appearance as though I had my life neatly put together. If would have met me then, you would not have known I was an alcoholic. I had periods where I would drink very heavily, sometimes moderately and, at other times, I wasn't drinking at all.

After leaving my second husband, I began drinking very heavily. Shortly after that is when I met my fiancé and it escalated from there. It began to influence every area of my life. Now, reality was starting to sink in. I knew alcohol was one of the main reasons for my poor decision making. I really wanted to stop, but I couldn't. I wanted to be free; I just didn't know how to attain it.

Every day, I would wake up and say to the Lord, *"Today I am not drinking."* And every day, I would drink. *"Tomorrow Lord, tomorrow I won't drink."* In my heart, I meant what I said. I wasn't going to drink but, no matter how much I meant it, daily I would find myself drinking. And then, as you would imagine, I would feel like a failure. Repeatedly, I told the Lord, *"Tomorrow is going to be different."* I felt trapped.

I remember looking in the mirror with tears streaming down my face, *"Lord,"* I cried out, *"I don't want this anymore!"* The alcohol no longer tasted good to me yet, notwithstanding, I drank it anyway. I felt I needed it to help me cope. It helped me deal with life, or rather, *not* deal with life. At that juncture, I knew it was controlling my life and I desperately wanted to stop. Even when he and I started attending church, I was still drinking every single day. Some nights, I would drink before heading to Bible Study. My fiancé would tell me I was a hypocrite because of it. He would always try to shame me out of going. Nevertheless, I would still press my way to church, regardless of the drinking.

One day, I decided to set up a meeting with my pastor because I was so tired of living in shame and guilt. During that meeting, I fearfully shared with him that I was struggling with alcohol and that I wanted to be set free. I even told him that, some nights, I was drinking even before coming to church. With such grace and compassion, he looked me in my eyes and said, *"Don't stop coming."* He quickly reminded me of the church theme for the year which was "totally committed." He reminded me to stay committed no matter what I was going through or that with which I was struggling. Shortly after that meeting, that is when the choking incident happened and my fiancé left. One Wednesday night, while attending Bible study, the praise team began to sing a song entitled *"Tomorrow"* by the Winans:

> *Jesus said, "Here I stand*
> *Won't you please let Me in?"*
> *And you said "I will tomorrow*
> *Jesus said "I am He*
> *Who supplies all your needs."*
> *And you said, "I know but tomorrow.*

Ooh, tomorrow
I'll give my life tomorrow
I thought about today
But it's so much easier to say tomorrow."
Who promised you tomorrow?
Better choose the Lord today
For tomorrow very well might be today.

The words pierced my heart as I recalled my words spoken to the Lord. It was always the elusive *tomorrow*. I began to cry and, with each tear, I felt a release. I felt like it was just me and the Lord in that place. It felt like Jesus himself was singing that song to me. I felt safe. I felt loved. I felt forgiveness. In that moment, I was delivered from alcohol. It was gone. It had no more power over me. It's hard to explain in the natural, but I knew I was set free. It was very similar to when I felt the spirit of depression leave me. I knew I was set free yet, in my mind, there was nothing wrong with drinking every once in a while. I was free, so I decided to set the conditions of my freedom by saying I could drink sociably or occasionally. I was the one in control now instead of the alcohol.

Although I still had a few beers and a bottle of wine, it had been a whole week where it didn't touch my lips; I didn't even think about alcohol. I spent the week praising God for setting me free. The following week, since I had determined the terms and conditions of being able to drink for special occasions, I decided I was just going to drink the little which was left in the fridge. The conversation I had with myself went something like this: *"There's nothing wrong with drinking every once in a while. I am just going to drink it so there won't be any more in the house. I won't buy any more."*

Corinthians 10:13 tells me that God will show me how to escape temptations and powers so I can bear up patiently against it. The conversation I had with myself was the temptation and my way of escape was to just pour it out. I, at the time, didn't even know I was being tempted, much less that my way of escape was to just pour it out. Sure, I had a thought to pour it out, but I quickly dismissed it with internal reconciliation, *"I don't want to waste it so it's okay for me to drink it this time."* I allowed the thoughts of consuming the alcohol take precedence over dumping it.

The next morning, I woke up feeling deathly ill. I could barely lift my head off the pillow due to pain. As I sat up, the room began to spin and I became very nauseated. I barely made it to the bathroom when I started vomiting with diarrhea. I felt so horrible as if I was dying—or rather, I wanted to! My first thought was that maybe I had a hangover, though I quickly dismissed it. I only drank three Bud Lights and a bottle of wine, which was nothing for me to drink at one time. By no means do I say this to brag, but rather to share the seriousness of my addiction. I was drinking up to a 12-pack a day. Some days, I would drink that and a bottle of wine along with my prescribed medications. I was taking a muscle relaxer or two, a pain pill or two, a sleeping pill or two, and I can't forget about the Xanax bars for my anxiety.

What I took and how much I took mostly depended on how well my fiancé and I were getting along. More often than not, things were not well between us. I used alcohol and my prescription drugs to zone out and numb the pain. It helped me go into a place of nothingness. I would have memory loss. I would wake up with evidence of having had sex but, I would have no recollection whatsoever. Prior to this, never did I get sick nor have a hangover—this sickness wasn't my norm. Surely this was *not* a hangover! I made a doctor's appointment and drove myself there. Getting there was a blur. Of course, the first thing they do is check your weight, blood pressure, and ask a million questions, questions I didn't feel like answering. I just wanted relief.

When the doctor finally made it to my room, he looked over my chart, listened to my heart, and then asked more questions. He said my blood pressure was extremely low, almost dangerously low. Looking over my chart again, he asked a few other questions which I don't remember and then he asked about my alcohol consumption. With that question, I felt a little burst of energy as I told him how God had, over a week ago, delivered me from alcohol. He seemed disinterested and asked if I had continued to take my blood pressure medication, as if my deliverance was unimportant. As quickly as that burst of energy came, it was gone just as fast.

I hadn't had any alcohol in my system for the past week, other than the night before, which I purposefully didn't mention. How could I tell him God had delivered me from alcohol but drank last night? Since I had been on high blood pressure medication for the past few years, he began to explain that my blood pressure had returned to normal being that I went from drinking everyday to no alcohol in a week. When I was first put on blood pressure medication, I was told my alcohol consumption and stress were the cause of my high blood pressure and I was instructed to eliminate as much stress as possible and stop drinking.

The drinking only continued to get worse. And, for the life of me, I couldn't figure out why the doctors thought it was caused by stress. I didn't feel like I was stressed. Naturally, there were moments of being stressed but, for the most part, life was good. It sounds crazy to me even as I tell my story but, when I was in my stressful life, I did not believe I lived a stressful life. Like I said, I had moments but, to me, those moments were brought on by arguments or mistreatment by my fiancé. When I did encounter these moments, I tried my best to control it. Generally speaking, my method of controlling it was masking it with more drinking and using prescription drugs.

The doctor told me to stop taking the blood pressure medicines and check my blood pressure at my local pharmacy for the next few weeks. Moments later, he walked out and the nurse returned with my papers instructing me to check out and to call if anything changed or symptoms got worse. Was she serious? Was that it? How could they just send me home? The way I felt, I wanted him to admit me to the nearest hospital! I literally wanted to be transported from his office by ambulance to the hospital where I could stay until I felt better. That's how horrible I felt.

Reflection Activity

Have you found yourself "delivered" from a situation but you still feel bound? Has God released you yet you continue in chains?

_____
_____
_____
_____
_____
_____
_____
_____
_____

CHAPTER FIVE

Saved from Myself

"I sought the Lord, and He answered me; He delivered me from all my fears (Psalm 34:4)."

Getting home was another blur. What should have taken me thirty minutes took about an hour and thirty minutes. I prayed the whole way home to God, *"Just let me make it home in one piece. I promise I will NEVER DRINK AGAIN!"* I kept saying this over and over. Unfortunately, this was not a statement that the Lord was hearing for the first time. I can't begin to tell you the countless times I have said this. I finally made it home and, not long after, I heard a voice in my head. I guess it is better explained by saying that I had a "thought" in my head but this "thought" had a voice and it wasn't mine.

Inside, I knew it was the Lord. This is another one of those things that's hard to explain in the natural, much like being delivered from a spirit. I know now that God speaks to us in countless ways. I believe we just haven't been taught how to *hear* His voice. Most times, it's not necessarily an audible voice when He speaks. Sometimes it can be a thought. It could be explained as intuition or something told to me or a "knowing" inside. We also may get a vision, a picture, or an analogy of some sort. This thought or voice said to me, *"Are you ready to get rid of the prescription drugs?"* At that, I began to weep. *"I won't abuse them anymore, I will only take them if I really need them,"* I replied. Then the internal battle began. *"Lord, you know I can't sleep without sleeping pills. Oh yeah, my back, You know I've had two back surgeries. What if my back starts hurting? I'll need my pain pills and muscle relaxers."*

I continued to plead with the Lord, *"I will only take them if I need them."* I heard the voice again, *"Are you ready to get rid of the prescription drugs?"* This time the voice was very stern but kind and loving. I began to have a dialogue with myself which went something like, *"I will take them all to the trash and throw them away." "No, you will only get them out of the trash." "I will just give them away." "Really? So you're going to cause somebody else to be in bondage?"*

I started weeping uncontrollably. *"I'm afraid,"* I said out loud. The same kind and loving voice said to me, *"What are you afraid of?" "I'm afraid!"* I shouted while crying. Again, the question was asked, this time the voice was full of compassion. It was loving, kind and thoughtful and full of concern. *"I don't know,"* I whispered as I continued to cry. I got up and began to gather all the different pill bottles throughout the house. I was ashamed as I sat at the commode with countless bottles of different prescriptions. I was ashamed of what I saw before my eyes. I never thought, not even for one second, that I had an issue with prescription drugs. I thought I was in control over them. It wasn't like I was taking them every day. Or was I? Alcohol was my battle. I knew I wasn't in control of my drinking anymore. It's funny how we always feel like we are in control when, in fact, we aren't in control of anything. I had been addicted to illegal drugs for many years prior and, when I wanted to stop, I just stopped. No rehab, no withdrawals, I just stopped. With the prescription drugs, it was a different matter because I felt justified in taking them. They were mine, they were from my doctor, and they were prescribed to me. It wasn't like I was going out buying this stuff.

I sat in front of the toilet surrounded by bottles of pills. Overwhelming thoughts of despair and fear gripped me. *"I can't,"* I thought to myself. The bathroom walls felt as if they were closing in on me and I found it hard to breathe. I was so dizzy as the room began to spin. I vomited a few times while begging the Lord to help me. *"Lord, please, make the spinning stop! I can't do this!"* I said out loud as I cried uncontrollably. Ever so slightly, the spinning stopped as I opened the first bottle of pills. I emptied the contents into the water. The second bottle, the third bottle, the fourth bottle, the fifth, sixth, and seventh bottle. I got to the sleeping pills. *"Lord, I won't be able to sleep without these. Just let me keep these,"* I begged.

Fear gripped me tightly as I thought of not being able to sleep without them. For years I had become dependent on them. My hands began to shake uncontrollably as I tried opening the bottle of pills. Finally, I got them open and dumped them. As I did, I felt a sense of peace and calmness. I got to the last bottle of pills. I hadn't thought about them until they were in my hand. *"Lord, I really need these. I don't even take these. Please let me keep them,"* I begged. I heard the same sweet voice in my head but, this time, the voice had urgency mixed with passion. *"You're killing him."* The Lord said the person's actual name but, for purpose of keeping his identity concealed, I will refer to him generically. I burst out in tears. It was true. I was killing him! I was shaking and crying as I emptied the newly filled prescription into the commode. I sat for the next few minutes in disbelief while I cried. I was overwhelmed with emotions of shame and guilt.

Eventually, I made it back to my bed. As I lay there, the room was spinning as I broke into a sweat but feeling extremely cold with uncontrollable shaking. I thought to myself, *"This reminds me of withdrawals,"* though withdrawals were something I had never personally experienced. *"I can't possibly be going through withdrawals. These pills aren't even out of my system. I know I continued to take a few different pills during the week. I took my sleeping pill every night, though I didn't drink alcohol,"* I recounted to myself.

I'm getting ready to try and explain another one of those hard to explain things. In that moment, I knew I was going through withdrawals for someone else. It was a knowing inside. God said, *"You're carrying this for someone else. You are going through withdrawals but it's not about you. It's for somebody else."* The voice continued to share with me, *"When you share with others how I delivered you or whenever someone reads about your deliverance, I will deliver them from their addictions and they will not have to go through withdrawal symptoms because you have carried it for them."*

Revelation 12:1 reads, *"They defeated him — the enemy — by the blood of the Lamb and by their testimony."* Jesus reminded me of what He did for me. He endured death on the cross for the penalty of my sin while I was still a sinner, even when I didn't want anything to do with Him. He took the penalties of my sins so that I could not only be free, but have eternal life through Him. Witness the beautiful story explained in the Scripture references below:

> "For the wages of sin is death but the free gift of God is eternal life through Jesus Christ Our Lord (Romans 6:23)."

> "He died for our sins and rose again to make us right with God, filling us with God's goodness (Romans 4:25)."

> "So that anyone who believes in Me will have eternal life. For God loved the world so much that He gave His only son so that anyone who believes in Him shall not perish but have eternal life. God did not send His Son into the world to condemn it, but to save it (John 3:15-17)."

I don't know about you, but I needed to be saved. Not just from my sins and hell, but from myself. My friend, are you struggling with an addiction? I dare you to believe that Jesus can and will deliver you. It doesn't matter what that addiction is. It can be drugs, alcohol, sex, shopping, food, gambling, pornography, or anything else. There is no addiction from which God cannot deliver us. The question is, do you really want to be free? If you truly want freedom, you must surrender your will to His. You must stop trying to do it on your own and on your own terms as I tried doing. It must be God's will in His way.

Remember, I told you that every day I would say, *"I'm not going to drink today,"* yet, without fail, every day I ended up drinking. It wasn't until I changed what I was saying that I stopped trying to do it in my own strength. I went from saying, *"Lord, I'm not going to,"* to, *"Lord, I don't want to drink anymore. I can't but You, Jesus, can. I want to be set free."* Despite my drinking, I was staying in the word of God. I continued to go to church, to *The Circle* every Tuesday, and I even started taking a small group class at my church called *Making Peace with Your Past*.

Food for thought: there are many disagreements about drinking, especially in the Body of Christ. Some people are totally against it and some people feel like there's nothing wrong with it. I just ask that you meditate on these thoughts: *"So then, whether you eat or drink or whatever you do, do all to the glory of our great God* (I Corinthians 10:31).*"*

How is drinking alcohol bringing God glory?

And no, Jesus did not drink wine. What He drank was unfermented grape juice. Don't take my word for it, do your own personal word study as it can be very powerful. Keep your heart open as you seek truth for yourself. Whether or not you drink alcohol is between you and the Lord. I'm merely sharing my personal experiences and the devastating affect I know alcohol has caused. Look at the world in which we live and you can see the devastating aftermath of alcohol. Why do you think alcohol is called "spirits" and why are some liquor stores called "spirit stores"?

Pray this prayer with me: *Jesus, I want freedom from _____. I know that I cannot do this in my own strength, but I can do all things through You. Spirit of addiction, you are no longer welcome in my life or my family's life. In the name of Jesus, with all power and authority of the Lord Jesus, He rebukes you. Spirit of addiction, you have to leave. You are commanded to loosen me _____ from the stronghold of _____. Jesus, show me the way of escape when temptation comes knocking. Fill me with the fullness of who You are. Pour out Your love on me in a tangible way and save me from myself. Cause me to be anchored in Your truth, no longer tossed around by the lies of this world. I believe, today, I have been set free from this day forward. Teach me to walk in my deliverance and to be obedient to Your Word, in Jesus name, Amen.*

Reflection Activity

Have you found yourself utterly dismayed by yourself, your own actions, words, or thoughts? From what would you like to be delivered?

_____
_____
_____
_____
_____
_____
_____
_____
_____
_____

CHAPTER SIX

The Residue

Definition of Residue: a small amount of something that remains after the main part has gone or been taken or used

I was in awe that God was going to use my testimony to set others free, that I was actually going through withdrawals for someone else. It's weird, but that knowledge made it a little easier. As I lay in my bed shaking, I thought about others and what they would not have to go through. I started praying for addictions to be broken in the lives of those I knew and those I was yet to meet. When I took my eyes off me and the physical pain I was in, it helped me to draw strength so as to press my way through. It made it all worth it.

    Finally, I was able to fall asleep and, to my surprise, I slept like a baby—no sleeping pill. The next morning, I got up and I was good. My head wasn't hurting, no dizziness, no shaking, no nausea, no spinning, nothing. I literally felt like a new person. *"Thank you, Jesus,"* was all I kept saying. Shortly after waking, I made my way to the bathroom. I was shocked to find the last set of pills—you know, the ones I didn't want to let go of because I wasn't taking them. Well, they were all caked up and stuck on the side of the commode; they hadn't dissolved like all the other ones. I flushed and nothing happened; they still remained.

Why didn't they dissolve like the rest of the pills? Let me explain about not wanting to let go of this particular prescription. It was 80 mgs of Oxycontin with a street value over $100 per pill. I was *not* addicted to taking them. I *was* addicted to the money I was making selling them. I was only selling them to one person. I felt justified in selling them since it was only one person and it was someone close to me. In fact, he was the one that told me to ask my doctor for them so he could buy them from me. I agreed. As I was begging the Lord to let me keep these pills, I clearly heard God say, *"You're killing him. What's more important to you? His life or the money?"* Of course, the answer was his life.

A few days later, this person called so as to buy some pills knowing full well I had just gotten a new refill. I told him I didn't have them anymore, that I had an encounter with Jesus and He had delivered me from drugs and alcohol. I told him that Jesus said I was killing him by selling him these pills and I couldn't do it anymore. To say the least, he was not happy. He stressed how he needed them and that, without them, he would go into withdrawals. I shared about God allowing me to take the withdrawal symptoms and that Jesus would deliver him just as He had done for me. I tried to plead and convince him he wouldn't go through the withdrawal symptoms.

He wasn't trying to hear that. He called me every name under the sun. He told me he was going to call the police and have me arrested. He even went as far as threatening my life. Although I knew it wasn't the real him talking, it was his addiction, still, the words hurt me deeply within my heart. A part of me was fearful as to what could happen to him—and to me. If only I could get him to surrender to Jesus as I had, he too would be set free. I couldn't believe the mess I had gotten myself into. I was afraid of the consequences I was facing. This time, I had no one to blame. It was the fallout of my own poor choices.

Guilt and shame consumed me. I tried not to think about it. All I could do was pray, pray that the Lord would be with me no matter what happened. I prayed for the Lord to show me a way out of this mess and to forgive me. I took full responsibility for the situation I was facing. Every time fear would try to set in, instead of focusing on myself and the trouble in which I could easily find myself, I would begin to pray for him. I would pray that God would deliver him from this bondage of addiction.

To this day, that relationship is still strained. I don't know if he has been delivered or not, but I continue to pray for his deliverance. I want nothing more than to see him living in the liberty of the Lord. Even as I share this part of my journey, my heart still hurts over this situation. My prayer is that God would not only restore that relationship, but that the Lord would set him free. Free from the pain of his past and free him from himself. Will you pray with me for his healing, deliverance, and restoration? Pray he would surrender his life to the Lord and become the mighty man God created him to be. Thank you. There is power in prayer.

Now, back to the toilet bowl . . .

God told me to clean the commode. I searched for the scrub brush to no avail. I heard, *"Use your hand."* My internal response was, *"No way, that's disgusting! I'm not going to use my hand."* You would think I would get it by now that, when God tells me to do something, I should just do it. Eventually, I realized God wasn't asking but telling me. So, I got an old washcloth, but not without an attitude, I might add. I mean come on, my hand in the toilet bowl? Really? I sprayed it with bleach and began to scrub. I scrubbed 'til it was all off the sides. I flushed and down it went—spotless. This was what I felt like the Lord was sharing with me. I quickly got a pen and started writing:

The Residue

"Everything I ask of you is for your own good. Some things in your life, when *you* decide to let go of them, that's it. They will just dissolve. There will be no resistance. There are other things in your life which have left a residue. It won't be as easy as simply letting go and flushing. If you will trust the process, together we will scrub all the residue of your childhood, your failed marriages, your past relationships, and the pain. By My hand, you will become spotless. There will be no evidence of the residue once I lovingly clean you from the inside out. I got you. I just need you to trust me and trust the process. I AM making all things work for your good."

Reflection Activity

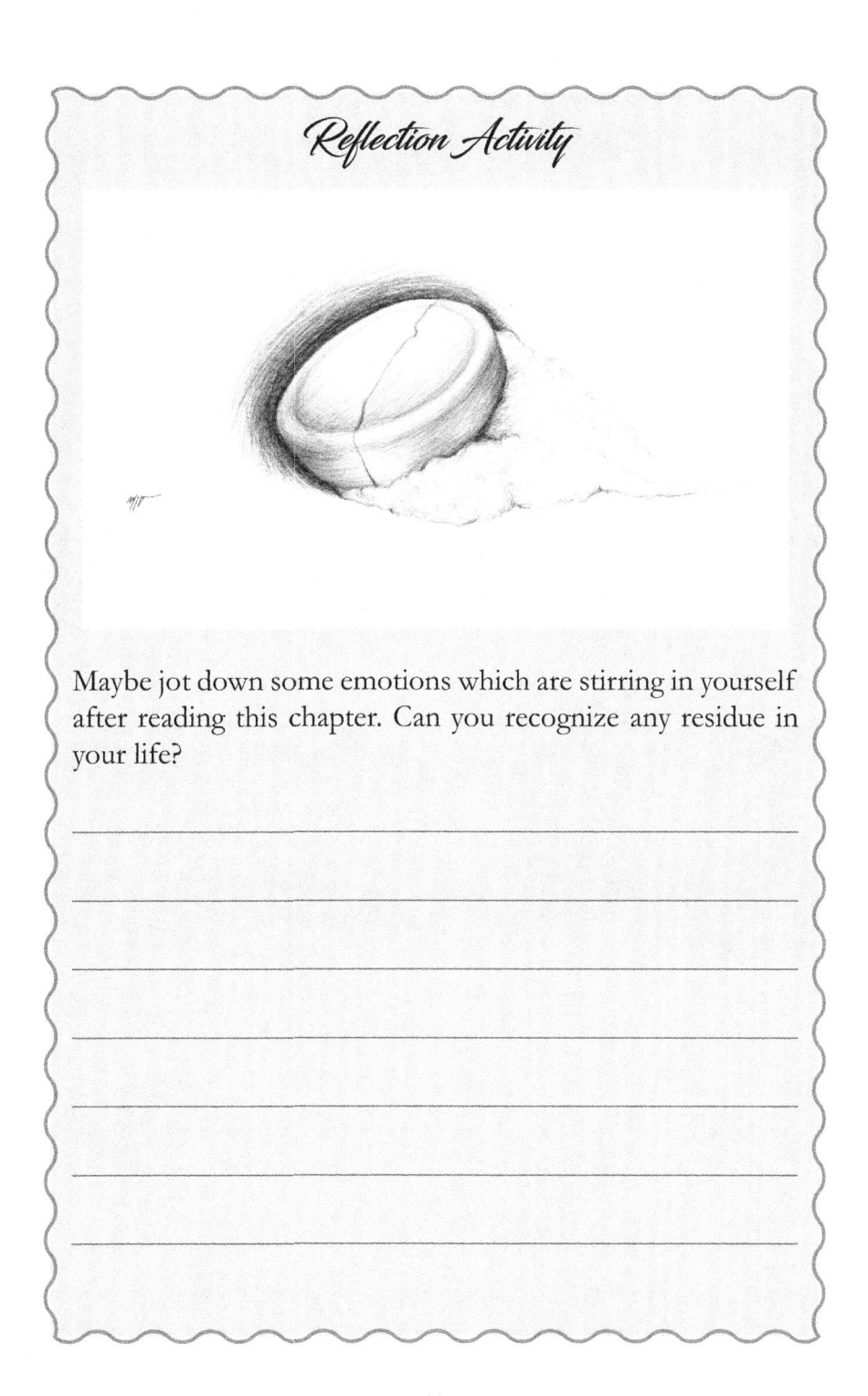

Maybe jot down some emotions which are stirring in yourself after reading this chapter. Can you recognize any residue in your life?

_____
_____
_____
_____
_____
_____
_____

CHAPTER SEVEN

Making Peace with My Past

"We cannot change the past but if we go through the process of recovery, we will gain more than we ever lost."

As I told you, I started taking a small group class at *Life Living Ministries*. This class was facilitated by Valerie and Darryl Lane who later became my mentors. This study is a biblical workbook by Tim Sledge, entitled *Making Peace with Your Past*. The workbook is divided into twelve units and each unit is broken into five days of work. Our group would meet once a week for twelve consecutive weeks to discuss each unit. This workbook is a powerful tool that only works if you are diligent in the process.

The very first time I took this class was approximately ten years earlier with the same facilitator. It was right before I married my now ex-husband, but we'll get to him soon enough. The first time I took this class, I thought to myself, *"I'm good. I don't really need this class."* My primary focus was getting married and making plans for our new life together. Needless to say, once again, I was distracted with my current relationship.

One night, while in class, a lady shared her story about coming home and finding her daughter lying in bed crying. She pulled back the covers to discover she had blood on her. Her husband had just raped her eight-year-old baby. I thought, *"This is way too much for me! My story is nothing compared to this. I don't need this class."* I don't think I finished the twelve weeks and I surely didn't work my workbook.

As a side note, you should never compare your story with someone else's. We all have been hurt to some degree, and we have all experienced some type of trauma. The enemy will use what he can to keep our eyes blinded. While going through pain, the evil one will make it seem so much worse than what it is. Furthermore, when we try to recover, he will diminish what happened as though it wasn't too terrible. I felt guilty as I heard that woman's story—guilty for even considering I needed to make peace with my past, a past which wasn't really "that bad." Don't fall for it. We all need to make peace with something unless we've already done so. Making peace is not a one-time event. It is an ongoing process.

"Making Peace" Class the Second Time

Let's travel back to the time shortly after the incident when my fiancé choked me. Let me remind you that it was before God delivered me; therefore, I was still addicted to alcohol and using prescription drugs. I wanted to make peace with my past, but my present was chock-full of dysfunction and distractions. I would like to say that I walked away from that relationship and never looked back. Suffice it to say, breaking all ties with him took several months. Although we were no longer living together, we were trying to work things out and trying to do it God's way. Our relationship was massively unhealthy and we were both still so broken. One day we were together and the next we weren't.

The relationship had me feeling like I was on a roller coaster ride and I was tired of riding it. I told the Lord, *"I just want to sit on the park bench and enjoy life without all the drama."* God showed me the analogy of, every time God gets me out of the relationship, that's me sitting on the park bench. Then my fiancé walks by smelling, talking, and looking good and, before you know it, we're walking hand-in-hand through the park. *"Life's good,"* I tell myself, but paying no attention that we are headed straight back to the roller coaster. We stand in line laughing and joking with each other. Happily in love, we sit down, buckle our seatbelts, and take off—that's when I decide I want to get off. Too late now! As I'm being slung to the right and to the left, I pleaded with God to get me off this thing. And He does, only for me to go right back.

Does any of this sound familiar in your life? The difference between my first time taking the *Making Peace* class and this time was my commitment. No matter what I was going through, I was staying committed to making class each week and I was working the workbook. Although, I must admit, it was very difficult. The workbook was bringing up stuff from childhood I had long since forgotten. I began to see how childhood issues I didn't think affected me was, in fact, impacting my life in tandem with my current relationship. One night after class, it was just me and Valerie, the facilitator. I said to her, *"I've never shared this with anybody before,"* and I poured out my story to her about the first time I remembered being molested.

I was between three or four years old and some guy was visiting our family home. I don't remember very much about him other than he was in a wheelchair. I don't know who he was or why he was at our house. At some point during his visit, he was out of his wheelchair sitting on the floor with me. While sitting with him, he put his hand down into my panties. When he stopped, I remembered vividly taking his hand and guiding it back down into my panties. I did not want him to stop.

Not too long after the man left our home, I told my mom and step-dad that the man in the wheelchair had his hands in my panties. There was something in me that knew this was wrong, his actions and mine. I told only what he had done, not my participation, and my step-dad took off after him. I didn't want this man to stop touching me. It felt good. I felt both wanted and loved. Adversely, it felt wrong, I felt dirty and shameful for wanting him to touch me. I also felt bad that I told on him because, I not only wanted him touching me, but I encouraged him to continue to touch me. But, as soon as he left, there was something in me that wanted to see him punished.

As I told my mom and step-dad, my step-dad became upset. As he stormed out the house, he said he was going to find him. At that moment, I remembered feeling love and a sense of protection from my parents. I don't remember whatever happened to him or if my dad even found him. I have no other memories of the rest of the story. Recalling this experience, however, brought up many more childhood memories which I wanted to stay hidden and buried. For example, learning how to masturbate at the age of seven. I clearly remember my age because of the hit song which had just been released in 1983 by Cyndi Lauper, "Girls Just Want to Have Fun."

I learned about masturbation while spending the night with a friend. God only knows how she knew, but it opened a door I wish for both of us it would have never been opened. We would sneak Playboy magazines which, eventually, led us to sexually experimenting with one another. As I started thinking back to my childhood, I realized it wasn't just her. My parents were friends with a couple who had a daughter around my age. When we would send time together, whatever we played, whether with Barbie dolls, house, or doctor, it was always sexual in nature.

A few years later, I started spending the night with a couple who was friends with my parents. This couple was older and didn't have any kids. Both he and she would molest me at different times. I never told on either one of them and I continued to go back to their home. Recalling all these memories was way too much for me. I shifted my focus back to making this dysfunctional relationship work. I tried sharing with my fiancé the things I had discovered about the molestation and the masturbation while taking this class. I thought it would help us become closer. I thought he would understand this was a portion of my issue with seeking attention from other men. I thought he would see I was really trying to get better. For me, for him, for us.

While sharing with him, he seemed to care and be concerned. He asked questions and I answered them truthfully. But then, when he became angry with me, the problem then became enduring him screaming insults at me about the intimate details I had shared with him. He used it to shame me, to add guilt to all that was already there. Talk about a hurt that can't be described! I continued to press in. *"Jesus, help me,"* was all I could say most nights and days as I tried my hardest to stay sober and complete my workbook. Most days, I would cry until nothing was left.

I finished my twelve weeks of the *Making Peace* class. I was very grateful to have had such an amazing support group while going through the childhood memories, the battle of letting go of the dysfunctional relationship, and wanting to be free from the addiction of alcohol. The class, along with the workbook, was so intense and painful. Numerous times, I wanted to quit, but I knew it was for my good. I also knew there was still a lot more work to be done.

Right after completing the class, during my "park bench" time (when we were apart), I started reading a book by Joyce Meyer, *Battlefield of the Mind*. This book was life changing for me and I highly suggest others reading it; you can also watch "Battlefield of the Mind" video teachings on YouTube. I began to understand that my thoughts and emotions were controlling my life. I had to think about what I was thinking about. I was told that, if I didn't control my emotions, my emotions would control me. Yes, this was my life story—I was controlled by my emotions. *"I can control them?"* I asked myself. I did not know this. I realize it sounds crazy, but I never knew there was such a thing. I found quotes which helped me fight the war against my own emotions such as:

"Emotions will tell you to go back even though experience has told you to break the toxic cycle and move forward."

"Feelings are like waves. You cannot stop them from coming but you can decide which ones to surf."

"When wrong people leave your life, right things will happen. Keep it moving."

I started writing things like these quotes and putting them all over the house. I found Scriptures which told me who I was in Christ. I would write them on index cards and read them throughout the day. By doing this, I was learning how to control my emotions. I was online daily, watching, reading and researching anything I thought would help me. With everything in me, I desperately wanted to stay off this roller coaster. *"Please Lord; keep me off the roller coaster!"*

Reflection Activity

Making peace with your past can be intensely tricky. What is lying open from your past from which you need to release yourself?

_____
_____
_____
_____
_____
_____
_____
_____

CHAPTER EIGHT

O Lord, I'm Codependent!

"You stop attracting certain people once you heal the parts of you that needed them."

One night, while spending time with the Lord, I was reminded of something I had read and highlighted in my *Making Peace with My Past* workbook. I quickly picked it up and flipped through the pages to find the section that I had not only highlighted, but around it I had drawn a whole bunch of stars. It was a small paragraph explaining codependency. I read over it again as if reading it the first time. I felt an excitement on the inside of me and I sat at the computer and typed "codependent relationships."

I was planted in front of the computer for hours. The more I read, the more I knew this was it. This was the place which had the strongest hold on my life. This was God answering my question from the night I fell to my knees and cried out, *"God what is wrong with me that I continue to attract these types of men?"* Suddenly, I became aware I was codependent. I was excited, yep excited! I was thrilled about the newfound revelation. For the first time ever, I was able to understand why and how I had become this way. I was elated because I knew God was going to set me free from this thing. I knew he was going to deliver me just like

He did with drugs and alcohol. I spent countless nights up late. Some nights I didn't even go to sleep. I was so engulfed reading about codependency that I ordered every book I could find on the subject.

I found it intriguing that some research suggests that people who have been abused, in any capacity, and/or neglected in their youth, are more likely to enter codependent relationships. However, anyone at any time can become codependent. Codependency is an emotional and behavioral condition which affects our ability to have a healthy, mutually satisfying relationship. It's when we love someone so much that we ignore our own personal well-being.

For me, "codependent" meant I was dependent on the approval of a man for my self-worth and identity. My sense of purpose in life was wrapped up in pleasing and taking care of the person with whom I was in a relationship at that time. I also had an unhealthy clinginess to this person as I would feel lost when I wasn't in their presence.

Additionally, when I wasn't with them, I would be worried they were cheating or they were going to leave me altogether. I would have separation anxiety when we weren't together. I needed to make sure I knew where they were and what they were doing at all times. I was dependent on their love and affection for my own fulfillment. As a side note, codependent relationships are not always abusive nor are they exclusively between romantic relationships. It can be between a parent and child, teacher and student, employee and employer, and so on. It can potentially be any relationship in which we seek to please and care for a person when, all the while, how we feel about ourselves is determined by how they feel about us.

If we are validated by this person on whom we are dependent, we may feel good or proud about ourselves. If, on the other hand, that person expresses they are not pleased with something we have said or done, we take it to heart. We feel like a failure and begin to feel badly about ourselves. One key sign someone is in a codependent relationship is when their sense of purpose in life is wrapped up in making extreme sacrifices so as to satisfy the other person's needs.

All the information I was discovering was bringing much healing and understanding. I was gaining strength. God was showing me that the only person upon whom I needed to be dependent was Him. One of the books which helped me the most was *Codependent No More* authored by Melody Beattie. I recommend this to others who are possibly codependent. As I read, I felt as though someone was in my head articulating my thoughts, feelings, and struggles. The more I read, the more I felt the chains being broken. I thought loving someone, even when it hurt, was doing the "Christian thing." I based that idea on Matthew 22:39 which states, *"We are to love our neighbor as ourselves."*

I thought that, by staying in these kinds of relationships, I was properly "loving my neighbor." And what about the passages which teach us to forgive and be kind to others as in Ephesians 4:31-32? It instructs us to, *"get rid of all bitterness, rage, anger, brawling and slander, along with every form of malice. Be kind and compassionate to one another, forgiving each other, just as in Christ God forgave you."* I would read Scriptures like this and feel guilty for getting angry when treated wrongly. I was not being kind, compassionate, loving or forgiving. I needed to love more and forgive more. Now I understand I was trying to give what I didn't have—that thing called love. I had no clue how to love myself, much less someone else. And how could I possibly get from others what they didn't have to reciprocate? Love doesn't tear down. Love builds up.

We Attract What We Are

When we're broken, we attract broken people. Two broken people do not equal wholeness. Broken people produce broken children. Just for the record, every relationship I was ever in was never in the plans of God for my life (Jeremiah 29:11-13). These were relationships I chose. Also, for the record, I chose to ignore all the warning signs.

The world tells us that, in order to heal our life, we just need to think positively—positive in, positive out. It is a lie. We need so much more than just positive thinking. We need healing and deliverance from the strongholds the enemy has created in our minds; healing from the bad things which happened to us and the lies we have believed about ourselves. We need God's Word and a determination in our hearts to want to be set free. We need willingness to do whatever it requires so as to live that freedom. The woman with the issue of blood is an excellent example of such a "want to."

Psalm 119:105 states, *"Your word is a lamp to my feet and a light to my path."* We need the light of God's Word to guide us and to expose the darkness. By default, any time we remove light, darkness prevails. Growing up, I didn't have the light of God's Word so, by default, darkness prevailed. My parents didn't have the light of God's Word when they were growing up. In turn, darkness prevailed.

Ed Hardy came out with a perfume called *"Love Kills Slowly."* Not only was this my favorite scent, but it was one of my most quoted sayings. I had home decor with Ed Hardy's design, *"Love Kills Slowly"* with skulls and bright colors. I had his logo on my phone case and, at one time, it was my Facebook profile picture. Love kills slowly. With all my heart, I believed this was a true statement. What I thought to be love was killing me slowly. Every man I had ever met took something from me, used me, and/or abused me, sometimes, all three simultaneously. I was slowly dying inside.

Then, I was told about God's love and how very different it was. I was told to read 1st Corinthians 13:4-8 which speaks about God's love and what it truly means. I began to pray to experience this kind of love, God's love. The more I prayed this and the more I read about God's love, something started happening on the inside. I began to realize God's love was the very thing that was bringing real life to my dead existence. Love wasn't killing me slowly, I was. I was killing myself slowly through the choices I had made, the circumstances I created, and the lies I had accepted as truth. My distorted view of love was destroying me. God's love was causing me to live.

I began to clean my house. I got rid of all the Ed Hardy stuff. I even threw away my favorite and expensive perfume. It went along with everything else I thought was a hindrance to my new walk with Christ. I was getting stronger on the inside with each passing day. My pastor used to say, *"What you feed grows. What you starve dies."* As I continued to feed my spirit-man, I became internally stronger. I was getting more and more confident in the Lord. My spirit-man had been deprived all these years. I couldn't get enough.

Oh, don't get me wrong. I was still going through, still trying to break free from the dysfunctional relationship. Nevertheless, I was getting stronger and saying "no" came a little faster. Not falling for the temptation to go back into toxic relationships was getting easier. I was on a journey from being a woman who loves someone else so much it hurts into being a woman who loves herself enough to stop the pain. I was on my way to being codependent no more.

Reflection Activity

Do you feel as if you have any codependent tendencies? Read the list and see if you can identify with any of these statements:

1. Difficulty making decision in a relationship

2. Difficulty identifying your feelings

3. Difficulty communicating within a relationship

4. Value the approval of others more than valuing yourself

5. Lack of trust in yourself and having poor self-esteem

6. Fears of abandonment or an obsessive need for approval

7. Unhealthy dependence on relationships at your own cost

8. Exaggerated sense of responsibility for the actions of others

Whether you can identify with one or all of these, here are some tools from which you can, hopefully, benefit:

Practice self-care. Too often, we lose sight of ourselves, especially in codependent relationship because the majority of our time and energy trying to fix the other person. To move forward and create healthier relationships, it will be important for you to take time to explore yourself. Explore your likes, dislikes, needs, desires, thoughts, and feelings. It will be detrimental if you do not take the time to understand what you need from a relationship. If you do not take the time, you will slip back into the pattern of taking care of someone else.

Take a moment to add your thoughts here:

Practice being alone. The most powerful, yet hardest, thing for me was learning to be content with being alone – it was worse than fearing it! Share your thoughts:

Set realistic expectations. If you have unrealistic expectations on your relationships, you will be let down. Expecting someone else to fulfill you is only setting yourself up for heartbreak. Learn to set realistic expectations. Share your thoughts:

_____

_____

_____

_____

_____

_____

Practice setting boundaries. It is important to learn how to say "no" to people or situations that are not healthy. Saying "no" does not mean you are being selfish or disrespectful. It means you are looking out for your well-being. Share your thoughts:

_____

_____

_____

_____

_____

_____

_____

Make peace with your past. Though painful and uncomfortable, it is most necessary in order for you to be able to move forward. Share your thoughts:

CHAPTER NINE

Addicted to Love

"In the end, we all just want someone that chooses us over everyone else, under any circumstances."

In 1985, Robert Palmer had a hit song entitled *"Addicted to Love."* I never imagined this was a real thing; I just thought it was a cool song, one with which I loved to sing along. Who would have thought being "addicted to love" was real? Research suggests that those who are codependent fall into such an addiction, also known as "relationship addiction." People with codependency often form and maintain relationships which are one-sided, emotionally destructive, and/or abusive.

Have you ever heard the statement, *"Women who stay in abusive relationships like being abused"*? It is the stupidest statement I have ever heard. No person *likes* getting abused. I've been asked, *"Why don't you just leave?"* That's like telling an alcoholic to *"just stop drinking."* There is a stronger and deeper force at work in the lives of these individuals. Codependency and love addiction are much like an addiction to drugs and alcohol.

If you have never experienced any type of addiction, it may be difficult to understand. My prayer is that, as you read, you will become more aware of what life is like for someone who is codependent and/or has a relationship addiction. The first step to changing unhealthy behavior is to understand it. When we gain understanding, it gives us hope for victory and teaches us how to fight for freedom, either for ourselves or for others.

Speaking from my personal experience of being codependent, at the core of my behavior, existed a refusal to acknowledge I had a problem. I thought my love, concern, and affection was enough to cause the man—whomever he was at any given time—to change. I believed my needs should have been sacrificed for his regardless of the negative consequences. Repeatedly, I would find myself stuck in relationships which were extremely unhealthy, destructive, and often abusive. If not physically, they were emotionally and mentally abusive.

Love addiction, aka relationship addiction, is a compulsive, chronic craving and/or pursuit of romantic love in an effort to get our sense of security and worth from another person. During infatuation, we believe we have that security only to be disappointed and empty again once the intensity fades. The negative consequences can be severe, yet we continue to hang on to the belief that true love will fix everything. The causes of love addiction could include, but certainly are not limited to:

1. Inadequate or inconsistent nurturing
2. Low self-esteem
3. Absence of positive role models for committed relationships
4. Indoctrination with cultural images of perfect romantic love and happily-ever-after endings

Those who have been molested and/or abused during childhood are likely to become codependent, leading to having an addiction to love. Looking back at my childhood, I was a prime target for both codependency and relationship addiction. Pretty much all the above applied to me. Not only was I molested at a very young age, I had no self-esteem and I was indoctrinated with cultural images of perfect romantic love. My understanding of love was based off *Playboy* magazines, secular music videos, and romantic movies which portrayed sex and living happily ever after.

I'm not sure how old I was the first time I found the forbidden cabinet full of *Playboy* magazines. I would sneak them one at a time and hide in my closet as I flipped through each page, soaking in the vivid details. To this day, I can still recall the images from those pages. It is as if they were forever branded in my memory no matter how hard I tried to forget them. I spent most of my time watching music videos and listening to music with sexual content such as Vanity 6, Prince, Madonna, and more. At the time, I had no idea it was sexually explicit. I simply liked the music and it was what everyone else was listening to.

I remember thinking very early that, if I could just look a certain way or act a certain way, I would get a man to love me. I wanted to be just like the women in the magazines, the music videos, and the movies. As I was writing this, I was reminded of my favorite music album from that era, Vanity 6's "Nasty Girl." The album was released in 1982 when I was six years old. As I pulled up the lyrics to quote, I decided not to do so because they were too explicit.

I can recall that, when this album was released, I begged my mother to buy the cassette tape for me. She had no idea what kind of music it was. If she would buy it, I promised to keep my room clean and do all my chores. My mother, being assured by my older sister it was appropriate, bought it for me. So, at six years old, I was not only singing the lyrics, but they were shaping my thoughts and destiny.

Just as the images from the *Playboy* magazines were branded in my mind, so were the lyrics to this song and worse. What we watch and that to which we listen affects what we do and who we become. Take, for instance, my favorite movie growing up, *Pretty*

Woman, a 1990's romantic film. A prostitute is hired by a wealthy businessman to spend the weekend with him; they end up falling in love and living happily ever after. Oh, how I wanted to be just like Julia Roberts who played the prostitute in this hit movie! If only I could have had curves like her, breasts, hair, lips, then I too could find a rich man to love me and take care of me. Again, what we entertain shapes our thoughts and imaginations. The ideas we entertain in our imagination, the things we think about, becomes who we are.

Proverbs 4:23 says, *"Above all else, guard your heart, for everything you do flows from it."* Most places in the Bible, when the writer uses the word "heart", it's referring to our mind. It could read, *"Guard your mind, for everything you do flows from it."* Always remember, the mind is where the real battle takes place and, I assure you, the enemy wants to influence and control our minds. We must never underestimate the power of what we allow into the gates of our eyes—what we watch or entertain—and the gates of our ears—that to which we listen—because it influences our destiny and it shapes our identity.

Proverbs 23:7 states, *"For as he thinks within himself, so is he."* I have no memory of wanting to be Cinderella, a ballerina, or a princess as a young child. I wanted to be a sexy waitress in a bar or a dancer in a club; therefore, I spent hours behind a locked door, playing dress up listening to Vanity 6 and mimicking those I wanted to be like. All these things, the magazines, the music and the movies, were influencing my life. They were shaping my desires and destiny, albeit, I had no idea that was happening. I was being indoctrinated with lies and deception. All these things portrayed women as sexual objects, but it was conveying to me, at a very young age that, if I looked

IN CHRIST, I WAS ALREADY LOVED, TREASURED, VALUED, AND ACCEPTED.

a certain way, acted a certain way, and performed a certain way, then and only then, would I find true love. I would be treasured, valued, and accepted.

What I so desired to be and do was the very opposite of who God had created me to be. In Christ, I was already loved, treasured, valued, and accepted. Unfortunately, it would take many years before I understood that.

Reflection Activity

Share your personal thoughts after reading this chapter:

_____

_____

_____

_____

_____

As you read the questions below, examine your relationship patterns.

1. Could you be addicted to love?
2. When you're not in a relationship, do you feel desperate and alone?
3. Do you find it unbearable or emotionally difficult to be alone?

4. When you are not in a relationship, do you find yourself craving and searching for a romantic relationship?

5. When in a relationship, do you find yourself being desperate to please the other person and fearful of rejection or abandonment?

The partners you attract

6. Are the partners you attract emotionally unavailable and/or verbally or physically abusive?

7. With the partners you attract, are they demand a great deal of your time, attention, and caretaking yet do not meet your mental, emotional, or physical needs?

Being addicted to love causes one to search for something outside themselves so as to find significance. Whether it be in a person, relationship, or sexual experience. Share your thought below about any or all of these questions:

_____

_____

_____

_____

_____

CHAPTER TEN

Hoarders Buried Alive

"Hoarding can destroy the lives of the person afflicted and their loved ones."

In all my research, I found two books which stood out the most during my journey. These two books brought so much understanding, healing, and deliverance from love addiction. The first one was *Women Who Love Too Much* by Robin Norwood. The second was *How to Break Your Addiction to a Person* by Howard Halpern. Literally, I was addicted to men just like I was addicted to drugs and alcohol. I was chasing this imaginary high. I would leave one dysfunctional relationship and get right back into another. I didn't understand why this current relationship was so much harder than all the others from which to break free. In the book, *How to Break Your Addiction to a Person*, I was able to plainly understand.

With each man, it was like a new drug. Normally, people who use drugs don't just start using a hard drug. For instance, most people don't just start smoking crack. They may start with pills, then marijuana, then cocaine, and then crack. This current relationship was like crack and, by no means, do I say that lightly. I've smoked crack before so I know what it's like and how addictive it is. It's nothing like pills, marijuana, or cocaine, all of which I've used at some point in my life. Drugs such as the aforementioned are way more addictive and destructive. Needless to say, this relationship was far worse than any previous relationship.

My biggest take-away from that book was to write a relationship log. There, I was to include why we shouldn't be together. It included events, in detail, that happened such as infidelity, physical, mental, and verbal abuse, etc. When I started feeling withdrawals of loneliness or wanting to go back, I was to get out the relationship log and read through all the reasons why I shouldn't go back. Man, was that powerful for me!

It was a very long and painful process. So many times, I wanted to give up or give in. I can't tell you how many times I had to read that log. Some days, I had to read it multiple times because the feelings of wanting to go back were intense. I would like to tell you this process was quick and easy, but it took several months to break free from that relationship. As I stated previously, in the beginning of this breaking free process, we would talk about getting back together. We would then start spending short amounts of time together which would, once again, open the door to sex. This was that roller coaster ride on which I was always finding myself.

Attending the same church was a huge distraction for me and it certainly made it much harder to let go. The Sundays he did come, I was distracted by his presence and, the Sundays he didn't show up, I couldn't focus on the message for door-watching just waiting for him to walk through. Although we weren't having sex often, when we did, it created this false sense of hope and security for me. I felt wanted, loved, and valued, but afterwards, I would feel used, disappointed, and ashamed. He only wanted sex—I wanted a commitment. Although he was saying he wanted us to be together, his actions always told a much different story. In my mind, when we would have sex, we were back together.

With this false sense of "togetherness," I would immediately become clingy and controlling. I didn't want to be apart from him. I wanted to constantly be in his presence. And when that wasn't possible, I wanted to know where he was, what he was doing, and with whom he was doing it. After a few months of us being apart, he invited me to his house one Friday night. He said he wanted to cook dinner for me and talk about us. I agreed, although everything inside me was screaming not to go. We had dinner and talked. Predominantly, it was him doing the talking. He told me how time apart had helped him prioritize and he wanted to try and make things work between us. I felt all the strength leaving my body. I knew I should not have been there. I wasn't strong enough. I wanted so desperately to believe him, to trust him.

I told myself that, maybe, God had changed him. We ended up sleeping together and, afterwards, I felt horrible all over again. I had let myself down and, more importantly, I felt as though I had let God down. Nevertheless, a part of me was still praying God would bless this relationship. Besides, we had heard countless testimonies of relationships like ours God had restored. I was back on the rollercoaster; it would only be hours before I started repenting and begging God to get me off the cycle again for the umpteenth time.

After all that pillow-talk of how he loved me and wanted to be together, the following Sunday he showed up at church with another girl. I could not believe what I was seeing. So many emotions were coursing through my brain. I felt numb and, as I continued to watch them, the way they were slightly touching each other during service, I became overwhelmed with anger. I was desperately fighting to stay focused. I went from wanting to get up to leave to wanting to get up and punch him in his throat! Thoughts of murder and suicide flooded my mind. Anger and rage tried to consume me. I felt as though I was drowning, and I had no one to save me. Looking back, I am so grateful that it happened at church. Had it been anywhere else, those thoughts and emotions could have easily overtaken me.

Needless to say, this was one of the events written in my relationship log. Sadly to say, the physical abuse wasn't what opened my eyes to finally letting him go—it was this incident. Eventually, he stopped going to that church altogether and it definitely helped me through the healing process. Every time I would see him, it felt like a wound was being ripped open. I was told he had joined another church and I was so thankful. I felt like I was finally in the healing process. It was crazy that, even after all that transpired, I had times where I wanted to go back. This is where the reading of that relationship log helped me stay off the rollercoaster and, eventually, out of the amusement park all together.

For the first time in my life, I was celibate. I never even dreamed that could be possible. I started having sex around the age of 12 and, from then on, I was with countless men. If I didn't have a boyfriend or a husband, I had someone with whom I was sleeping. This was my first time being completely alone and it did not feel good. There were nights I just cried. There were nights I had temper tantrums. I was angry at God. I felt abandoned and forgotten. I wanted desperately to hear God, to feel God, to see God. I wanted God to speak to me like He did when He was delivering me from the drugs and alcohol. But nothing. Just silence. No thoughts, no visions, no voice. It was as if God had abandoned me. That's how I felt.

I was told I must trust God even when I can't trace Him. I had to trust the process and press on. An important truth is that our relationship with God is *not* about feelings. It *is* about being anchored in His Word. He speaks to us through His Word. I had to get into the Bible and believe that, what I was reading, it was for me. I didn't hear Him because I wasn't listening the way He was speaking. His Word clearly says He will never leave nor forsake me. This is what fighting for my freedom looked like, allowing God's written Word to become my anchor. Finally, the chains which held me captive for so long were broken and I was delivered. I made it out. I survived.

If you're reading this and can see yourself, then you're a survivor too. You *can* make it out as well. With God's wisdom, knowledge, and understanding, you too can make it out. At long last, I was free. I was no longer codependent, no more drugs, no more alcohol, no more relationship addiction. In my mind, I felt like I was now ready for a relationship. One night, while meditating and praying, my conversation with God went something like this: *"God I want a husband. You have healed me and set me free. I'm good now."* I heard a laugh in my head and I knew it wasn't mine. The laugh I heard wasn't a sarcastic laugh. It was more like a tender-loving father laugh. I knew it was God and, immediately, I busted out crying and started having one of my 3-year old tantrums. *"You just don't want me to be married!"* I cried. In that moment, a vision came to me.

When I was a child, my mother would tell me to clean my messy room. *My* way of cleaning consisted of both clean and dirty clothes lumped together because I didn't feel like putting the clean ones away. As a result, in the dirty basket they went. I would shove stuff under the bed, throw stuff in the closet, hide stuff in the drawers, and pile stuff on top of the dresser. Then I would go and announce to my mother, "It's clean." When my mother walked in to check my room, it *looked* clean.

It had the appearance of being clean but, the reality was, it was far from clean. I don't know how my mother knew but, somehow, she did. She would get down on her knees and begin to pull out all the junk from under the bed. Next, she opened the closet and started pulling everything out that didn't belong. She would then dump all the contents of the dresser drawers in the middle of the floor and take her hand and knock all the stuff off the dresser onto the floor. After she was done, she would look at me and say, "Now, clean it up the right way," and walked out.

God was showing me I still had "stuff under the bed," junk hidden in the closet and dresser. Although I appeared clean, there was a lot more work which needed to be completed. Thankfully, I wouldn't have to do it alone. Right after that, I got another vision. This one was of the reality TV show "Hoarders, Buried Alive." God was showing me that being set free from the drugs, alcohol, and men was just so He could get in the door of my house. God was letting me know that my addiction to drugs, men, shopping, alcohol, and a lot of other things, was just surface issues.

There was still so much more to deal with, to uncover, to clean out, and to get rid of. Yes, I was delivered, but still I was very damaged. Residue from my past remained. I still had behaviors and habits that needed to be broken. I still had an old mindset that needed to be renewed. My identity needed to be restored. I needed to know who I was and how valuable I truly was. As for me, the process continued. I had to get to the root of the problem so, back to making peace with my past I had to go.

Reflection Activity

How does this make you feel? Are you a metaphoric hoarder? Can you see similarities in your own life?

_____
_____
_____
_____
_____
_____
_____
_____
_____

CHAPTER ELEVEN
New Negative Labels

"What we don't deal with has a way of dealing with us."

I committed to taking another twelve weeks of the *Making Peace with Your Past* class. This time around, I was delivered from the aforementioned. I was no longer codependent, nor was I addicted to love. I was okay with being single. My self-esteem was being built up in Christ as He was teaching me who I was in Him. It was just me and the Lord, no distractions. I was focused, determined, and I was totally committed. The picture of my so-called "clean room" kept coming to mind and I was finally ready to take on the task of cleaning it correctly. I worked the workbook. I spent time saying my affirmations as well as meditating on the Scripture focus. I continually prayed for the members of my current support group, all of which is outlined in the workbook.

Unit one was about discovering self-esteem, along with understanding the characteristics of a dysfunctional family. Allow me to reiterate that, no matter how awesome our family is or isn't, we all have some type of family dysfunction. Remember, the enemy's job is to steal, kill, and destroy as stated in John 10:10; therefore, the enemy will use any and everything he can to do just that. He will cause us to feel and think about things which may not actually be true. That which is bad, he will use to intensify the pain and hurt we have experienced. Regardless of how we were raised—good home, great home, bad home or horrible home—he will use it to his advantage. Satan will highlight hurtful events in childhood, no matter what it was, in order to plant seeds of doubt, fear, and insecurity. He will use manipulation and deception so as to inflict more pain. He will use what he can to feed us lies, which eventually become our truth *if* we allow it.

As an additional thought, I would be envious of people who were raised in a Christian home, those who had a foundation built on Jesus and His love. In my mind, they had this perfect life about which I could only dream. One day, God allowed me to hear a testimony from a young man that I assumed had a perfect life because of his Christian upbringing. His parents loved the Lord and each other very much. This young man said that, growing up, he and his siblings were nurtured in the love of God. They were deeply caring and it was evident to those around them they were loved. His parents lived the Christian life to the best of their ability.

When this young man was around eight or nine, he got lost in the amusement park where the family was visiting. It took a while before anyone in his family realized he was even missing. He was scared and terrified as he frantically looked for his family. Eventually, he was reunited with the help of the park staff. After that vacation, his family would tease him about getting lost. They would say things like *"We didn't even miss you."* Both his parents and siblings used to tease him and make jokes about the incident. This caused the spirit of rejection and abandonment to set in. Did his parents or siblings abandon and reject him? Absolutely not, yet, because of the lies the enemy was telling him, in his mind, it became his truth. He said that every time he was teased about getting lost, the voices in his head confirmed what he was feeling—feelings he was not loved and no one cared about him. He felt unwanted and unvalued. Even as a grown man, he said the fear he felt on that day became real all over again every time the incident was brought up.

Unfortunately, this young man grew up and experienced many broken relationships full of hurt and pain because of his insecurities, fears, and doubts, all of which were seeds planted that day. He said it wasn't until he began to seek Jesus for healing and getting to the root of the problem that all the lies were exposed. The Lord showed him that, from that particular incident during childhood, he had allowed feelings of rejection and abandonment to become his truth. He said that, as he continued to stay in the process of allowing God to heal him, he was able to gain freedom as he filled his heart and mind with the truth of God's Word. *"Whom the Son sets free is free indeed," states* John 8:36. This is just a small example as to how the enemy works in our lives regardless of our upbringing.

One night in class, I was sharing about how rebellious I was growing up. I couldn't understand why I was so angry and rebellious. I was asked by Valerie to seek God so as to show me the root of my issues. The next several nights, I continued to ask God to reveal the core. While working my workbook, I felt prompted to get a piece of paper and begin to write a timeline of events in the order in which I remembered them.

I started writing things I hadn't even thought about until that point. I started this timeline with my birth and my parents' divorce, the first time I was molested at three or four years old, the exposure to alcohol, the Playboy magazines, being touched inappropriately by a family member at eight years old, learning to masturbate, the molestation by the husband and wife couple, and so on. Shortly after starting, I was awakened in my sleep and I heard, *"It happened."* Immediately, I knew what "it" was. Although I knew "it" happened, I was a little confused. I didn't realize then, but the Lord was exposing the root of my rebellion and anger. As I laid there thinking of the words "it happened," my mind took me back to that occurrence where I was eight and inappropriately touched by a close family member. Due to the nature of what happened and those involved, I choose not to go into intimate details of the event. I will, however, share this. We will call the unnamed culprit "XYZ."

I was eight when I felt XYZ run his hand just inside the top of my panties; I pretended to be asleep. Panic filled my mind. Fear tried to paralyze me. Still pretending to be asleep, I quickly rolled over onto my stomach to stop what was happening. It worked. XYZ stopped. I laid there for what seemed to be hours as my mind raced. *"Did that really just happen? Did I do something which suggested that type of behavior was okay?"* I asked myself. I began to feel guilty and blamed myself. Why didn't I say something when it happened instead of pretending to be asleep? The more I thought about it, the angrier at myself I became. The voices in my head shouted insults at me, *"This is your fault! You're nothing but a big punk. You should have said something! You should have confronted him in the moment!"*

I told someone in my family what happened and they reported it to the Department of Social Services (DSS). Then, something happened I did not want. A caseworker showed up to talk to me and my parents. I don't know why, but I felt so embarrassed and afraid. I was told XYZ was questioned as well. The next time XYZ saw me, he asked me, *"Did I really touch you like the caseworker had explained?"* I remembered being flooded with emotions. I became angry and then frightened as I mumbled, *"Yes."* I will never forget the look in his eyes. Such compassion and sincerity mixed with pain as he said, *"I'm sorry, if that did happen. I didn't know it was you."* To reiterate, the enemy will use whatever he can. Wordplay is one of his strategies. In my mind, I was like, *"What do you mean 'if' it happened?"*

I felt like I was being called a liar and that no one believed me. I immediately began to gravitate toward the one person who did believe me, the same person who called DSS. Whether or not she sincerely cared about me being touched, I'm not sure. What

I do know, looking back at the whole picture, is that she had an ill-will against XYZ and it wasn't at all about her concern for my well-being.

The devil began to use this person to whom I gravitated, as well as others, so as to intensify the situation, ultimately influencing my thoughts and behavior toward XYZ. Over the next several weeks and months after the incident, my emotions became uncontrollable. I felt abandoned, rejected, unloved, and unworthy. I had feelings of shame, guilt, anger, depression, and rage. I hated myself. I was to blame. I was so stupid and I was nothing but a punk for not speaking up in the moment. This is what my self-talk sounded like on a daily basis.

Because of my behavior, I was immediately placed into psychiatric counseling. I don't remember much about those sessions other than telling my counselor on several occasions that I just wanted to run away and live on Skid Row in California. This is where Guns N' Roses, my favorite rock group, lived. This was the dream of a very lost, disturbed, and broken little girl. The influence of the music to which I was listening wasn't helping either. All the counseling I received was from a secular standpoint and nothing spiritual was ever addressed.

I was told I was a victim, so *victim* became a label. I accepted it and used it as an excuse to act out. I was medicated with antidepressants, which made matters worse. I became suicidal and full of rage. At one point, I attempted to kill myself by taking a bunch of pills. I had to be taken to the hospital where my stomach was pumped—a truly horrible experience. I remember having to drink this chalky stuff which made me vomit and the nurse was so mean to me. What was the reason for my suicide attempt? An older guy at school, whom I liked, did *not* like me. Once again, I felt rejected and I was devastated. I wanted him to like me and, since he didn't, I didn't want to live anymore.

I was told I was depressed, yet another label I wore and another excuse I could use for my bad behavior. The cycle continued and it grew worse. Shortly after the molestation incident, I started sneaking beer out of the refrigerator and hiding in my room to drink. I'm sure this had a huge impact on my emotions and behavior as well. I would also take canned sodas and mix it with liquor. I didn't care too much for the taste of liquor, but I really liked the taste of beer, so I stole it the most.

Reflection Activity

Have you ever graduated out of old labels just to have more attached to you? Make a list of some new labels which are unkind:

_____
_____
_____
_____
_____
_____
_____

CHAPTER TWELVE

The Power of Friendships

"Mind playing tricks on me..." ~ Geto Boys

Once I entered middle school, I began hanging with the wrong crowd. They were always much older than I. I often lied about my age telling people I was years older than I really was. I started cutting myself and writing dark poetry about death. I became obsessed with rock music, which intensified my anger and rage. I hated being home and I was always looking for ways to get out of the house. My mom had to confirm with my friend's parent where I could and could not go. That made me mad. I started hanging around a young girl in one of my classes. We'll call her "Stacy." I was only allowed to spend the night with her after her mom had met my parents. The times I was allowed, Stacy and I were left in the care of her older brother and his friends while her mom was out. I'm not sure where her mom was, I just know she wasn't home with us. We were both exposed to and started experimenting with popping pills and smoking marijuana in addition to drinking alcohol.

I was ten years old in elementary school when I was introduced to my first hard drug—powder cocaine. Stacy and I were hanging out at the skating rink, like we did most weekends, and one of the older guys gave us powder cocaine to try. School was such a struggle for me as I felt so stupid. I had no clue as to what was being taught. I felt dumb and kids would pick on me and call me "slow." I would act out so as to get sent to the office. I spent most of my time in detention hall. Collecting D-notes—disciplinary notes—was a game to me. The more I had, the cooler I thought I was. So long as I was getting in trouble, the less focus there was on my learning disability. I believe it was dyslexia, though I was never diagnosed. Even as an adult, I currently struggle with symptoms of dyslexia.

On the bus, I was being bullied by some older black kids, so I would purposely miss the bus so that my parents had to take me to school. That would only make my parents mad and caused added friction between us. Finally, I started skipping school altogether. My parents didn't know what to do for or with me. Eventually, I was put on probation for truancy, a fancy word for cutting school. I had an amazing probation officer who really cared about me. She would share words of wisdom with me, although, at the time, I wasn't trying to hear any of it.

"*Show me your friends and I'll show you your future*," I was told. I didn't understand what that meant, but I was sure to find out the hard way. She was a woman of faith and believed in Jesus. She made it well known and she was a praying woman. She not only tried her best to help me, but also she and my mother became really close. God moved through her during a very difficult time so as to encourage and give hope to my mom. To me, she was just another adult trying to control my life and I wasn't going for it. I wasn't going to let anyone control me or tell me what to do.

I thought I knew it all and that I was in control. I ignored the rules of my probation and continued to cut school, drink alcohol, use drugs, and be disrespectful to anyone who tried to force any type of rules on me. I ended up having to go back to court. I tried to act all tough on the outside but, on the inside, I was scared. My probation officer said they would, more than likely, extend my probation time and I would most likely have to do community service. Ultimately, it would be up to the judge to decide. As the judge heard my case, he asked if anyone else had anything to say. That's when my mother stood up and said, *"Yes sir, I do."*

She started telling the judge how out of control I was and that she and my dad couldn't do anything with me. As she was talking, I felt rage like I had never felt before. The judge looked at me and said *"Well, young lady, since you have a problem following the rules and submitting to authority, I am sending you to the department of juvenile justice for the next forty-five days."* You would have thought he said forty-five years the way I reacted. In my mind, it was her fault. If only she would have kept her big mouth shut. Rage filled me from head to toe. I wanted to kill her. With all my heart, I really believed that, if I could have gotten to her in that court room that day, I would have done just that—killed her dead.

That was the longest forty-five days of my life and it was unbearable. That place was beyond disgusting and unsanitary. I had absolutely no privacy. The bathroom stalls didn't even have doors. We were all required to take showers together, which was terribly embarrassing and degrading. My cell smelled horribly. I would complain to the officers almost daily. The smell was so bad it would make me nauseated. One day, during a mandatory shakedown to look for contraband, the source of the smell was discovered. My cellmate was placing her bloody pads under her mattress. As if that wasn't bad enough, I ended up contracting crabs because of the filthiness of the facility. That place was terrible and it was a place I definitely never wanted to return.

Faithfully, my mother would come to visit every weekend and she would always bring me outside food, which was only allowed during visits. You might think I would have been grateful for the visits and the food, but I wasn't. I still had so much anger and resentment against her. I blamed her for where I was and for every bad thing that transpired while there. It was all her fault.

At the conclusion of my forty-five days, I was released. I refused to go home and, in turn, was placed in a runaway shelter called *The Hope House*. This was the place where I met my best friend, Heather Pounds. We quickly became friends while sharing a room at *The Hope House*. We knew a lot of the same people from the streets and remained friends after leaving. After my time was up, I was sent back home. I continued to act out in rebellion, hang out with the wrong crowd, and began drinking and using drugs again. Seeing where this was going, my parents quickly had me committed to the state hospital for evaluation.

Now I was labeled "crazy." Once inside, I quickly learned how to manipulate the system. If I acted out uncontrollably, they would escort me to one of those padded rooms and, once inside, if I continued to act out, they would come give me one of the "feel good" shots in my butt. So, guess what I did? I acted out consistently. I don't remember any of the mandatory, daily counseling sessions. I just wanted to be in that padded room; besides, I was "crazy." Why not act crazy since that was my label?

I am not sure how long I was there but, I do remember the day I left. I was told my biological father had come to pick me up. I was filled with excitement that my real dad had come to rescue me, or that's what I thought. He picked me up and told me I was coming to live with him. I was so excited! Finally, someone to love me. *"See,"* I told myself, *"he really does care about me."* I had never been close to my biological dad. From the time of early childhood, I have memories of feeling rejected, unwanted, and unloved.

Even being around his side of the family, I never felt like I was good enough. I never felt like I belonged or that I was worthy enough to be part of his family. No one ever said that to me, it was just how I felt. My dad was neither an affectionate man nor was anyone in his family. There were never any hugs or words of *"I love you."* No birthday parties or grandparent's days at school. Everyone on my dad's side of the family, including my dad, seemed very distant, cold, stern, and unaffectionate. I thought something was wrong with me. I took it as rejection and it created a sense of unworthiness at a very early age.

I was just a little girl when my biological father started voicing his concern about my weight. He would tell me, repeatedly, that I was going to be fat just like my mother and my sister if I didn't watch what I ate. This created such a fear in me very early. I remember feeling so afraid of eating in front of him. I could eat an apple and feel as if I were eating a box of Little Debbie snack cakes. I felt like, no matter what I ate, he would warn me about getting fat. Instead of eating in front of him, I would hide food and eat it when he wasn't around.

Growing up, I referred to my stepdad as "dad." He and my mother married when I was less than a year old. My real dad remarried and had another child. Oh, how I dearly loved my little brother, but I was so jealous of him! I was jealous of the way my dad treated him because, in my mind, he loved my little brother and not me. In my thought process, my little brother got all the attention which I so desperately wanted from Dad. It left me feeling as though I wasn't good enough, smart enough, or pretty enough. Those were my thoughts and feelings, which became my truth; they were not necessarily the actual truth.

I felt like, *"Wow, NOW my real dad was coming to rescue me,"* but my excitement about being rescued quickly changed. I realized the love and acceptance I so desperately desired from him was not a reality. He was still that cold, unaffectionate, and distant man he had always been. Moving in with him, I had to change schools. I made new friends and I wasn't using drugs or drinking that much, other than the wine I would sneak from the refrigerator from time to time. Wine and liquor was not my thing. My first year of high school at my new school was when I lost my virginity. I started dating a guy at my school who was much older than I. He had his own car, so he would come see me when my dad wasn't home.

I continued to feel rejected by my biological father. A couple of events happened which caused me to no longer want to live there, so I made plans to run away with a group of friends. We were only gone about three days before we were caught. My dad was furious that he had to drive to Aiken, South Carolina to pick me up; it is approximately 45 minutes to an hour away from where we lived. He drove me straight to my mother's house, knocked on the door and, when my mom opened the door, he said, *"Here is your child,"* and got in his car and drove away. One more time, I had to change schools.

My first day of the new high school, I met the coolest girl ever; we'll call her "Buffy." We quickly became best friends. Our moms met and I was allowed to spend the night. As protective as my mother tried to be, she still had no idea of the things I was doing or what I was becoming. What my mom didn't know was, Buffy's mom had a drug addiction and she was never home, although she would make up all kinds of stories as to what we were going to do while I was at their house.

For instance, I remember one weekend she told my mom she was taking us to the beach for the weekend. She dropped us off at home and we didn't see her until Sunday evening. She would tell my mom whatever she wanted to hear so that I could stay with them. Even when she was home, she let us do whatever we wanted. We would drink alcohol, have boys over, and smoke weed. Her mom was dating a drug dealer and he was the one who would give us weed. One night, unbeknownst to us, he put crack cocaine in our weed. You'd better believe we knew as soon as we smoked it!

Us being so young and naïve, we had no idea this is how drug dealers would get people hooked. This was someone we thought we could trust and it was a hard lesson to learn. After that incident, I started smoking crack, although Buffy didn't know it. When she found out I had been smoking, she told me she wasn't going to be my friend anymore unless I stopped. Her friendship was everything to me. As crazy as it sounds, I stopped and I never wanted to do it again. Looking back, I know it was nothing but God. He used the power of our friendship to save me. Only the Lord knows where the enemy would have taken me in that addiction. Surely death or incarceration would have been my destiny.

Reflection Activity

Take a moment to ponder the friendships of your life. Which have been beneficial, healthy, and good? Which have been negative, unhealthy, and bad?

CHAPTER THIRTEEN

Men and Children

"Self-pity is easily the most destructive of the non-pharmaceutical narcotics; it is addictive, gives momentary pleasure and separates the victim from reality."
~ John Gardner

With my first physically abusive relationship, I was only fifteen and dating a much older man. To this day, I don't know how my mother knew it. It just so happened that she was coming to get me from this place I was staying, and she showed up with the police. She had no idea I was being abused. I don't know why she thought to have the police escort her, but I am so very thankful she did. I didn't tell her, at the time, and it was years after I was grown before I shared the fact that, when they arrived, I was seconds from being raped. I had a kidney infection and I was in so much pain. My abuser didn't care. He had needs to be met. He told me that, since I couldn't have sex, he was going to have anal sex with me. I was terrified as I was fighting to keep my pants up. That's the moment the police knocked on the door and announced themselves. I have never been so happy to see the police and my mother as I was that day!

I started attending and living on the campus of Wil Lou Gray Opportunity School. My abuser began to come to the school stalking me. One day, while standing outside talking to a group of friends, he came out of nowhere and slapped me to the ground. I was so humiliated, embarrassed, and scared. Soon after that, my mother got me enrolled into Job Corps in Morganfield, Kentucky. I was thankful to get away from this man. I spent the next few years attending Job Corps where I attained my General Equivalency Development—GED—and a job skill.

Initially, I hated Job Corps and I called home crying every day. It didn't help that, the first week I was there, someone stole all my money and personal items. My mother encouraged me to hang in there. In her mind, I'm sure she was thinking there was no way she was going to allow me to come back home after all the things I had put them through. I honestly can't say I blame her. I was a selfish, angry, rebellious teenager with no direction, concern, or care for anyone else.

I soon got adjusted and started to enjoy it. It was like living on a college campus. Everything we needed was right at our fingertips, including a bowling alley and movie theater. My best friend, Buffy, joined me after she graduated high school. Heather, whom I met at the runaway shelter years earlier, came as well. We were having a ball. Although we had authority and rules to which we submitted, we found ways to sneak to do the things we wanted. We would sneak out of our dorms on the weekend so as to drink, smoke weed, and have sex with our boyfriends. We did the things we were required to do, but we found ways to get around the rules.

Heather left Job Corps before me and went back home. Shortly thereafter, she called to tell me she was pregnant. Buffy and I graduated from Job Corps in the following weeks. For graduation, my mom and stepdad surprised me with a used car they had fixed up for me and I was very grateful. Shortly after returning home, I contacted Heather who was living in a one-bedroom apartment for which her grandmother was paying. Although my relationship with my parents had gotten better while I was away, I did not want to live with them. I moved in with Heather and her small baby.

Heather's tiny one-bedroom apartment was the party spot. We had all kinds of people in and out, drinking and smoking weed. We both attained fake I.D.'s so we could get into the clubs and hang out with our much older friends. You couldn't tell us anything—we were living the life. When I left for Job Corp, smoking weed was a common thing. When I got home from Job Corps, all my weed-smoking friends had started snorting powder cocaine. Remembering my experience at ten years old in the skating rink bathroom, I was like, "*No thank you!*"

That quickly changed as I began doing it privately and then with friends. This became my drug of choice. In the midst of all the partying, drugs and alcohol, I started working. Heather and I started falling out with each other and I decided it was time to find a place of my own. I was doing well for myself, my own job, car, place to live, etc. Working, partying, drinking, sex, and drugs were my life and I didn't see anything wrong with the way I was living. Besides, I was being responsible, which justified my lifestyle and choices. As I saw it, at least I wasn't some bum on the street. I was the one in control.

I became pregnant with my first child at the age of eighteen. I met her father when I was fourteen. He was much older than me and I was crazy about him, or more like infatuated with him. I had dreams of us getting married and having a family together. When I got my own place, he spent a lot of nights with me. In my mind, we were living together, even though all he'd really do is use my house as a crashing pad after he left the club. It was convenient for him to stay with me rather than going home and waking his mother in the middle of the night. I lived in a fantasy world, ignoring the reality of my situation. I had no clue how to be a mother—what was I going to do with a baby? She was just a month old and I was already leaving her with a babysitter so I could go to the club.

Our daughter, Jazmine, was only two and a half years old when her dad, Joe, died of a cancerous brain tumor. His death sent me into a very dark place. I used his death as an excuse to go deeper into my drug and alcohol use. *"Poor me, I just lost my child's father."* I went from using cocaine and alcohol on the weekends to using almost daily. After an all-nighter in the club, I couldn't sleep. I called one of my male friends to come and get me so I wouldn't be alone. By this time, Jazmine's grandmother had dropped her off so she could go to work.

When my friend arrived, I told him I couldn't go because I had my daughter with me; he assured me it was okay. He said that where we were going, those people had a daughter around the same age and she would be fine. I agreed. I was still high and I didn't want to be alone. Shortly after arriving, my homeboy told me that he and the guy who lived at the house were going to make a "drop" and they would be right back.

My daughter and I were left at this house with the guy's wife and their small child. After an hour or so, I started getting worried that something had happened. The wife assured me they were fine and that they were probably spending the money since the drop was at the mall. Not long after that, Richland County Police Department busted down the door, guns pointed straight at us and told us to get our hands up. I was scared to death and Jazmine became hysterical while screaming, *"My mommy didn't do anything!"* over and over again. I got sober real quick. I can't explain the fear that gripped me.

As they searched the house, they began pulling out dope like I had never seen before. I knew this was it for me. I was going to jail and I was going to lose my daughter. *"I should have stayed home,"* I kept telling myself. As I was being questioned, I told the officer I had just lost my child's father and that was why I was there. *"I had no idea about the drugs,"* I pleaded with him. Although it was true, I was using my famous victim card of "poor ol' me, I just lost my child's father."

The officer said the house had been under video surveillance for several months. I replied, "*Well then, you know I have never been here, ever; check the surveillance.*" He left me standing there alone while he talked to other officers. I felt like time was standing still as I stood there waiting. Finally, he came back and said that Jazmine and I could leave. He sure didn't have to tell me twice. This was before cell phones, so I had no phone and no car. I grabbed my baby and took off walking as fast as I could. The whole time I was praying and thanking God for letting me go. The reality was sinking in that I almost lost my child and my freedom from this one poor decision. I was so thankful to get out of there that I stopped using powder cocaine on the spot.

I, however, continued to drink and party with my girlfriends. One night, my girls and I were at a local hang out spot when I met a guy with whom I immediately fell "in love." It was an instant attraction. "Love at first sight" was what we called it. After sharing with him the loss of Joe, he became very involved. One day, he took Jazmine and me to visit the gravesite. He even bought flowers for us to leave there.

After a few short weeks of dating, he asked me to marry him. I quickly said, "*Yes.*" I was so emotionally attached that I truly believed he loved us. He was the first man to really show me any affection or attention. We got married at a Justice of Peace and, that night, we headed to the club to celebrate. By the time we made it home, I was throwing up everywhere as I drank way too much. I spent the night on the floor puking my guts up. Some honeymoon!

That following Monday, when I came home from work, I felt like something wasn't right when I walked in my house. The closet in our bedroom was opened and all of his clothes were gone. I noticed the phone book lying on the bed opened to the Greyhound bus station page. I was devastated—he had left me. I started going through the house taking inventory and that's when I realized all mine and Jazmine's jewelry was gone. No longer was I devastated—I was infuriated. My mind began to race and then I remembered he had my ATM card. I quickly called to check my balance which confirmed what I already knew: all the money was gone. Not only was I enraged with him, but I became furious with myself. I had been played; I felt like a fool. I was so hurt wondering how I could be so stupid. Although embarrassed and humiliated, I was determined I would get the last laugh.

Rage began to rise in me as I plotted how I was going make him pay for what he had done. I was going to show him he had crossed the wrong woman. In my anger, I made some really bad decisions as to getting revenge. I did some really horrible things and told some pretty horrible lies. This was my first husband. I called him my *"weekend husband."* Even after I was divorced, I didn't acknowledge being married because I was so humiliated and embarrassed. Many, many years later, I asked the Lord to forgive me for what I had done. God also allowed me the opportunity to apologize face to face and I was able to ask him to forgive me as well.

After the devastation of this failed marriage, I started seeking relief. I thought of Joe's mother, my daughter's grandmother, who was a woman of faith. She was always attending church. Before Joe died, he started going to church with his mom until physically he wasn't able. I do know he accepted Christ before he died; I vaguely remember a conversation we had about this. I can still hear the Kirk Franklin song "Stomp" being blasted in his car and room. He was always playing that song. Yeah, I liked the song, but I wasn't trying to hear about this God or "getting saved" thing. What kind of God would allow Joe to suffer the way he did? I was angry at God. My life was good. Besides, I was having fun running the streets and doing me. Going to church was for old boring people.

It's funny how life has a way of breaking us down. After the devastation of Joe dying, my drug use almost landed me in prison, I nearly lost my child, I married a man I thought loved us, that husband robbed us, and I was finished. I knew something in my life had to change. When I thought of change, I thought of Joe's faith-filled mother. I needed what she had. I started going to church with her. It wasn't that boring and, to my surprise, there were some young people. I thought to myself, *"Maybe I can find a good Christian man and then I would finally find the love I so desperately wanted."*

One service, the message was about Naomi, the widow who had two daughters that had been married to her two sons, both of whom had died. After her sons had died, Naomi told her two daughters-in-law to go back to their own countries and find a husband. Ruth, one of Naomi's daughters-in-law, refused to go back. She wanted to go with her mother-in-law. Ruth told Naomi, *"Your people shall be my people and your God shall be my God."* As I listened to the story unfold, I felt like God was talking straight to me. This was how I felt about Joe's mother: *"Her people shall be my people, and her God shall be my God."* After that Sunday service, I went to the altar where I gave my life to the Lord. Don't get excited—I still had a very long journey ahead of me. By January 2000, I was baptized and started attending church regularly. I wanted to know this God to whom she was so faithful and committed. I was reading my Bible but I was flooded with questions. I felt like I didn't understand any of it. I remember reading a passage that said women shouldn't cut their hair and they should cover their head while praying. I felt convicted because I had short hair.

It all seemed so overwhelming to me. I reached out to the deacon assigned to me as a new believer. He did his best to answer all my questions. It made more sense to me once he explained the answer to the specific question I was asking. I was trying so hard to change my behavior that I pretty much stopped going out, albeit, I was still smoking weed and occasionally drinking. I would get up in the morning, smoke marijuana, and watch preaching on TV. Although I was saved from eternal hell, I had not been delivered. I was full of baggage I didn't even know I had.

After just a few weeks of going to church with Joe's mom, I did meet a man. He and his two children were visiting our church. This would soon be my second husband. More about that relationship is in upcoming chapters.

Reflection Activity

Can you relate to any of this story? Does it stir anything within you?

_____
_____
_____
_____
_____
_____
_____
_____

CHAPTER FOURTEEN

The Root of the Problem

"Unless you heal the root of the problem, the pain will not go away. You can hide from it, but the problem stays until you dig deep."
~ Leon Brown

"It happened" were only two words, but they had so much meaning to me. Remember in chapter eleven when I heard those two little words? I knew, in that moment, in a very powerful way, God was validating my feelings and my understanding of what happened with XYZ. It was so much bigger than the incident itself. It was the seed which took root that night. This was what God was showing me. When I heard in my head, *"It happened,"* I knew God was solidifying that I wasn't crazy; it really happened. Now, as to whether or not this person knowingly did it was not the issue being addressed. The issue was how the enemy gained access and used it to try to destroy me.

I spent years feeling like my mind was in a battle of tug-of-war. My emotions would go back and forth. Did it happen, did it not happen, was it my fault, was it not my fault? I often felt like I was crazy and that maybe it didn't really happen. Then I had thoughts of questioning whether or not I did something to warrant it. The enemy told me that, if I hadn't been where I was, it wouldn't have happened. To reiterate, it wasn't so much the incident itself, it was all the mental torment that came from it. The enemy was having his way and he used others to intensify the uncontrollable emotions going on in my head.

I was being consumed with thoughts of rejection, abandonment, depression, anger, suicide, shame, and guilt. I felt like my parents had let me down, like they didn't love me. I felt like they didn't want me and they didn't care about me or what I was going through. I often wished I would have never been born. The enemy started infiltrating his plan to destroy my life from the time I was conceived and it continued until he finally had his hooks in me. When "it" happened, this was the point where the enemy's seeds took root—those seeds he had been planting all my life. Seeds of molestation at three or four years old, the seeds of sexually explicit music, the movies, the Playboy magazines, masturbation, and more, began to grow as do all weeds.

Satan used this particular incident to his advantage. I was left to fight an internal battle I didn't know how to fight. I was placed in institutions and was seen by many different counselors who didn't know how to help me fight. Medication was their answer. What I needed was light to expose the darkness. The night the Lord woke me up and said those two words, "*It happened*," I cried as though I had been holding tears all my life. It was as if a dam had broken. I cried for what seemed to be hours and, as I cried, I was being released from the mental torment I felt as a child.

Because I was seeking Light—God—the darkness, aka the plot of the enemy, was being exposed. I lay in bed that night with my spiritual eyes opened. I thought about all I had been through or, rather, all through which I had put myself. As I cried tears of release and then tears of joy, I knew God had been with me through it all. All the hurt, all the disappointments, and all the self-inflicted wounds were being healed. As I lie there, as inexplicable as it may be, it was as though I felt the love of a father for the very first time—love which I had never known before and love which could only be experienced. All the love I so desired from those in my life who did not or could not grant it, God was fulfilling. I was reminded of a Bible story about a woman who was healed by touching the hem of Jesus' garment.

I imagined this was how she felt. The moment she touched the hem of Jesus' robe, she was healed and made whole. Oh, but the beauty of the story was Jesus calling her "daughter." With that one touch when her identity was restored, she was His daughter. She wasn't just some woman who touched Him; He let her know she was His. She left that experience with Jesus with so much more than a physical healing. Then He said to her in Mark 5:34, *"Daughter, your faith, your personal trust and confidence in Me, has restored you to health; go in peace and be permanently healed from your suffering."*

I cried until my tears dried up and I fell back to sleep. My heart was full and I was content. I went to sleep knowing God was my Father and I was His daughter. I went to sleep knowing I was loved, valued, and that He cared for me. When I got up in the morning, I grabbed my Bible and my daily devotional and headed outside to spend some quiet time with God. For a few minutes, I sat in amazement of how real God was and all He was doing in my life. It was like I had been seeing in black and white all my life and, finally, I was able to see in color for the very first time. I just kept thanking the Lord for His love and grace toward me. I kept thanking Him for healing me and making me His daughter.

As I read the devotion of the day, the story was of a young girl who had felt like she had been abandoned by her mother and father, how she never felt like she belonged anywhere and felt all alone. She felt no one understood her until, one day, she was introduced to Jesus and she started following and trusting in Him. That's when her life began to turn around. As I read the story, it seemed like my own story.

When I got to the end, the Scripture for the day was Psalm 27:10 which reads, *"Although my father and my mother have abandoned me, yet the Lord will take me up and adopt me as His child."* I wept uncontrollably. This was a defining moment for me. This is truly how I felt as a child: abandoned by my father and mother. God was validating how I felt and also restoring my identity by letting me know I was His child. It was as if God was putting healing ointment on a wound which had just been exposed. I lost it. I was an emotional wreck the rest of the day. I worshipped and cried that whole day. God was uprooting the lies and replacing them with truth; truth about who He was to me and truth about who I was in Him. I was His daughter and I could actually feel His love in a tangible way as never before.

Identity is such an important key in our relationship with our heavenly Father; something changes on the inside when you know you're a son or daughter and that your Father loves you. Knowing this changes how we see ourselves, our perspective, and definitely our position. No longer do we live like orphans. The orphan spirit has to leave when we take hold of this truth. Don't forget, Jesus came that we may live life to the fullest and we will never walk in our true calling or purpose until we understand who we are in Christ.

Somewhere, within each of us, lays a root the enemy has planted. Never forget, he comes to kill, steal, and destroy. Until this point, I had spent my life surviving, never really living. The enemy had stolen my identity. At such an early age, he began to make me feel and think things about myself which were rooted in lies and darkness. We have all had bad things happen to us, whether big or small, but what we do with those experiences will determine the course of our life.

My questions to you are:

1. Are you living life to the fullest?
2. If not, why?
3. What is stopping you?
4. What roots do you have which need to be uprooted?

We must not continue to allow the lies of the enemy to plant weeds of destruction in our lives; let's get to the root of the issue. Let's begin to dig it up so we can start to plant different kinds of seeds, life producing seeds. We can live life to the fullest as God intended. Jesus paid a price none of us could have ever paid so that we could be free. Let's learn to walk in that freedom.

1. What lies has the enemy caused you to believe about yourself?
2. What is the origin of the lies: parent, teacher, friend, sibling, circumstance, etc.

The Keys to Exposing the Lies

When we walk into a dark room, the lights don't automatically come on. We have to actually turn on the light switch. Unless we do so, we will remain in the dark. In other words, we must be intentional about flipping the switch. The same is true for our spiritual lives. We must seek truth in order to expose the lies.

God's Word = Truth
Lies = the seeds planted by the enemy

Satan will do whatever he can to keep us in the dark. He will try and keep us busy or distracted as much as he can. I am sure you have already witnessed that while reading this book. He does not want you or I to be free. Don't be fooled or intimidated by his schemes. Continue to keep pressing. Exposure only happens as we continue to seek the Light of God's Word. It doesn't just happen. We must seek after it.

The questions now are, *"How badly do you want it? Do you want it badly enough so as to press past the distractions and the chaos?"* The choice is solely up to you. We must be willing to give up some things. It may be a relationship, staying off social media, letting go of that TV show you love so much, cutting your phone off while spending time in God's Word, or it may be giving up your free time. You know, that time we just need to be alone and do nothing. This is another trick of the enemy because, as long as we stay in the nothingness, nothing will ever change.

The definition of insanity is doing the same thing over and over again but expecting a different result. Don't fall for the traps of, "*I'll do it later*" or "*I'll start tomorrow.*" Again, how much do you want it? Will you press through all the obstacles and distractions? Will you become a freedom fighter, one who will fight for liberty or will you stay stuck in the cycle of dysfunction all because it's what's familiar to you? The choice is yours. No one can make you want to do what's necessary so as to live a life of freedom. You have to make yourself. I must warn you, as you make a decision to seek after the truth, everything in this world will fight against you. Nevertheless, I encourage you to allow truth to become your anchor.

> "Be strong. Be courageous. Do not be afraid of them. For the Lord your God will be with you. He will neither fail you nor forsake you (Deuteronomy 31:6)."

> "I have told you all this so that you will have peace of heart and mind. Here on earth you will have many trials and sorrows; but cheer up, for I have overcome the world (John 16:33)."

> "But you belong to God, my dear children. You have already won a victory over those people, because the Spirit who lives in you is greater than the spirit who lives in the world (I John 4:4).

As you make your own personal commitment to seek truth—to expose the lies and dig up the roots—remember the words found in Matthew 7:7-8 which read, *"Ask and keep on asking and it will be given to you; seek and keep on seeking and you will find; knock and keep on knocking and the door will be opened to you. For everyone who keeps on asking receives, and he who keeps on seeking finds, and to him who keeps on knocking, it will be opened."* Healing may not come over night, but keep seeking, keep asking and keep knocking. God will show you. My sweet friend, you've got this. I believe in you. You're not alone. Trust the process.

Reflection Activity

Can you reflect on your life and figure out the root of your problems? Are you willing to dig up that which needs removal? How desperate for God are you? How desperate are you to live a life of liberty?

_____
_____
_____
_____
_____
_____
_____
_____
_____
_____

CHAPTER FIFTEEN

Abused but Not Abandoned

"Do not fear, for you will not be put to shame, and do not feel humiliated or ashamed, for you will not be disgraced. For you will forget the shame of your youth (Isaiah 54:4).*"*

We live in a fallen and broken world; bad things happen to *all* people. That certainly doesn't mean God doesn't love us. The difference for the children of God is this—we have a place we can turn where all the pain can be surrendered and exchanged for something far greater. We are all from God, but we are not all God's children. We choose whether or not we are His by our own personal decision to follow Him. John 8:44 states, *"You are of your father the devil, and you want to do the desires of your father."* For those of us who choose to follow Christ and surrender our lives to Him, He will turn our pain into purpose and our misery and mess into a message. It's up to us what we do with our deepest hurts and pain. We can choose to allow it to make us better or bitter.

For example, let's say there is a father who has two teenage sons. Both are being bullied in school. One child goes home and shuts down. He doesn't want to talk to anyone and he hides in his room. While thoughts of sadness, anger, depression, suicide, and rage become his constant companion, his father tries, to no avail, to get him to open. Through the door, the loving father pleads for him to open the door. With the door still closed, the dad tells him he loves him and he cares. The boy, full of anger and bitterness, refuses to let him in. The boy puts on an outward mask which says, "*I am okay,*" but inside, it's a different story. The father continues to attempt to get through, though unsuccessful.

The other boy is deeply hurt and has all the same negative emotions as his brother, only this son comes home and runs into the arms of his father. The teenage boy crawls into his lap and cries his eyes out. The father holds him tightly as he expresses his care and concern about what he's going through. He affirms his unwavering love for his son and reminds him who he is, that his identity is not what others say and do to him. The father assures his son he is greater than what he is going through. The father gives him hope and courage.

In this, the boy has chosen not to allow the hateful words of the other kids to define who he is. He knew he was safe and secure in the arms of his dad, despite the emotional turmoil he was battling. In his father's arms, he gained strength to face another day. Day after day, he faced the same abuse at school, but continues to crawl in his father's lap and allow his father to help him through the pain, anger, and bitterness. This scenario is a depiction of our heavenly Father and our personal response to His Love. Love is the strongest force in existence. I have to be honest, seeing God as a loving father was really challenging for me. For so many years, my perception of God was influenced by my relationship with my earthly fathers, both dad and stepdad. I saw God as hard, harsh, distant, and unaffectionate. I saw Him as a mean Judge waiting for me to mess up just so He could punish me.

I grew up feeling rejected and abandoned by God just like I did with my dad. This process of trying to see God for who He really is was not an easy journey for me. Every time I would hear about Him being a loving Father, I had thoughts of desperately wanting the love of my natural father, which I never received. But, like the analogy above, when I came out of my metaphoric room, once I finally allowed Him in, I began to see God for who He really is—loving, kind, gracious, tender, forgiving, and patient.

This happened when I started allowing truth to fill my heart as I read His Word; truth that God loves me with an everlasting love and, with that love, He draws me to Himself. His posture toward me is not just of everlasting love, but of unfailing kindness as found in Jeremiah 31:3. This is true about you as well, my beloved friend. God is full of an everlasting love and He is full of unfailing kindness toward you. His love and kindness aren't based on our good or our bad behavior. It doesn't matter where you've been, what you've done, or what's been done to you. The enemy doesn't want you to believe that. This is why he continues to throw insults and accusations at you about the things you have been through as well as the things you have done. The enemy often says things like, *"If God really did love you, why did He allow that to happen to you?"* or *"There's no hope for someone like you, God doesn't love you."*

Why does God allow bad things to happen? I had to make a decision to stop asking the *why* questions. Instead, I chose to believe His Word concerning me. *Why* kept me stuck. *Why* kept me in my room with the door closed. *Why* caused me to be bitter. When I decided to let go of the *why*, the doors of my heart began to open. Instead of *why*, I began to ask *what*: "What do I do with this? What must I do to be healed?" We must shift from *why* to *what*. Isaiah 61:3 is full of promises which God desires for us. He wants to give us beauty for ashes, the oil of joy for mourning, and the garment of praise for the spirit of heaviness so that we will be called trees of righteousness planted of the Lord so that He will be glorified. In order to live in the promises of that Scripture, we must be willing to give up the ashes; the *why* questions keep us holding onto the ashes.

Beautifully Broken

Think of a glow stick. It was made to shine but, in order for that to happen, it must be broken. In my experience, if you start at one end and work your way to the opposite end, breaking it in several places and shaking it up will cause a much brighter and lasting light. My broken life has produced something so beautiful and, although the breaking was painful, it produced a light in me which can never be put out. I never imagined hurt, disappointment, and pain could have ever been exchanged and used for a greater purpose. But, all because I chose to sit in my Father's lap, it has. No longer do I sit in my dark internal room listening to the lies that say I am nothing and I deserve nothing. No longer do I choose to wear the mask which says everything is okay when everything is *not* okay. I chose to be open and transparent with my heavenly Father as well as those around me.

I know that, whatever that thing is on the inside of me I don't want to share because of the guilt and shame, is the very thing the enemy is using against me to keep me in a place of bondage. I chose to be broken and unashamed. I chose to fight for my freedom instead of surrendering to the lies that scream so loudly in my head. Fighting for freedom means we will have to fight the thoughts which constantly remind us of the hurt. Our thoughts and attitudes play a huge part of our healing process. We have to take ownership over our thoughts and attitudes.

I'm sure you have heard this statement before, "*Life is 10% what happens and 90% how we react to it.*" There is so much truth in this statement. It's not so much *what* happened to me that matters as much as how I responded. The way I react will determine whether the circumstances make me better or bitter. I can view everything as an obstacle or an opportunity for growth, a stumbling block or a stepping-stone. Read and meditate on James 1:2-4.

Reflection Activity

What does James 1:2-4 stir within you? What does this bring to mind?

CHAPTER SIXTEEN

Changing Our Reaction

"The Lord is close to the brokenhearted and saves those who are crushed in spirit (Psalm 34:18).*"*

Let us begin to allow God to change our reaction by leaning in closely to Him, crawling into His lap, and allowing Him to do what only He can do. In His loving presence, our attitudes and thoughts begin to change as we keep our minds stayed on Him. Let's look at Isaiah 54:4 again which reads, *"Do not fear, for you will not be put to shame, and do not feel humiliated or ashamed, for you will not be disgraced. For you will forget the shame of your youth."*

What do you fear about your youth? What about your youth has caused you to feel humiliated and shameful? Maybe it's not something from your youth but from adulthood, or maybe both. Spend some time asking the Lord to show you and then write them down. The Lord wants you to know you will not be disgraced and you will forget the shame. I am living proof that this Scripture is true. God has made these very words come alive in my own life.

First, you must be honest with the humiliation and shame. Is it from an abusive situation or is it from a personal choice you have made such as an abortion? God wants to heal you and to let you know you are forgiven. The enemy wants you to stay imprisoned by the guilt and shame. He wants you to feel like you will be humiliated if anyone ever finds out your secret. The enemy is a liar, but God's Word is Truth. As you give it to God, His promise to you is that you will not be disgraced and you will forget the shame. Do Not Fear. Fear stands for *False Evidence Appearing Real.*

You, my beloved friend, must make a choice, a choice to continue to believe the lies or seek the truth. Will you choose to stop asking the *why* questions? Ask yourself which *why* questions you need to stop asking. Will you choose to take off the mask and be transparent? What are some of the masks you wear? No matter your age, race, social background, etc., every one of us has had bad things happen and they have affected us in some form or fashion. When something bad happens, you have three choices. You can let it define you, destroy you, or strengthen you.

The enemy wants you to be defined and destroyed by those lies. The truth is that God defines you by His Word. You are who He says you are and, obviously, you haven't been destroyed because you are still here. Now, you must choose to let it strengthen you. Here are a few nuggets of truth from which you can draw strength:

1. You can do all things through God who gives you strength (Philippians 4:13).
2. God gives strength to the weary and increases the power of the weak (Isaiah 40:29).
3. Look to the Lord and His strength; seek His face always (1 Chronicles 16:11).
4. Be strong in the Lord and in His mighty power (Ephesians 6:10).

Were you abused? Did you speak your truth and no one believed you? Did you speak your truth, yet experienced the pain of someone doubting you? If you were abused, know that I do believe you. I stand with you and for you. Speaking the truth after being abused takes incredible courage and strength. I want you to know, I am pleased with you and I support you. We can be victorious together as survivors. I am a survivor. You are a survivor and we are strong for having survived. Today, we stand on the truth of God's Word. We stand together triumphantly and we move forward in truth. We are freedom fighters. We are no longer victims and we stand victoriously.

If you have been abused or are currently a victim of abuse and have not yet spoken out, I urge you to reach toward a safe person and speak your truth. Get help. Your abuser is sick and you are not his or her cure. Love yourself enough to let go. I pray for your strength and for you to see the way out for which God has made. You are strong and courageous. I speak life into your very soul. I declare with the power and authority of Jesus Christ, you *will* survive, you *will* find freedom, and you *will* be victorious. With God and me, stand in agreement with this declaration. His Word will not fail you.

You, my beloved, are not forgotten. Just as a mother could never forget a child from her womb, God could never forget you. You are His child. With all the hurt, disappointment, shame, guilt, and fear, run into His widely open arms and allow His healing love to embrace you. You are safe in His arms, you are loved in His arms, and you will be healed in His arms.

Prayer: *Father, some of us feel broken because of the abuse we have endured. Some of us have been physically, sexually, emotionally, and spiritually abused. Father, only you know the depths of what we have been through and what we are currently enduring. We are hurting and feel abandoned. Your words say you will never leave us nor forsake us and that you are near to the brokenhearted. It's hard for us to trust that to be true because of what we have experienced. Show Yourself to us in a real and tangible way so that we may gain hope and strength for the journey ahead. Cause us to know the power of Your presence and healing. Help us to see You for who you really* *are and let us see ourselves as You see us. We want to surrender all of our ashes of abuse, pain and disappointment; we desperately want the beauty You have for us. We cry out for Your help. Father, we can't, but you can. May we find all we need and more as we commit ourselves to Your loving care. Teach us how not to live by our feelings but by the Truth of Your Word. We have been abused but we are not abandoned. We will rise and become victorious in Christ. We will stand up in Your strength and fight for our freedom. We declare that You are a merciful Father, and the source of all our comfort. Today begins a new journey toward freedom. Today we walk in the beauty which You have bestowed us, no longer do we wear the ashes of our past. We take off the spirit of heaviness and put on the garment of praise You've made available to us. In Jesus' name we pray, Amen.*

Reflection Activity

_____ (your name)

"Do not be afraid or discouraged, for the Lord will personally go ahead of you. He will be with you; He will neither fail you nor abandon you (Deuteronomy 31:6).*"*

Take some time and write your story of abuse, abandonment, disappointment, abortions, and/or pain. Whatever your story is, write it. Don't be ashamed; don't be afraid of someone seeing it. It is okay, trust me; this will be vital to your healing. Once you are finished, burn it. Don't rush through this, take your time and be intentional about trying to remember every single detail.

1. What happened?
2. What were your thoughts?
3. Who was there?
4. Where did it happen?
5. How did you feel afterward?
6. Did you tell anyone?

7. What was their response?
8. How did their response make you feel?

Now that the memories are fresh in your mind, I want you to complete this exercise. I have witnessed many people get set free by doing this. Jesus wants to heal you. He wants to set you free.

I want you to relax, take a deep breath, and then blow it out. You are not alone. Jesus is right there with you. Now, I want you to go back into the story, close your eyes, and experience what's going on as you are in the story.

Look for Jesus as the abuse is happening—He's there. It's okay if you don't see Him right away. Keep your eyes closed and stay in the story. Ask God to show Himself to you. Be patient, He is there. Finding Him may look different for everyone. You may see a physical being, you may hear a voice, see a face; you may get a feeling or a thought, you may even get a picture or an analogy of some sort. *If you get something condemning, it's from the enemy and not the Lord. Keep looking for Jesus.*

You are brave and you are strong and I support you. I encourage you to do this exercise with every painful memory you have no matter what it is. God wants you to know you are forgiven. He does not want you living under the guilt and shame any longer. God is not mad at you; He wants you to experience healing and deliverance. You are forgiven, now forgive yourself. Together we stand as freedom fighters. We have fought for our own freedom and now may we fight for the freedom of others. We survived so that we can help other's find the freedom that is now ours.

God is our merciful Father and the source of all comfort. He comforts us in all our troubles so that we can comfort others. When others are troubled, we will be able to give them the same comfort God has given us. Read and meditate on 2 Corinthians 1:3-5.

CHAPTER SEVENTEEN

Bag Lady

"The time has come to lay that baggage down and leave behind all the struggling and striving. You can be set free as you journey forward into a balanced healthy and rewarding future."
~ Sue Augustine

I had spent years collecting and carrying baggage. My baggage had become a part of me; it was who I was. Now that I had completed a timeline of events, the Lord began to show me this analogy. I saw myself carrying four sets of luggage.

1. the first bag was labeled "adolescent years"
2. the second was "teenage years"
3. the third was "adulthood baggage"
4. the fourth was "parenting bag"

Each set of luggage had labels written all over them. God was showing me this was what I, and so many others, looked like in the natural. I spent time meditating on baggage and I wrote all the words the Lord had given me. I gathered different size bags and, on each bag, I wrote labels so as to bring the visual to life. I often use these bags when ministering at speaking engagements.

I want us to look at the different stages of life and see what it looks like. Of course, each person's baggage will look different depending on their own personal experience. The following are some examples.

Adolescent Baggage

You may have heard statements like these, either directly or indirectly:

1. No one will ever love you.
2. You will never amount to anything.
3. Do as I say, not as I do.
4. You make me sick.
5. You're stupid.
6. You act just like your no-good father and/or mother.
7. What goes on in this house stays in this house.
8. No one will ever believe you.
9. You made me do it.
10. It's your fault.

Some of us have experienced the loss of a loved one, such as the death of a parent or a close relative. We may experience the separation or divorce of our parents. We may have been adopted or placed in foster care. We may have been brought up in a home where one of our parents was an alcoholic or had some type of addiction. Maybe we experienced one of our parents being physically or mentally abused. Perhaps we knew of an adulterous affair in which one or both was engaging.

We may have experienced rape, molestation, incest, bullying, verbal, sexual, physical, and/or emotional abuse. Because of what we experienced, we began to develop insecurities which resulted in abandonment issues, loneliness, low self-esteem, drugs, alcohol, instability, malnourishment, rejection, and so on. One can become caretakers, loners, or emotionally detached. There are eating disorders, jealousy, resentment, anxiety, emptiness, suicidal thoughts or attempts, and much more.

Because of our experiences, it is highly likely we developed various fears and negative emotions. A lot of it is based on what our parents do and don't do, good and bad. The music to which we listened and watched on TV or at the movies also plays a big part as well. Keep in mind, the enemy will use whatever he can to plant lies such as fear and rejection. Each one of us has a deep longing to be accepted, valued, and loved. We all need words of affirmation and healthy physical touch to some degree—some more than others. When we don't receive these things, the enemy uses it to communicate that we are the issue, that something is wrong with us. As children, most of us began early stuffing negative emotions into our bags, which starts the cycle.

Teenage Baggage

While still carrying our childhood bag, those fears and negative emotions heighten based on our experiences. We begin to attract those to whom we can best relate. Most likely, we attract those with similar experiences. We may experience more rejection, depression, anger, death; therefore, we may become promiscuous, rebellious, or codependent. We become exposed to more things which keep us in bondage such as sex, pornography, drugs, and partying.

Some of us may not have experienced molestation or rape in our adolescent years, but we experience it in our teenage years. Some have even been sexually exploited by someone they trusted. Some may have been involved in bisexual or homosexual relationships. The more the negative experiences, the deeper we fall into a black hole of depression and the lower our self-value becomes in our own eyes. We may become a bully or we may be the one that gets bullied. It is insecurities rooted in fear that causes one to become a bully.

We may become the abuser because we were abused. We learn how to wear masks and ignore the pain. One may become pregnant and have a child or an abortion. We lie, cheat, and steal. We may become full of shame and guilt which develops a shame-based identity. We start wearing labels others have put on us. We may even seek help because we don't know what to do with all these negative emotions. We may get diagnosed and medicated for things like ADHD, ADD, bipolar, depression, or something of the like. We may experience the loss of a loved one and we don't process the grief in a healthy way. Most of us become controlled by our unhealthy emotions, which we don't know how to properly channel.

We may act out in rebellion causing negative consequences. We may find ourselves comparing our lives to others, desperately wanting to be like someone else. We build up walls refusing to let others in. We have a false sense of being in control. We tell ourselves we will never let anyone else hurt us ever again which, in turn, causes us to have control issues. There is always a *why* behind the *what*.

Adult Baggage

While carrying our childhood and teenage bags, we continue to pack our adult bag full of the same junk, only now it is intensified. We start to feel weighted down and tired and rightfully so. We are full of disappointments and soul-wounds. We have learned to suppress—deny—our emotions. We want to be in control of everything or, on the other end of the spectrum, we want no type of responsibility. We may find ourselves in abusive relationships or marriages. We may be codependent caring more about others than we do about our own well-being. We may be alcoholics, rage-aholics, or workaholics.

Adultery, eating disorders, anxiety, high blood pressure, sickness, unforgiveness, rage, and bitterness have become our best friends. Our addictions escalate to pornography, shopping, gambling, drugs, alcohol, sex, food, etc. We may even find ourselves in the lifestyle of our addiction such as prostitution, sexual exploitation, stealing, being jailed, or even trafficked. We become overachievers or underachievers. Some of us will put forth too much effort and others won't put forth any effort at all. We will spend the rest of our lives in fear and desperately trying to keep on our mask, intensely attempting to make others like us.

Some of us will give all of ourselves to others while others will continuously practice social distancing. We become closed, afraid we may get our hearts broken again. We become hard and unaffectionate or even needy and clingy, possibly unable to show affection toward others. We don't know what being affectionate or loving is. Our only means of expressing this could be through the things we buy for others. Most times, I see this in husbands as they have no clue how to love their wives, but they may buy expensive gifts as an expression of their love. Everyone, at any age, needs security. They need unconditional love, acceptance, support, words of affirmation, and approval. This is not communicated in buying stuff. It's communicated by our words of affirmation and physical touch. Our bags, no matter what negatives we have collected, need to be emptied so as to learn how to be free.

Reflection Activity

What baggage have you been carrying? Has your baggage weighed you down to the point of being unable to function in everyday life? Are you an overachiever in the attempt to prove your worth? Are you an underachiever because you are overwhelmingly defeated?

_____

_____

_____

_____

_____

_____

CHAPTER EIGHTEEN

The Parenting Bag

"Unpack your baggage so your kids don't have to carry it."
~ L.V. Hanessian

No matter what age we begin to have children, I call this our *parenting bag*. This bag isn't really ours. Rather, it belongs to our children. All thoughts of fear, disappointment, abortion, adoption, whatever the mother goes through during pregnancy, gets placed inside this parenting bag. The parents determine what goes into this bag, which will eventually become our child's. This becomes the first of many bags that they too will begin to collect and carry as they go through life. Even as early as conception, we start to fill this bag for them with things such as our own bags of rejection, abandonment, low self-esteem, pride, anger, manipulation, gossip, cheating, lying, drugs, alcohol, denial of emotions, codependency, ingratitude, low self-image, varying addictions, control issues, bitterness, and a tremendous amount more

My Birth Story

This is my mother's side of the story as it was told to me, though I have never felt comfortable enough to ask my dad his side. At this point, it doesn't really matter. Again, this is more about me than either of them. My sole intention is to paint a picture of how the enemy plots, at the time of conception, to infiltrate his plan of destruction for our lives. This is not about making my parents look bad. I recognize they were both young and each had their own unresolved baggage.

My mother and father were high school sweethearts and married very young. They already had two other children together prior to my birth. Before my mother became pregnant with me, she suspected my father was having an affair. He spent lots of time away from home, only coming around briefly so as to shower and change clothes. When questioned by my mother, he always had some excuse. She knew he was cheating, she just didn't have proof; she said she knew instinctively. Some would say it is a women's intuition, but I say it is warnings and revelations from Holy Spirit.

Shortly after my birth, she obtained the proof and filed for divorce. I am sure, given the circumstances, I was an unwanted pregnancy. The actions of my father proved it to be true on his part, although my mother would never admit it. I am sure, if she were honest, she didn't want another child either. She suspected his cheating, she was worried on the nights he never made it home and, even when he was home, it would turn into a screaming match as she questioned his whereabouts. Needless to say, she was stressed out and feeling unloved and rejected by her own husband.

So, yeah, I'm sure having a third baby only added to the already stressful situation. Infidelity can cause emotional and physical distress. During my mother's pregnancy with me, she experienced both, so much so that, on two occasions, she was hospitalized and given medication so as to stop early labor. At nearly seven months pregnant, her second time of active labor, once again, she was given medication to stop the labor. This time, however, as soon as my mother was getting ready to leave, her water broke.

The doctor informed my parents that, because her water had broken, they would have to induce her and the chances of me being born alive were not good. Furthermore, if I was born alive, the chances of me surviving were minimal. My mother was devastated and an emotional wreck. She spent the next sixteen hours in hard labor. One bad set of news after another. The ultrasound showed that my hand was on top of my head. The doctor stated that, if I was born this way, my arm would break during delivery. The only option was inserting his hand into the uterus and removing my arm from my head. My mother said that procedure was one of the worst kinds of pain she had ever experienced; it was indescribable.

Shortly after the doctor removed my hand from my head, I started having irregular heartbeats. Again, the doctor informed my mother that he did not think I would be born alive. My dad stood at the door with his hands crossed, emotionless, as tears ran down my mother's cheeks. Vividly, my mother recalls the doctor saying to my dad, "*You sorry son of a b***h. If you can't be of any help to her, get your a** out of here and send someone else in here that can be.*"

Mom said, at that, my dad turned and walked out of the room. The doctor was furious at my dad for his lack of empathy or sympathy. I was supposed to be a boy and she was going to name me *James* after her doctor. It turned out I was a girl, so they decided *Jami* was as close to James as they could get. Sixteen hours of distress and emotional trauma, thoughts of not knowing if her baby was going to live or not, sixteen hours of painful labor with no support from her husband, and I was born alive weighing four pounds twelve ounces. They said I was so tiny I could fit in the palm of my doctor's hand. I was born June 26, 1976.

My parents' divorce was finalized December 1976, six short months after my birth. I share that story to show how the enemy already has an assignment for our lives at conception. His plan is to do what he can to keep us from the truth. At conception, he assigned rejection, fear, and abandonment to my life. As I grew, they grew. The voices in my head were assigned to keep me from

God's truth. The enemy, along with his army of demons, will use people, situations, and experiences to keep us from our true identity. He will take what is true and manipulate and lie to make things seem one way or the other. He wanted me to believe my parents didn't want me. It wasn't even about me because they didn't know me. They may not have wanted another child, but it wasn't me personally they didn't want.

I don't look at my dad as the villain and my mom as the hero. In my eyes, they were both victims. Both of them were full of their own baggage. Don't forget, two broken people don't equal wholeness—broken people produce broken children. They were victims of their own past. Through the eyes of grace, I now see them as survivors and I love them dearly, including my stepdad.

Born Alive

"For I know the plans I have for you," declares the Lord, "plans to prosper you and not to harm you, plans to give you hope and a future (Jeremiah 29:11)."

"And he knows the number of hairs on your head. Never fear, you are far more valuable to Him than a whole flock of sparrows (Luke 12:7)."

God's Word is full of *intent* (our birth was intentional), *power* in which we can walk, *promises* for us to claim, and *purpose* which is abundant life. My parents didn't know me at conception, but God did. Any male and female can have sex, but life can only come from God. In fact, Jeremiah 1:5 tells me that God knew me before He formed me in my mother's womb. And He knew *you* too. As I have said so many times, the enemy will do what he can to keep us from our true identity. He will try everything he can to feed us lies which will eventually become our truth if we allow it.

Reflection Activity

What comes to mind after reading this? Were you wanted at birth? Were you rejected in the womb or after you were born? Be honest. Think about the truth of the matter and write your emotions about that. Acceptance of truth is the beginning of healing.

_____
_____
_____
_____
_____
_____

CHAPTER NINETEEN

Baggage Check

"Previous journeys have taught me the danger of taking too much stuff."
~ Tahir Shan

Let's mentally take a trip together to an airport. Those preparing to take a flight must first wait to have their luggage checked, weighed, and tagged. They have all kinds of restrictions such as weight, size, and contents. Let me give a real visual of what it looks like for me at the airport: I get all my baggage unloaded from the car onto a rolling convenient cart. Before I make it inside, I'm already tired from having to load and unload the car. While waiting my turn, my mind is racing wondering if I have everything I need. I quickly shift to, *"Why in the world did I bring all this stuff? I probably won't even need it or use half of it. Next time, I'll do better."* I begin to silently pray, *"Lord please don't let these bags be overweight."* As I finally make it to the counter, I frantically try to lift each piece so as to be weighed. I intensely pray for it to not go over the limit. Then I hear the words, *"Overweight."*

I tried desperately to pull out some small items and stuff them in my carry-on bag, which is already bulging at the seams, so that I can get it at the 50 lbs limit. My chance of getting it under weight was slim to none. Got it. 50 lbs. I'm feeling a little better now that the heaviest of my bags was checked and on the way to the plane. My focus shifts to all the stuff still in my hand.

With me, I have my bulging-at-the-seams carryon bag, pocketbook, blanket, and pillow. My praying continues as I am fearful my carry-on luggage is too big or I have items not allowed for travel. And, Lord, what if someone put something in my bag and I didn't know! I struggle to quickly get everything on the security belt where it will all be scanned as I remove my shoes. Once I am free of all my belongings, I am motioned to walk through the metal detector. No weird beeps, so I'm good.

As I go to collect all my belongings, I notice the TSA worker has pulled my carryon bag and placed it in a separate section for further inspection. She begins to take out the contents. Are you kidding me? Do you know how long it took me to get all that in there? My mind starts racing. What if someone slipped something in my bag when I wasn't looking? She holds up a bottle of perfume, *"Mama, you can't have this, it's not allowed,"* as she tosses it into the trash can. I immediately become angry as I thought about how much money it cost and they just tossed it in the trash as if it were nothing. Now I'm upset. Why did they have to throw it away? Oh, well. At that point, I have to suck it up as a lesson learned.

I was told I could go ahead and put the rest of the stuff back in the bag. I was thinking, *"You were the one that took it all out, you should be the one to get it all back in there."* I spend the next ten minutes getting all my junk back in the bag. I load my arms, once again, with all my belongings and head toward the departure gate. After waiting several hours, it's finally boarding time. It never fails. I am always the last zone to be called. I hear, *"Now loading zone three."* I grab my stuff and make my way to the plane. Now comes the tricky part—trying desperately to make my way down the long narrow crowded space to my seat, all the way in the back, zone three.

I frantically begin an attempt to get what I can in the overhead bin so I can take my seat. Out of breath and tired, I squeeze into this cramped little space with the things which couldn't fit overhead and the things I needed during flight such as my pillow and blanket. Finally, now I can rest, but that idea quickly goes out the window as I become consumed with worry about my checked baggage. What if it gets lost? What if they didn't load it on the plane? Thoughts fill my mind of things I have to have. I won't be able to survive without all my necessities like clothes. What am I going to do without my clothes? Worry, worry, worry until I land and retrieve the checked luggage; then I am thankful everything made it safely.

Layovers

Do you know how hard it is to maneuver through an airport with all that junk? Going to get something to eat or just being able to walk around is a challenge. There's nothing fun about being weighted down with a whole bunch of baggage. When I do travel, I often wish I could leave my stuff somewhere securely until it's time to board the next flight. Unfortunately, you have to keep your bags on you at all times. Oh, let's not forget about going to the bathroom; this can get quite complicated with so much stuff. I hope you're getting this visual because, the truth is, this is what we look like with all our baggage.

What God wants us to realize is that He has a much greater destination for us, but we are our own hold-up. We are so focused and consumed with all our baggage that we can't enjoy the journey. We're bogged down and distracted trying to keep up with all our stuff. We're stuck at security not wanting to let go of things we have put in our bags. We are too worried about our baggage and the things within that we feel we can't do without. When we hold on to and refuse to let go of our baggage of life, we're missing out on the greater God has for us.

Fancy Bags

Let's talk about my "fancy" bags. They are the ones with the matching bags, hats, shoes, pocketbooks, etc. This was me. I covered all my garbage in my name brand bags and clothes looking as if I had it all together. I was a dressed-up mess. I was going to church and all, but I was a mess on the inside. From the streets to church, all I did was change clothes, so to speak. I took off my street clothes and was given some church clothes.

The church clothes were another form of mask. The clothes concealed the real issues which were brewing inside of me while the outside was dressed up really nicely. I learned how to play the part. I was told I needed to wear white on 1st Sundays, so I went out and bought white. I thought that complying was going to fix the mess I was experiencing on the inside and the mess I was experiencing in my marriage.

Nope, that didn't fix anything. No one was addressing the grave clothes, the dead stuff in my life—my thinking, actions, and character. I was full of dead stuff. I was trying to clean up the outside, but it was an inside job that had to take place. Once that happens, the outside stuff will begin to change. It's time to expose all the dead stuff, but first, we have to take off the street clothes *and* the church clothes. It's time to deal with what's really going on internally, in our spirit, soul, and mind. It is time to stop hiding behind our fancy bags and clothes.

Ladies, how many of you can relate with the fact that, no matter how often we clean our pocketbooks, the next time we clean it, we always find junk and trash? Every time I clean out my bag, I think to myself, *"How in the world did all this get in here? I just cleaned this thing out!"* It doesn't matter what kind of bag lady you are, we all have those secret compartments, you know, the ones in which we hide things. While cleaning out our metaphoric bags, we often discover things we forgot we had or we find things we thought we had lost. You know what I'm talking about.

I Know I'm Not the Only One

Are you tired of carrying the weight of all those bags? Are you ready to let go? Please note that, whether or not you deliberately unpack your baggage, it does and it will have an effect on your life, the people around you and your personal and spiritual growth. One of my friends posted a picture of a lady with a bunch of bags and the caption was, "*We all come with baggage, the key is finding someone who will help us unpack them.*" Well, here is your someone to help you. I gladly share the steps I took in my own journey.

Reflection Activity

Can you relate to my dilemma? Are you heavily weighted by your baggage of life? Do you need relief from the stresses of too heavy a load? Write some things you know you need to release. Ask the Lord to reveal things you need to release but are not yet aware.

_____

_____

_____

_____

_____

_____

CHAPTER TWENTY

First Things First

*"Let us not look back in anger, nor forward in fear,
but around in awareness."*
~ James Thurber

Step 1: Self Awareness

We must become aware of what we are carrying and then become intentional about getting rid of it. I spent years in counseling. I was told that, if I just talked about it, I'd be okay. Healing, unfortunately, does not take place by simply talking about the problem. We have to acknowledge it and we do so by touching that place of pain and then releasing it to Jesus. Do you remember the exercise in a previous chapter of mentally going to that place of hurt? We all need to mentally open and unpack our suitcases. Meditate on it; this isn't something which should be rushed. Ask God to help you and remember that you are not alone. Ask God to show you what things need to be unpacked, exposed and healed.

Step 2: Stuffing

We are always stuffing "stuff." We have to stop putting stuff in our bags that doesn't belong to us. Let's look at some practical examples. When we text someone and they don't respond, we automatically feel offended or rejected. Or, we may feel anger toward this person and a grudge against them starts building in our hearts. We don't take into consideration the possible scenarios of, they may have lost their phone, the battery was dead, poor reception, or simply they were busy and forgot to respond. We make it about us and begin to think crazy things like the aforementioned. That leads to the thought, *"They must not like me."* This kind of thinking could be rooted in a shame-based identity and/or low self-esteem.

What about when we feel overlooked when someone doesn't acknowledge us? Jada, my youngest daughter who was ten at the time, and I were at a women's conference. She was standing with my best friend, Heather, along with a young lady we all knew. This lady came up, gave Heather a hug, and started chitchatting with her. Jada walked away because she felt like the lady had purposely ignored her. When she told me what happened, I assured Jada that was not the case. I later spoke to the lady and she felt horrible Jada felt that way and immediately apologized. They became inseparable the rest of the day.

Had I not addressed the issue, Jada would have missed all God was doing at the conference because the enemy would have continued to plant seeds of doubt, disappointment, and rejection. Do you see how the enemy tried to trap her in her mind? What if Jada hadn't shared her feelings with me? She would have held onto all that stuff, and you best believe the enemy would have made a mountain out of a molehill. How often do we hold onto to the hurt, rejection, doubt, and worry over false issues?

Let's just say, for instance, that this young lady purposely ignored Jada. That would be on the her, not Jada. This is when Jada had to change her perspective. Whether or not she meant to ignore her, it was solely up to Jada to decide what she was going to do with the negative feelings. She was either going to cram them in her bag or throw it out. So many of us, in our hearts, carry offenses against people based on the way we have been treated by them or how we think they have treated us. If someone hurts you, *that person* does not know who they are in Christ. If we become offended, *we* don't fully understand who we are in Christ. This is why it is imperative to have our identity secured in Christ. We have to know who we are in Him. We have to be God-confident instead of people pleasers. People will always let us down. That's why our hope must be found in God and God alone. We must become anchored in truth so that, when the lies, hurts, disappointments, and offenses come, we shall not be moved.

Step 3: Evaluate and Take Captive

> "Casting down imaginations, and every high thing that exalteth itself against the knowledge of God, and bringing into captivity every thought to the obedience of Christ (II Corinthians 10:5)."

The way we feel affects the way we think. Just because we *feel* it, doesn't mean we have to react. Feelings are *indicators* not *dictators*. Evaluate your thoughts or, in other words, follow your thought process. Ask yourself, *"Why do I feel this way? How is feeling this way helpful to me? If it's not helpful but harmful, what must I do to replace this feeling? Where did this feeling come from?"* When negative emotions come, evaluate them and, afterward, decide where they need to go. If they are unhealthy and/or do not belong to you, throw them out. Do not put them in your bag.

Take every thought captive. In August 2011, God sent Heather back into my life. We had been apart for many years. This time, we were both saved and living for the Lord. At that time, Heather was spiritually more mature than I. Shortly after we reunited is when God delivered me from my drug and alcohol addiction and the codependent relationship I was in. God used our friendship in an amazing way. Proverbs 27:17 reads, *"As iron sharpens iron, so one person sharpens another."* I thank God for her. You can read her personal testimony in her book, *Behind the Bars: One Woman's Journey to True Freedom.*

Heather used to always say, *"Take every thought captive and bring it into the obedience of Christ."* It used to make me angry because I didn't understand what that meant, and she would say it all the time. *"Bring it into the obedience of Christ? What does that even mean?"* I would continually ask myself. Because I didn't understand it, I began to let it aggravate me when she would say it. Now, years later, I understand the reason the enemy wanted me to be aggravated. He did not want me to understand this Scripture because this is where he had a stronghold in my life. He knew it was going to be a wrap for him and the mind games; he was used to playing with me.

This was my personal revelation and it has changed my thought-life drastically. When I have a thought in my imagination, I snatch it and I ask myself, *"Does it line up with the Word of God? Is it true or untrue?"* Then I have to decide where it goes. God's Word must become a filter through which I run every imagination—thoughts. Take, for example, a water filter on a faucet. The dirty water is made clean because of the filter. The filter is in place for the sole purpose of removing the impurities and chemicals which could be harmful to use. Using the Word of God as a filter for our thoughts has the same purpose. Philippians 4:8 reads, *"Now, dear brothers and sisters, one final thing. Fix your thoughts on what is true, and honorable, and right, and pure, and lovely, and admirable. Think about things which are excellent and worthy of praise."* We are to set our minds on those things, as it doesn't just happen. We have to seize—snatch, grab, or take hold of—the negative thoughts and bring them into the obedience of Christ. Then, we have to set our minds on the things of God. This requires effort on our part.

Here's how seizing in action functions. We may have a thought that we are not loved. Grab hold of it right away and run it through the filter of God's Word. The Word says in Ephesians 2:4-5, *"But God is so rich in mercy, and he loved us so much, that even though we were dead because of our sins, He gave us life when He raised Christ from the dead."* It is only by God's grace you have been saved. This is the same thing I have shared with you in previous chapters about replacing the lie with the truth. The enemy wants us to maintain our negative thoughts so they will become our truth. Remember, the battle is in our minds. The enemy will plant thoughts, but we don't have to entertain them.

Let's look at negative thoughts as little orphaned children running around in our head. They are orphans, they are not ours. However, if we pick one of them up and begin caring for it, feeding it, changing its diapers, and altogether attending its needs, it becomes ours. Essentially, by entertaining bad thoughts, we have adopted them and made them our own. I've also heard this analogy, *"We can't stop the birds from flying above our heads, but we can stop them from building a nest."* Proverbs 4:23 reads, *"Guard your heart above all else, for it determines the course of your life."* I don't know about you, but I am sick and tired of following my heart. The reason is because the heart of man is vile, wicked, and deceitful above all things according to Jeremiah 17:9. Following my heart has caused a whole lot of brokenness and pain from which would require years to recover.

Unpacking

> "Therefore, since we are surrounded by such a huge crowd of witnesses to the life of faith, let us strip off every weight that slows us down, especially the sin that so easily trips us up. And let us run with endurance the race God has set before us. We do this by keeping our eyes on Jesus, the champion who initiates and perfects our faith. Because of the joy awaiting Him, he endured the cross, disregarding its shame. Now He is seated in the place of

honor beside God's throne. Think of all the hostility he endured from sinful people; then you won't become weary and give up (Hebrews 12:1-3)."

Definition of Endurance: the ability to do something difficult for a long time; the ability to deal with pain or suffering that continues for a long time; the quality of continuing for a long time

Erykah Badu's song "Bag Lady" pretty much sums it up. Check out some of the lyrics:

> *Bag lady you gone hurt your back*
> *Dragging all them bags like that*
> *I guess nobody ever told you*
> *All you must hold onto, is you, is you, is you*
> *One day all them bags gon' get in your way*
> *One day all them bags gon' get in your way*
> *I said one day all them bags gon' get in your way*
> *One day all them bags gon' get in your way, so pack light,*
> *Pack light, mm, pack light, pack light, oh ooh*
> *Bag lady you gon' miss your bus*
> *You can't hurry up, 'cause you got too much stuff* (end lyrics)

Pack lightly, ladies and gentlemen. The Lord is doing a new thing. Let's be ready. You have purpose and destiny. Don't allow your baggage to keep you from experiencing all God has for you. I pray this has been useful to you and your journey. From here on out, may we all pack lightly.

Reflection Activity

Is there any baggage, of which you are aware, that was passed down at birth (e.g. unwanted pregnancy, drug or alcohol use, adoption, wanted a girl instead of a boy (or vice versa), or something of the like)? Now, write out truth found in God's Word concerning your life and your existence. Spend some quiet time with the Lord and allow healing to take place. May we run this race with endurance! You can't run while carrying baggage. Let's get to unpacking! I support you, I believe in you, and I love you. You *can* do this. It's time for a baggage check:

Childhood Baggage

_____
_____
_____
_____
_____

Teenage Baggage

Adult Baggage

Parental Baggage

CHAPTER TWENTY-ONE

Unpacking and Forgiving

"To err is human, to forgive is divine."
~ Alexander Pope

What is *forgiveness*? It is to release, to let go completely. It is to lay it all down at Jesus' feet—to grant freedom and blessing to those who have hurt us. Forgiveness is to let go of our own view of justice and punishment. It is finding compassion in and through the pain. What is *unforgiveness*? It is holding on to or not releasing unresolved hurts, disappointments, anger, offences, and bitterness. Unforgiveness is like cancer. Although it can't be seen with the natural eye, it slowly eats away everything it touches. I once heard a statement that unforgiveness is like drinking poison expecting the other person to die. Unforgiveness causes *us* to suffer, not the person who has actually hurt us. When we forgive someone, we are not denying the wrong done to us, nor are we allowing the person to be a part of our lives where they could continue to hurt us. When we forgive, we are simply choosing not to allow it control over our lives. It sets *us* free, it makes *our* load lighter. It's removing all that junk from our baggage that doesn't belong to us.

What does forgiveness look like? Jesus is our perfect example. Forgiveness looks like Jesus hanging on a cross after being rejected, mocked, spit on, and beaten beyond our human understanding. It looks like Jesus standing in my place, dying for my sins, your sins, and the sins of those who have hurt us. I was the guilty one, they were the guilty ones, but Jesus, being fully aware of all our guiltiness, took our place. It should have been me on that cross. Instead, He hung there in unimaginable pain and He cried out for His Father to forgive all mankind—past, present and future—because we knew not what we were doing. You may read the full story in Luke chapter 23.

If you're anything like me, during my journey through forgiveness, my thoughts were, *"Oh, they knew good and well what they were doing."* Let's explore that mindset as it is so very important to understand that hurt people, hurt people. Yes, we have been hurt. The flipside is that we have hurt others as well, whether intentionally or unintentionally. It may not be in the same manner or magnitude, but we are guilty as well. The question is, *"Will we be the ones to stop the dysfunctional cycle?"* My parents didn't mean to hurt me, they didn't mean to hurt each other. They did the best they could with what they had.

My abusers didn't mean to hurt me. It's what they knew and it's who they had become because of the hurt done to them. They were just as much the victim as I. By no means does it excuse what was done and by no means does that mean we should stay in a romantic, platonic, parental, or any other relationship where any form of abuse is taking place. The sickness of codependency says to stay, that it's the "Christian thing" to do. Love and forgive. You know how many men, women, and children have been destroyed all in the name of love and forgiveness because they stay in such relationships? Neither do I because the numbers are countless.

God is a loving Father, right? Absolutely! What parent in their right mind would want their child to stay in any type of abusive relationship, be it sexual, physical, mental, spiritual, or emotional?

We can trust that our heavenly Father doesn't either. Forgiveness is a choice not based on feelings or emotions. When we make the choice to forgive, our feelings will eventually catch up. Remember what I have said about controlling our emotions and taking every thought captive? Here's where you will have to continually do them both.

Unforgiveness is like little demonic emojis running around freely in our head. They will continue to wreak havoc until we decide to evict them. Often times, we think they are gone but, as soon as someone pushes the right button, it's like the floodgates are opened. We can't sleep or all we want to do is sleep. We can't eat or we can't stop eating—we're an emotional wreck. These little demonic emojis have power over us; they control us because we have allowed them to take space in our heads and in our hearts.

Here's a practical example. Let's look at two different girls who were both, for years, sexually abused by their father. One child grows up having emotional issues. She becomes addicted to drugs, alcohol, sex, etc. She never deals with the pain of her childhood, nor does she forgive her father. She never seeks Jesus in the healing that could only come from Him. The second one has a pretty tough start, but she is determined to not let her past control her life any longer. She seeks help. She sits at Jesus' feet and allows Him to heal her from the inside out. She understands the power of forgiveness and, although it hurts, she relies on Jesus' strength in her to release the pain. Releasing is acknowledging to Jesus what she feels instead of dwelling on or entertaining the thoughts of terrible memories. *Secondly*, from her heart, she asks Jesus to take away the hurt, anger, and bitterness. No matter how many times the thoughts keep coming up, each time she turns her focus back to Jesus. *Thirdly*, she takes those thoughts captive and replaces them with the Word of God. This woman decides to use her pain to help others. She is able to freely speak about what her childhood was like, but absent of the pain. She has fought for her freedom. She has become a wounded warrior who reaches back to take the hands of those still trapped in their past.

The next example is of two different men, both hit by a drunk driver. Both men end up losing their legs in the tragic accident. One refuses therapy, becomes depressed, and very angry. He becomes difficult to be around, always hateful and refusing any type of assistance. He blames his terrible life on the drunk driver. The second guy presses his way through the pain of the recovery process. He welcomes any help he can get. He learns how to use prosthetic legs. He uses this tragedy to speak to high school students about the importance of drinking and driving. Through Jesus, he learned the power of forgiveness, extends it to the driver, and is grateful to be alive.

Reflection Activity

Can you think of any unforgiveness in your life? Are there people who you have not forgiven? Make a list and begin to meditate on God's Word so as to lead you successfully into lasting forgiveness.

_____
_____
_____
_____
_____
_____
_____

CHAPTER TWENTY-TWO

Same Experiences, Very Different Outcomes

"Choose whom you will serve (Jeremiah 24:14)."

Definition of Infirmity: a bodily ailment or weakness, a condition or disease producing weakness; a failing or defect in a person's *character*.

Definition of Character: personality, nature, disposition, temperament, temper, mentality; the mental and moral qualities distinctive to an individual.

The power of choice is the answer to why people can have the same experience with different outcomes. Each individual made a choice and each one of us must make our own choices every day. Will you choose to walk in the freedom of forgiveness or will you continue to walk in the bondage of unforgiveness? Your destiny is not a matter of *chance,* but of *choice.* It's not something for which you wait to happen; it must be achieved. What you and I make of our lives is solely up to us, it's our choice. It's time to take back what rightfully belongs to us.

Another question is, *"Do you want to be healed?"* Sounds like a crazy question, right, but it's really not crazy at all. Some people choose to hold on to their pain and baggage. They feel justified in holding on and they use it as an excuse, much like the examples in the previous chapter. People become comfortable in their pain instead of pressing through the initial hardship of recovery. Jesus asked a lame man that question, *"Do you want to be made well?"*

Let's look at that story in John 5:3-9:

> "In these lay a great multitude of sick people, blind, lame, paralyzed, waiting for the moving of the water. For an angel went down at a certain time into the pool and stirred up the water; then whoever stepped in first, after the stirring of the water, was made well of whatever disease he had. Now a certain man was there who had an infirmity thirty-eight years. When Jesus saw him lying there, and knew that he already had been in that condition a long time, He said to him, "Do you want to be made well?" The sick man answered Him, "Sir, I have no man to put me into the pool when the water is stirred up; but while I am coming, another steps down before me." Jesus said to him, "Rise, take up your bed and walk." And immediately the man was made well, took up his bed, and walked. And that day was the Sabbath."

Now, let me explain how this story directly related to my life. In verse three, there were a great multitude of sick people. It was a bunch of sick folks talking about sick stuff. When I was an alcoholic, I would sit around other sick folks and talk about sick stuff. I was going nowhere in life; I was stuck. In verse four, we see that whoever stepped in first was made well. The key here is *first*. I was never first. I was always last. I was always overlooked. So why try?

Verse five reads, "*Now a certain man was there who had an infirmity thirty-eight years.*" Thirty-eight years! As for me, I definitely had an infirmity and my character needed a serious makeover. Verse six goes on to say, "*When Jesus saw him lying there, and knew that he already had been in that condition a long time, He said to him, 'Do you want to be made well?'*" Just like the man in this story, I had been in that condition a long time, but I never did what I needed to do to get well. I was stuck.

Verse seven reads, "*The sick man answered Him, 'Sir, I have no man to put me into the pool when the water is stirred up; but while I am coming, another steps down before me.'*" Here again, just like this man, I had an excuse of not having a man in my life and I blamed my not getting well on others. My focus was on what I had been through, what someone had done to me, or what I was currently going through. If my husband wasn't cheating, if Joe wouldn't have died, if I wouldn't have been violated as a child, mentally abused, physically abused . . . if, if, if. The list goes on and on. Let us recall verse 4 which says, "*Whoever steps in first, gets well.*"

If he *wanted* to be well, the answer would have been much different. He says that, "*…while I am coming, someone cuts in front of me.*" This lets us know he wasn't paralyzed, as he had means of coming, but he had excuses and he blamed others for not being well. For thirty-eight years, someone has cut in front of him. Clearly, he had a victim mentality just as did I. Besides, that's what I was told by the therapist: I was a *victim*. I believe this man had become comfortable living this way and his mindset, or rather his character, kept him that way. And, yep, that was me.

His way of thinking kept him sick. When we get sick and tired of being sick and tired, by any means necessary, we are going after our healing. When we change our thoughts, we begin to change our life. Remember the woman with the issue of blood? She thought to herself, "*If I can touch the hem of His garment.*" When we change how we view ourselves, when we change what we say and what we do, this is what it looks like, "I am *not* going to live like this, I *will* be healed, and I *will* be victorious by any means necessary."

No longer do we live in the excuses of why we can't do or achieve something. When we want to be healed, our thinking becomes, *"I am going to be the first one in the water. I'm not waiting for the stirring, I'm getting in now and I'll wait in the water until the next stirring."* Unfortunately, there is a reality that many people do not want to see about their situation and that is *change*. Change means work. Change means doing something we have never done before. Change means leaving the familiar and stepping into the unfamiliar. Change can be painful and uncomfortable. This is not a desired reality.

While studying different commentaries on this particular story, this is the conclusion to which I came. This man probably made a living begging. If he was to be healed, he would be responsible to make his own living. One who is healed must change and take responsibility for his or herself. This is where I found myself; I had to take responsibility for myself. One of the hardest things in this journey was forgiving myself. After taking the *Making Peace* class and God showing me all my baggage, I was able to gain compassion for others. I saw my parents, my ex's, I saw all those who had hurt me, abused me, disappointed me, rejected me, etc. through the lens of Jesus. I saw each of them with their own baggage.

It wasn't mine to carry, it belonged to them. They became who they were because of their baggage. I was able to have grace toward them. That does not, adversely, mean I allowed them back into my life. Now I just had to find that same grace and give it to myself. One day, I was sharing my story with someone and I said to this person, *"If I could go back, I wouldn't change a thing. Today I am a better woman because of it. It was all worth it."* Sounds good, doesn't it? It may even sound noble and it may even sound spiritual, but it is not.

The more I thought about this statement, the more I took my thoughts off me and I thought about all the damage I had done to others. I think it's our innate selfishness to think about what we have been though, our pain, our hurts. We don't tend to think about the damage we have caused with our own words and our own actions. The more I thought about the statement, "*I wouldn't change a thing,*" I saw the faces of those I had hurt, those I had abused, those to whom I had lied, cheated, stole from. The truth is that, if I could go back, I would change everything.

Reflection Activity

Would you change your past? Do you want to change your future? What can you see in your life where, if you change, you'll have to take responsibility? Does the idea of accountability scare you?

_____
_____
_____
_____
_____
_____
_____
_____

CHAPTER TWENTY-THREE

I Would Change Everything

"It is human nature to want to go back and fix things or change things we regret."
~ John Gray

Saying, *"I'm sorry"* can never fully erase the pain I have caused my parents—the disrespect, disobedience, rebellion, words spoken in pure anger. The *"I hate you,"* the *"I wish I were never born,"* *"you're not my real dad,"* and so many more unpleasant words caused them so much pain. I think about the times I ran away and they didn't know where I was, what I was doing, or if I would be found alive. Having children of my own has made it more real to me how my behavior must have devastated my parents and broken their hearts. I can't imagine the pain I caused. I can't imagine the tears and the thoughts of failure which flooded their minds. Oh, if I could go back, I would do it all differently. My heart grieves thinking about the damage I caused as a child.

As you know, I had my first daughter, Jazmine, when I was eighteen years old. I had no clue who I was. I was full of baggage. I was caught up in a lifestyle of drugs, alcohol, men, and partying. I often chose my lifestyle over her. To me, she was this beautiful little baby to show off, but I had no clue how to love or nurture her. I am so very thankful for her father's side of the family as his mother and sister played a huge part in molding her into the amazing woman she is today.

It hurts my heart when I think about the situations in which I placed her such as using drugs, selling drugs, drinking, and having different men in and out of my house all in her presence. Shame often tells me I failed her as a mother, but the truth in God's Word has worked it all out for my good (Romans 8:28). She has seen her mother go from death unto life. She has witnessed firsthand what God has done in and through me. My heart grieves thinking about what I wasn't able to give her growing up.

Remember the church-guy? Well, I eventually married him and gained legal custody of two of his children. Because I was hurting, I ended up hurting them. Remembering what I put them through as I type these words breaks my heart. By no means do I offer this as an excuse. I was lost, broken, and full of even more baggage when I became involved with their father. I was looking and longing for the same thing they were—acceptance, unconditional love, security, worth, and value. I was controlled by this need. I ignored all the warning signs that this was not a healthy relationship for either of us. My desperate neediness to have a husband and family blinded me from seeing the reality of my situation.

The reality was that I had no clue what love was. I had no clue how to be a wife, much less a mother. Because of my codependency, I was desperately trying to fill a void which caused me to focus on getting *my* needs met. When my need for love, acceptance, worth, value, and security was filled, then I would be able to meet the needs of others. The thing is that my needs were never met because I was looking in the wrong places. I had unfair and unrealistic expectations of their father. I was looking for him to do what only God could do and, by doing so, I made him my god.

In my attempt to be a good wife and a loving mother, I failed miserably. I was not a good wife and I was not a good mother. In my endeavor to have the perfect life, I ended up causing more damage than good for them, me, and their dad. Although we were all going to church each week, sometimes two or three times a week, the way we lived displayed nothing which represented Christ other than some Christian rap music and church clothes. My husband and I were still drinking, listening to secular music, cursing at each other, and fighting. Oh, sure, we were trying. We were part of an amazing ministry at church. We did cookouts, small groups, and even went on family retreats together. We lived like that many years.

The problem was that we didn't have a real connection with the person of Jesus. We didn't understand the dynamics of a personal relationship. We heard the "personal relationship" part, but we totally missed it. We were so caught up in each other and the things of the world that we were saying we had a relationship with Jesus, but we did nothing to cultivate it. Neither one of us was pursuing intimacy with Christ, we were simply church goers.

I didn't know that everything I sought in this man could only be found in Jesus. I wanted my husband to complete me, heal me, and make me whole. I wanted him to love away all my pain and baggage—pain and baggage, mind you, I didn't even know I was carrying, but I expected him to know. My focus was on this man and this marriage and what he was and wasn't doing. Like I said previously, he had become my god. He was my idol. I worshiped him.

After years of trying, I wanted out. Since this man didn't want to act right, I was done. This is around the time I found out I was pregnant with my second child. I was so upset at God for allowing me to get pregnant. Did God not hear me when I said I wanted out? Shortly after I found out I was expecting, an incident happened with my stepchildren. Because of my own selfishness, I didn't stand up for them. I made some really poor choices which caused them both a lot of pain. I was only thinking about me and how to get out of this marriage. I saw this as an opportunity to have one less responsibility to worry about. Eventually, they went to live with their biological mother in a different state hours away. Additionally, their mother and I have a beautiful relationship. She was there for me during some really dark days. She was able to give me hope, encouragement, and strength when I wanted to give up. I thank God for her. I admire and honor her journey as well, a beautiful woman of great strength and dignity. She is a survivor.

I put all the blame on their father. If he would have acted right, if he would have stopped drinking, if he would have stopped going out, if he wouldn't have been physically or mentally abusive, I wouldn't be in this predicament. Everything was about *him*; it was *his* fault we were going through all of this. The pain in my heart hurts as I relive the memories of these events caused by my own choices. My heart is saddened for my stepchildren, whom I love deeply.

By the time Jada was born, she and Jazmine were the only children in the house. Jazmine, being ten years old, became my babysitter. I wanted out of this marriage and I didn't want the responsibility of taking care of a baby. Shortly after Jada was born, I started drinking daily and using prescription drugs. Emotionally, I was holding onto much anger and bitterness toward my husband. In my eyes, everybody else was to blame; it was always someone else's fault for my life being so unhappy. I was so depressed. I really didn't want to live. What was the point? Life was dark and painful. My husband was still hanging out late nights and some nights he didn't make it home at all. I've heard excuses from, "*I fell asleep in the parking lot of the club*" to "*I lost my keys and phone*" to "*I fell asleep watching the game at my homeboys house.*"

I was so sick of it. I starred, waiting until he would leave, and then I would leave too. I was going to show him. What's good for the goose is good for the gander. I realize now that two wrongs don't make it right, but I sure was able to sleep better at night. He thought he was playing me but I was going to show him. *"I can play this game way better than you. Watch me,"* was my sick thinking. I was back to seeking attention from other men. I was hanging out at bars and clubs, while praying he didn't end up at the same location. One night, I didn't make it back before he did. We started fighting, it got really ugly, and the girls got involved. We were screaming, yelling, and cussing at each other.

Jazmine was pleading for us to stop, Jada was crying and, in the heat of the argument, he called Jazmine something ugly. The thing is, words spoken out loud can never be taken back and those words left an imprint only God can erase. In that moment, I saw myself taking his life. I knew, without a shadow of doubt, that one of us was going to end up getting killed. The police arrived and made us separate for the night. I took Jazmine and he kept Jada. I returned a few days later and asked him to leave, to which he responded, *"No."* Although the house was in my name, because of the fact we were legally married and living together, I could not make him leave.

My mind was made up. He could have it. I could care less if it burned to the ground. To me, this was a place of torture and bondage. It had become a prison cell to me. I told him I was leaving and he told me I couldn't take Jada. It hurts to say but, the truth was, I didn't care. I didn't want the responsibility of taking care of a four-year-old. I packed mine and Jasmine's stuff and we left. I felt guilty for leaving Jada, but it didn't stop me. I just drank more so I didn't have to think about it. I made sure to tell people how awful my husband was and that he wouldn't let me take her. Never did I share the real truth that I didn't fight for her. Putting the blame on him gave me justification for my actions, but it left me full of more shame and guilt.

So many things I did and said to my parents, children, and husband. To say I wouldn't change a thing was incorrect. So many things I did and said to myself. I had become my own worst enemy. I had to learn how to forgive me. I had to learn how to extend grace to myself. Through this process, I have learned the power of prayer and the importance of letting go of my baggage, baggage that started with rejection, abuse, neglect, disappointment, soul-wounds, anger, bitterness, and rage. All of which eventually turned into unforgiveness. I learned the importance of getting to the root of the problem.

I have forgiven those who have hurt me. I have forgiven myself for the hurt I caused others and myself. I can look back today and I am thankful and grateful for the relationships I have with each one of my children and grandchildren. Today, I love them without guilt and shame. Who I was is no longer who I am. As for each one of my children, it's up to them to choose; they will either choose to walk in bondage or they will choose freedom. They will either continue to carry their baggage created by others and themselves or they will decide to let it all go. They will have to choose for their own lives if they are going to take the necessary steps to get to the root of the problem or they can deny there is a problem and continue the cycle of dysfunction. A broken life full of pain will eventually pass down to their children. They must choose and I must pray, encourage, and love them right where they are in life no matter what they choose.

I pray fervently for each one of them, that they learn the power of forgiveness, that they too are able to make peace with their past. I pray each one of them chooses to make Jesus the Lord of their lives, that they come to know the depth and height of Jesus' love for them, and that they will be rooted and grounded in that love as described in Ephesians 3:18. I also pray the same for you, my sweet friend. It is important to let you know that the enemy doesn't stop. The closer I get to God, the louder the accusations the enemy yells in my ear. He reminds me often that I failed them as a parent. He still reminds me of past mistakes and choices I have made concerning them. Every time one of them makes personal decisions which end up causing their hearts to be broken, he lets me know that I taught them and that they are living the example I set.

The enemy reminds me often of the horrible way I trained my children. So many times, I have to fight by taking those thoughts captive and speak the Word of God back to him. The enemy is right. During my early years of parenting, I didn't raise them in the ways of the Lord. Regardless, Romans 8:28 tells me that God will work all things out for my good because I love God. God promises me that my children will be blessed. So, I choose to stand on the promises instead of feeding into the lies.

> "Train up a child in the way he should go, and when he is old he will not depart from it (Proverbs 22:6)."

Reflection Activity

What lies are you feeding your soul? Do you have someone reminding your of your past sins and indiscretions? Are you able to pull down those wrong thoughts and take them captive? What lies are you being told?

_____
_____
_____
_____
_____
_____
_____

CHAPTER TWENTY-FOUR

I Am Forgiven

"Darkness cannot drive out darkness; only light can do that. Hate cannot drive out hate; only love can do that."
~ Martin Luther King, Jr.

"If we confess our sins, He is faithful and just to forgive us our sins and to cleanse us from all unrighteousness (I John 1:9)."

"Be kind to one another, tenderhearted, forgiving one another, as God in Christ forgave you (Ephesians 4:32)."

"But I say to you who hear, love your enemies, do good to those who hate you (Luke 6:27)."

"Judge not, and you will not be judged; condemn not, and you will not be condemned; forgive, and you will be forgiven (Luke 6:37)."

He does not deal with us according to our sins, nor repay us according to our iniquities. For as high as the heavens are above the earth, so great is His steadfast love toward those who fear Him; as far as the east is from the west, so far does He remove our transgressions from us. As a father shows compassion to his children, so the Lord shows compassion to those who fear Him. For He knows our frame; He remembers that we are dust (Psalm 103:10-14).

I have confessed my sins. I have repented. This means I have turned from my sins and now walk in that forgiveness.

Prayer of Forgiveness: *Father, I acknowledge that my heart hurts because of the wrong done to me by others. My heart also hurts because of the wrong I have done to others as well as myself. I don't want to carry this hurt anymore. I want to forgive, but I need Your help. Teach me how to release all the pain, disappointment, rejection, abandonment, offenses, mistakes, ill spoken words, anger, bitterness, or anything else I may be carrying which keeps me from experiencing all You have for me. I willingly give it all to You. When the thoughts come to my mind, those which remind me of all of the hurt, help me to take those thoughts captive and replace them with Your truth. No matter how I may feel, remind me forgiveness is not based on feelings. Remind me it is a choice. In Jesus' name we pray, Amen.*

Reflection Activity

Today, I choose to forgive (*list everyone you need to forgive*).

Spend time with the Lord asking Him to show you if there is anyone you need to forgive. Sometimes we know immediately, but other times we need to spend time asking the Lord to reveal it because we have suppressed so much. Sometimes we truly believe we have already forgiven someone, but we haven't. Either way, spend time and ask the Lord to search your heart. Read and meditate on Psalm 139:23-24. Make a list. Start with, "Today, I choose to forgive myself."

_____

_____

_____

_____

_____

_____

Prayer: *I release it all to You, Father, and I know that, in Your perfect timing, You will cause all things to work together for my good if I love you (Romans 8:28). I thank You that You have not dealt with me according to my sins. I thank You for the compassion You have shown me and for Your steadfast love. I give You permission to move through me and my experiences so as to bring freedom to others. No longer can the enemy use my past to keep me in a place of bondage. God, as I receive Your grace, cause me to give it freely to those connected to me. I declare that, today, I have received Your forgiveness and I release forgiveness to others. In Jesus' name, Amen.*

I encourage you to listen to this song by Mary Mary entitled, "Forgiven Me." I kept this song on repeat as I went through my process of forgiving myself. I even wrote the words and kept them beside my bed. I pray this song brings just as much healing to you as it did for me. Here are the lyrics:

I hold a memory of myself
Reflections of what I used to be
These broken roads that got me here
Can't make it hard to face reality
But a new day is here
It's time that I embrace it
Can't wait another day
Right now I gotta face it

I never ever wanna press rewind
Never wanna go back in time
Not much glory
In that story but it's mine so I'm
Loving who I am today
The past has passed away
Finally I
Have forgiven me

Confessions of an X-Codependent

I hold a memory of myself
So young and foolish and not knowing
Careless decisions that I made
I wish somebody would have told me
But a new day is here
It's time that I embrace it
Can't wait another day
Right now I gotta face it

I never ever wanna press rewind
Never wanna go back in time
Not much glory
In that story but it's mine so I'm
Loving who I am today
The past has passed away
Finally I
Have forgiven me
The mirror on the wall
It makes me see today
That I'm, I'm not that foolish girl
Time has brought a change
A transformation
The old into the new
When I let go of me
And held on to you

I never ever wanna press rewind
Never wanna go back in time
Not much glory
In that story but it's mine so I'm
Loving who I am today
The past has passed away
Finally I
Have forgiven me

I never ever wanna press rewind
Never wanna go back in time
Not much glory
In that story but it's mine so I'm
Loving who I am today
The past has passed away
Finally I
Have forgiven me

Yes Lord, finally I have forgiven me
(end song lyrics)

The Topic of Abortion

Remember in chapter six when I talked about residue? Abortion is one of those things in our life that leaves a residue and God wants to clean it out and bring total healing! Unfortunately, we live in a world where it's not only widely accepted but, most times, it is encouraged to have an abortion. But what's *not* talked about is the aftermath of abortion—the shame, guilt, condemnation, accusations, and torment caused by it. I am here to tell you that God not only wants to make you clean, but also He wants to bring healing and for you to experience forgiveness in that area of your life. Sometimes, just like the residue, it takes time and effort on our part. Each person's journeys will look different, but here are a few steps I encourage you to do.

1. *Repent*
2. *Ask for forgiveness*
3. *Seek counseling or join a grief class.* There are many ministries out there that help people in the healing process of abortion. Also, there are many ministries that will help if you're contemplating abortion. You may have to do a little research to find one, but it will be worth it.

4. *Don't allow the fear to keep you stuck* in the place of tormenting thoughts and don't listen to the lies of the enemy that may tell you it doesn't affect your life or your emotions. Even if we are not consciously aware of it, it does, and you need someone who can help you walk through the process.

Reflection Activity

A lily is often used at funerals because it symbolizes that the soul of the departed has received restored innocence. You baby was always innocent. If you struggle to visualize your baby, visualize a pure lily. I want you to go on a mental journey with me. As you do this exercise, I want you to know that you are not alone. Picture God or me being in the room with you. Just know that you are not alone.

I want you to think of that child. Was it a boy or a girl? Some people know the gender, but others may not. If you don't know, that's okay—ask God to tell you. Remember, God doesn't always speak in an audible voice, so it may be just a gut feeling you have. After you know the sex of your baby, I want you to name your baby if you haven't already done so. You may need to spend some time thinking about it. You may even ask the Lord to help you name him or her if you have to. After naming your baby, I want you to hold your baby, spend some time with your baby, cry over your baby, talk to your baby, and then, when you are ready, hand your baby into the loving arms of Jesus. As you do so, I want you to release all the negative thoughts and emotions as well. No matter how many abortions you had, whether one or too many to count, I want you to know that Jesus doesn't condemn you. This allows you to stop condemning yourself. You are forgiven. Now you must forgive yourself! Release your baby or babies and let them go. They are in Heaven now surrounded by the perfect love of their Heavenly Father. I want to close this chapter with some very powerful tools God used during the forgiveness process in my life.

Misty Edwards is a very powerful and anointed musician used by the Lord to bring healing and deliverance to those who desire inner healing. You can listen to all these and more, but I definitely encourage you to listen to:

1. "I Knew What I Was Getting Into"
2. "What Does Love Look Like"
3. "Broken Men"
4. "Songs of Deliverance"

Jesus is asking, "*Do you want to be healed? Do you want to be made whole?*" Write whatever you're feeling and want to remember.

_____

_____

_____

_____

_____

_____

_____

CHAPTER TWENTY-FIVE

The Heart of the Matter Is a Matter of the Heart

"The heart is more deceitful than all else and is desperately sick; who can understand it (Jeremiah 17:9)."

What happened in 2000 when I got "saved"? I was trying to get close to God. I was reading the Word of God. But, as I told you before, I was focused on things like "women shouldn't cut their hair and wear a head covering." I know it may sound crazy, but I started feeling guilty and condemned because I had short hair. I tried reaching out to my assigned deacon because I had so many questions. I felt like I didn't understand anything I was reading. He tried his best to explain, yet I still didn't get it. I wanted so badly to understand. Unfortunately, I was still caught up in my lifestyle, so I had remaining destructive habits and addictions.

This was after the police raid, so I wasn't using powder cocaine anymore and I had stopped going out. I was still drinking and smoking weed, however. I used to get up in the morning, roll a blunt, and watch preaching. Being high on weed used to make me feel really intelligent and deep, and then I would get really hungry, eat everything in the house, and get super sleepy. I would go to sleep only to wake up and repeat. It was a cycle in which I was stuck. My twisted way of thinking was, "Marijuana was from the earth, so there was nothing wrong with smoking it, right?"

Prior to getting saved, Heather, myself, and two other girls had planned and paid for our Memorial Day Bike Week trip to Myrtle Beach, South Carolina, aka Black Bike Week. I told myself there would be no harm in going. *"I don't have to participate in the sinfulness I had in the past. I would just be going to people-watch and hang out. I am strong,"* was my thinking. After all, I wasn't drinking or smoking anymore. A part of me wanted to go and a part of me didn't. I reasoned with the part of myself that didn't want to go. *"I have to go,"* I told myself, *"It was already paid and everything is in my name, so I couldn't not go. The other girls wouldn't have a ride or a place to stay if I back out, plus they paid on the trip as well. I am obligated. I'm good, I got this."*

A week before we left, I ran into that guy from church. You know, the one who was at church with both his kids. We chitchatted for a while. He asked for my number and said he would call me later that night. He kept his word and we literally stayed on the phone all night. I felt like I was in high school. After our conversation, I didn't want to go to Bike Week. I wanted to stay so that I could spend time with him. I knew I wouldn't be right to back out on my friends since they were depending on me. I made up my mind to go anyway, but we promised to talk every day.

Heather and I were all packed and ready to go. We picked up the other two young ladies and headed to the beach. Now, when I say young, I mean young! We had no business even taking them with us to Bike Week. Heather and I were 24 and they were teenagers. We thought we were something big in our rented, gold Impala. You couldn't tell us we weren't fly! Until, that is, we saw the blue lights behind us. Was he pulling us over? Are you kidding me? I didn't even realize I had been speeding. *"I wasn't used to this car,"* was my excuse and I was sticking to it. The officer was nice as he asked for the usual information and I handed it to him. He asked where we were headed. Before I could answer, he said, *"Let me guess, Bike Week?"*

"*Yep,*" we all replied with excitement. He noticed the cooler in the back seat and said, *"You got Diet Coke and water in that cooler, right?"* We all busted out laughing. We opened the cooler, which was mine and, literally, water and Diet Coke filled it. All the other times, that same cooler was filled with Bud Lights, so I was feeling proud of myself. We all laughed. He still ended up giving me a speeding ticket, though. I thought for sure he was going to give me a warning.

As we pulled off, I was feeling some kind of way. I started talking junk about all the other cars that had passed us and they were going way faster than us. One car that passed us was so full of weed smoke you couldn't even see in the car. He should have stopped them. Oh, well, I would wait to worry about that added expense when I got home. The closer we got to the beach, the more excited we were. Once we got settled into our room, I called home to let my new friend know we had made it safely. This was way before the cell phone days. He was so sweet. He told me he missed me already and to be safe. I couldn't wait to get back home so we could spend time together.

I was impressed and excited by the fact he wasn't going to Bike Week—everybody went to Bike Week. He was different from all the other guys, or so I thought. Every year I went to Bike Week, I rented the same room. It was on the main strip with a connecting deck. All we had to do was walk out our door and we were right in the middle of all the action. We quickly got ourselves together and sat on the deck so that we could people and car-watch. We laughed and picked on people for everything from how they were acting to what they had on. We got excited over all the different pimped out cars and bikes. We ran into all kinds of people we knew from back home. We were chill'n and having a good time. We pretty much stayed close to the room our first day.

That night, I went to sleep feeling proud of myself for "staying saved." Day one and no drinking, no drugs, no men, no crazy conversations with men, no flirting. I was proud of myself; I could do it. Day two, we decided to venture out. We got in the car, pumped the music, and we were feeling ourselves. We soon met four really cool guys on bikes who were all staying together. They told us they were from Milwaukee, Wisconsin. I only remembered because Milwaukee was the name of a beer— the mind of an alcoholic.

They invited us to go swimming they were staying. Why not? They were cool, had bikes, and they were cute. It didn't take us long to decide we were all going. If one goes, we all go, was the rule. In that moment, we were all game. We followed them to where they were lodging and hung out for a while before heading to the pool. They offered us something to drink and I declined. I was sticking to my plan of no drinking. I really wanted a beer though, and everybody else was drinking. After hanging out at the pool for a few hours, we all made plans to hang out that night together. They each picked us up on their bikes and went riding. We were having a ball, you couldn't tell us anything.

They told us they worked together as police officers. I was thinking to myself, *"They sure do a lot of drinking and driving to be police officers."* Then again, I'm sure they were lying. We didn't care. We were living in the moment and having fun. I was just glad I wasn't snorting powder cocaine anymore because I probably would have had it with me. We ended up back at their place. This time, when they offered a drink, I accepted. It was already late and everybody was drinking, so they thought it would be best if we just spent the night and take us back in the morning. We ended up spending the night. Well, so much for being "saved." That only lasted the first day.

To me, being "saved" was following a bunch of rules and regulations. If I followed the rules and regulations, *then* I would be able to earn God's approval and *then* I would be saved. In order to stay saved, I had to work at being perfect. No drinking, no drugs, no partying, and no sex. As for the rules I was to follow, I felt like I already had a strike against me because I had short hair. As silly as that sounds, I really thought God loved me less because of my hair. So, already I believed a lie that God wasn't pleased with me. I remembered thinking how I needed to go home and "do good" so I could be saved again. I just needed to tell God I was sorry and do good so I could earn God's love, acceptance, and approval.

I also couldn't wait to get home to spend time with the church guy. *"Maybe he will be the one,"* was my thinking. I was excited about the fact I had met him at church, not some club, not at Bike Week, not in the streets. We met at church. This *had* to be a sign from God. I just knew for sure he was the godly Christian man for which I had longed. The day I got back, I called and he was excited to hear from me. He said he wanted to come over and spend some time with me. I went and picked him up from his sister's house where he was living.

He ended up spending the night and he never left, literally. I was quickly introduced to two of his children. On the weekends, we would pick them up so they could stay with us. In my mind, this was what I had always wanted: a family. We spent most weekends doing fun stuff with the kids from cookouts to spending the day on the lake, going to eat pizza together, and things of the like. He liked to drink and hang out with his friends. So, in my attempt to change him, I would plan family outings so that we could all be together. I thought if I could just keep his mind off hanging out, it would change him. But after the kids went to bed, he would say he would be right back. Sometimes "right back" would turn into the next morning. He would often times be drunk and belligerent. I continued to live in a fantasyland thinking I could transform him into the family man I so desperately wanted and needed.

Occasionally, we would all go to church together, but we were definitely not pursuing God individually. I had stopped doing all the things I had been doing right after getting saved such as reading my Bible, watching preaching on TV, etc. My focus was completely wrapped in this man and his children. I didn't have time for anything else. The truth was that I didn't *want* to have time for anything else. I was in love and I was determined to have the family I had always wanted. I was making my plans and then telling God what I wanted Him to do with my plans. Psalm 127:1 states, *"Unless the Lord builds the house, the builders labor in vain."* I had never even read the book of Psalms before, so I surely didn't know about Psalm 127:1. All my building was in vain.

I became excessively controlling and jealous. I thought every woman who looked at or spoke to him wanted him. I was so scared he was going to leave me. I saw how he would look at other women and it would make me feel intensely insecure. I never felt I was good enough. I was determined to make him love me. I would do more. I loved and looked forward to the times we all spent together as a family. I wanted that so badly. I would plan more trips, more outings, more anything I could so as to be together. I would do anything to show him how much I loved him by how much I loved and took care of his kids. We were going to make this work, I just knew we would.

I was the only one working so, during the week, instead of taking my daughter to daycare, I would leave her with him. It was part of my way of controlling things. If he had to watch her, he couldn't run the streets and do whatever he wanted. One day, I got off early. When I got home, my baby was outside playing by herself. No adults or other children in sight. He was nowhere to be found. I was furious! I knew he was cheating, I could feel it. The longer I stayed outside waiting for him to show up, the more enraged I became. About thirty or forty-five minutes later, I saw him coming out of one of the sets of apartments. The way the apartments were set up, I couldn't tell the exact apartment.

I was crying. I was so mad. I screamed and cursed at him calling him every name I could think, other than what his mama had named him, as I was throwing his stuff out the door. I was done. I couldn't keep doing that. I remember standing in the shower that night crying my eyes out telling the Lord to help me to not let him back into our lives. I asked the Lord to keep the hatred I felt in my heart. In my hatred, the guy couldn't get back in. It was when I had calmed down that he would come with the "I'm sorry. I love you. Just give me another chance." I was so tired of being disrespected, cheated on, and taken advantage. All I did for him, all I did for his kids—how could he do this to me, to us? I wondered, *"Why wasn't I enough? Why wasn't my love enough?"* Mary J. Blige's song, "Not Gon' Cry" stayed on repeat. All the sacrifices, all the hurt. Mary helped me be strong and not go back.

NOT KNOWING OUR TRUE IDENTITY WILL CAUSE US TO COMPROMISE AND TO COMPARE AND COMPETE WITH OTHERS.

There were countless stories and incidents. I could write a whole book about them alone. The point is, this was the reality of where I was. I was broken and so were the men I allowed into mine and my daughter's life. I didn't have low self-esteem—I had no self-esteem. It caused me to settle for less than God's best for my life. Not knowing our true identity will cause us to compromise and to compare and compete with others. This was where I was, although I didn't know it much less understand it. People would tell me I deserved better but, to me, this was the best it could get.

Remember, you attract what you are, whether you know you're broken or not. Dysfunction attracts dysfunction, drama attracts drama, and hurt people hurt people. By no means was I the innocent one. I used my mouth as a weapon and I would speak things that never should have been thought, much less spoken.

Reflection Activity

Where is your heart? Is God the center of your heart or is it men and/or women? Is it children, attention, career, money, or anything or anyone other than God? What are you attracting? Take a moment to reflect on this chapter and see if anything resonates with your life. Write what comes to mind.

CHAPTER TWENTY-SIX

Anyway, Back To the Drama

"Hope is being able to see that there is light despite all of the darkness."
~ Desmond Tutu

Back to the church guy—the one with kids—I can't tell you how many times we did the "break up and get back together" thing. Every time I would go back, it was always with a promise he was going to change; we were going to be a family. The anger in my hurt subsided and, once again, I fell for the *"I'm sorry"* speech. It's funny how we would rather believe a dressed-up lie than the buck-naked truth. This time, I gave him an ultimatum: either we were going to do it God's way or no way. I told him we had to start going back to church, that we couldn't keep living the way we were. I stressed to him I wasn't going to continue living in sin together. We were either going to get married or we weren't going to be together. He agreed to my terms. Unfortunately, there seemed to be two problems with this:

1. My thinking was warped
2. Church wasn't the answer, Christ alone was

First, going to church made me no more a true Christian than standing in a garage made me a car. Secondly, church folks love to tell people they are living in sin and they should get married, that in marriage, God would honor their commitment. *"God don't bless no mess,"* is what we were told. We were informed that marriage was the answer, that we needed to stop living in sin. Truth is, if both of us would have been taught who we were in Christ, we would have never been together to start with.

God was nowhere in that relationship, it was all us. What attracted us to each other was strictly lust. Plain and simple, we were drawn by a physical attraction. We had not a single clue what love was. Our sexual desire for each other and the promise of a family created a soul-tie, one which was codependent, dysfunctional, and very unhealthy for both of us. We were tied to each other. Instead of tying the knot, we should have been burning the ropes and breaking the chains which held us in bondage to each other.

I was back to my "doing all the right things" so as to be accepted by God and for Him to bless us. I just needed to clean up my act, get it together, stop drinking, stop wearing a certain type of clothes, stop cursing, stop listening to that music, go to church, stop living in sin, and get married. I spent eight long years in that marriage. The first several years, I tried so hard to live right. We were always at church. I felt good so long as I was there, but it seemed as if a black cloud was over me as soon as I left.

The only thing that had changed was us getting married and getting custody of two of his children. He was still going out on occasion, still drinking and being irresponsible. The first year or so, it wasn't that much but, soon after, it became more and more frequent. Again, I blamed him when I started drinking again. My theory was, *"If he wouldn't keep bringing it in the house, I wouldn't be tempted to drink it."*

At church, they talked so much about the importance of fulfilling your purpose. I desperately wanted to know what my purpose was, but how? I always felt like I wanted to help other women. I could give other people really good advice, I just couldn't apply that same advice to my own life. My own advice didn't work because I wasn't the problem—as stated previously—everybody else was. I felt like I was trapped in this cage like a hamster. There were times I thought I was moving forward but it was only an illusion. Much like the hamster on his exercise wheel, no matter how hard, , or slowly I ran, I wasn't going anywhere—I was stuck.

I just thought to myself, *"If my situation were different, I would be okay. If I had a husband that respected me, loved me, and cared for me, I would be okay. If he would treat me better, I would be able to focus more on the kids. He was always making me so angry. If I wasn't so mad all the time, I wouldn't lose my temper so quickly and curse at the kids."* It was entirely *his* fault; I was just a poor victim. I felt all alone in a house full of people.

Going to church, I wished I could have a different husband. I wanted a husband who was a pastor who followed God for real. If I could just marry a pastor, he would love me. He would treat me with respect. One weekend, my husband and I attended our annual tailgating at a football game with some of our church friends. Shortly after arriving, some of his "other" friends stopped by the tent, friends of which I didn't approve. He told me he was going walking with a group of friends and I thought to myself, *"No way was he going without me!"* I took that as my cue to get up and follow along. I had to make sure he didn't go smoke, drink, or flirt with other females. I got up and stood beside him and said I was going to walk with them too. Being bored was my excuse for wanting to tag along. He looked at me and said very harshly, *"No, you're not going with us."* He said it loudly and in front of everyone. I was so embarrassed and hurt.

It's hard to explain how I felt. The best way to describe it is that I felt like the annoying little "fat" sister trying to tag along with her big brother. And who wants to be bothered with your "fat" annoying little sister? I just knew he was going to holla at other chicks. I sat my fat self back down in that chair as I fought so hard to hold in the tears. A few did manage to slip out. I felt so disgusted with myself. If I were skinny and had this and had that, he would want me to go. It was my looks. My sadness quickly turned to utter rage.

I sat in that chair and made up in my mind that, this time next year I was going to be fine and was not attending tailgating with him. I was going to show him. I had always been so insecure about my weight. It was true, I was fat. Weight was an issue my whole life. When we married, I was a size 20 about 200 pounds but, over the years, my weight had increased. I was now wearing a size 22/24 weighing 235 lbs. I guess my dad was right. I was going to be fat just like my mother and my sister.

That day, as I sat in that chair, I was internally an emotional wreck. Anger was the emotion that drove the vehicle and it was in complete control. I was determined. I was going to change everything and I did. I started eating healthier meals and exercising every day. I would get out of breath just walking to the mailbox and back, but I kept doing it. For a week, I walked just to my mailbox and back a few times. The following week, I walked to the end of my road and back. Each week, I added more distance until I was able to walk three miles every day. I would sit at my desk and use hand weights and a Thigh Master in between customers. On my lunch break, I would walk. When I got home from work, I would walk.

I became obsessed. I felt like I wasn't in control, though, it felt as if a force greater than myself was fueling my obsession to look good. I was on a mission and nothing was going to stop me. The voice in my head said we could do this; we were going to get revenge. We were going to show him; we were going to make him jealous. *"If you were skinny, he would stop cheating. You see how he looks at skinny women,"* the voices would taunt me. Yes, this was the answer. I was going to get skinny, make him jealous by gaining attention from other men, and then he would want me and be faithful.

It took me about nine or ten months to get down to a size 12 @180 lbs from a 22/24 @235 lbs. You couldn't tell me anything. I felt free. I felt like I had been trapped in a fat suit all my life. I was getting compliments and it made me feel really good about myself. A year had passed and the football game rolled around. I kept my promise to myself—I wasn't going with him. A few days before the game, he asked me something about what time we were leaving and who was going to keep the kids. I said it just as nasty and as hateful as he had said what he said to me a year earlier, *"We ain't going nowhere together. I'mmmmmm going with my girl Tasha and the crew."* These were the ones with whom I used to run the streets.

At the game, I was having a ball with my home-girls drinking, and laughing. I felt alive again. I loved all the attention I was getting. It made me feel so good about myself. While hanging out, my husband walked up out of hundreds of people. How in the world did he find us? As we were standing there, he reached down for my hand and my heart skipped a beat. He was actually holding my hand; he wanted people to know we were together and that I was his wife. It made me feel like a princess and my prince had come to get me. We didn't come together but we did leave together. It worked, my plan had actually worked.

The next day at work, my co-worker called me and asked if my husband and I were still together. With excitement, I said, "*Yes*," but my excitement quickly turned to panic. Why would she ask me that? She began to tell me how she and her girlfriend were at the game and they ran into my husband. She told me he kept trying to holler at her friend to the point that her friend was feeling very uncomfortable around him. My co-worker spoke up and said something about me and he said we weren't together. What? We weren't together? My mind started racing. My heart felt as if it were going to come out of my chest like I couldn't breathe. *"God, help me, what's happening?"*

The room started spinning. I felt like I was going to throw up. As I desperately tried to calm myself, rage, from the bottom of my toes, began to rise up my entire body. The voice of rage was so loud in my head. *"Since he couldn't get with her, he came and found you, the stupid one; the one he walks all over, the one he continues to cheat on. I can't keep doing this. Lord, I just want out. I don't even want to live, I am tired, and I am tired of trying. I had been faithful to that man all those years and this is the thanks I get."*

In the weeks and months that passed, a deep darkness covered me. I felt almost zombie-like. I was numb. I drank more. I went to a doctor who would give me any type pill for which I asked. I got loaded up with all kinds of prescriptions and I began to take them all. Four years together and not once did I even dream of cheating on him. He was my everything. Oh, sure, I had a bad attitude, said some pretty awful things. I would get mad and break things or cut up something of his. I would threaten to put him out, but I never cheated. I was faithful. At one point, we even went to marriage counseling. At our first appointment, I gave the counselor the scoop about all my husband's dirt. I probably told the counselor about every single time I had caught my husband cheating or in a bald-faced lie.

It seemed as though I would catch him in a lie on a daily basis. Every time I would catch him in something, it would take me all the way back to the very first time he had hurt me. I could name dates, times, and places. I could remember what he was wearing and who he was with. It was as though a movie screen was playing the same horror movie in my head and I couldn't turn it off. The counseling session ended with the recommendation that I come back next time alone. The counselor said I was depressed and he wanted to put me on an antidepressant. *"Are you kidding me?"* I was beyond mad. I was not depressed, if this @%##*@**%$#@ would stop cheating on me, I would be okay. Needless to say, I never went back. That @%##*@**%$#@ counselor had no idea what he was talking about!

After my co-worker called me, I was so done. I had lost all my weight and I was feeling good about myself. I felt like I was finally skinny enough that someone else would want me now. My mind was made up. I wanted out of this marriage. I made another doctor's appointment and that's when I was told I was pregnant. I liked to have passed out. The room started spinning as I felt dizzy and nauseated. *"I can't be pregnant, this can't be! God, you've got to be kidding me. Why him? Why now, why God?"* I cried out.

That appointment left me in a whirlwind of emotions. A part of me wanted to be happy. I remembered the conversations of us wanting a child together. Then the horror story started playing in my mind; all the cheating, lies, and fighting flooded my thoughts. I cried until my whole body hurt. This was all I ever wanted, a family, but not like this. Depression covered me like a warm blanket on a cold night. Now I was *really* depressed.

This is when my anger at God became real to me. Had He not heard all my prayers? Why wouldn't He change my husband? *"God, if you would have just changed him, my life would be okay. I would be happy. You just don't want me to be happy. This must be my fate in life. God, why are You so hard and harsh? Why don't You love me? If you cared about me, I wouldn't be going through any of this. Why, God, Why?"*

Reflection Activity

How does this make you feel? What does this bring to mind? My life was a wreck and I blamed it all on God. Are you currently blaming God for your life's choice? Do you feel as though God has not come through for you in your mess?

_____
_____
_____
_____
_____
_____
_____
_____
_____

CHAPTER TWENTY-SEVEN

Which Ground Are You?

You shall have no other gods before Me. You shall not make for yourself an image in the form of anything in heaven above or on the earth beneath or in the waters below. You shall not bow down to them or worship them; for I, the Lord your God, am a jealous God, punishing the children for the sin of the parents to the third and fourth generation of those who hate me (Exodus 20:3-5).

My husband was my god; he was my idol. Just like every other man I had ever been with, they became my idol. Although I was going to church, saying my prayers, faithfully paying my tithes, I was saying with my mouth that I loved God, but my heart was far from Him and I didn't even know it. I made everything about my husband—the good, the bad, and the ugly. I allowed him and everything he did or didn't do to control me. How I felt and responded on any given day was predicated on how he treated me. I felt like a puppet on a string. When he treated me well, life was great. When life was great and I wasn't drinking, I was more relaxed, calmer, and I was involved with the kids and others. I was kinder and easier to get along with. If he was treating me unkindly, I would use alcohol and prescription drugs to help me cope. I would become depressed, short-tempered, withdrawn, angry, and everybody around me felt it.

All the times we sat in church listening to the pastor, I was praying and hoping he would get it. I would buy him little things to help encourage him so as to draw him closer to the Lord—e.g. a Bible just for men, just for men devotionals, etc. My prayers were always centered on him. "God change *him*, make *him* love me, make *him* stop cheating on me, make *him* respect me, make *him* stop lying, *him, him, him.*" It was all about him. Not once did I ask the Lord to change *me*. Not once was I praying or seeking the Lord for *me* to draw close to Him. I was too worried about my husband. My husband had my heart, mind, will, emotions, and strength. I just needed God to make my husband act right.

My relationship with the Lord was centered on God making my life better. I just wanted to be happy. I wasn't asking for a whole lot. I just wanted my husband to love me. If God would change my husband, my life would be perfect. Then I could be a good mother and we would be one big happy family.

Getting to the Heart of the Matter

> That same day Jesus went out of the house and sat by the lake. Such large crowds gathered around Him that He got into a boat and sat in it, while all the people stood on the shore. Then He told them many things in parables, saying: "A farmer went out to sow his seed. As he was scattering the seed, some fell along the path, and the birds came and ate it up. Some fell on rocky places, where it did not have much soil. It sprang up quickly, because the soil was shallow. But when the sun came up, the plants were scorched, and they withered because they had no root. Other seed fell among thorns, which grew up and choked the plants. Still other seed fell on good soil, where it produced a crop—a hundred, sixty or thirty times what

was sown. Whoever has ears, let them hear (Matthew 13:1-9).

This is my own personal interpretation of Matthew 13:1-9 and how it explains what happened when I got saved. The condition of my heart was the issue. Jesus often taught in parables so as to lend a visual for understanding. Parables were a natural story with a supernatural application. He would tell stories so that those to whom He was speaking could relate. It was to help them understand the things of the kingdom of God.

With the parable above, these people knew farming. They were very familiar with planting seeds and the type soil needed for the seed to grow. Producing their own food was how they were able to eat, unlike most of us. I know very little about farming. I would much rather get what I need from the grocery store. Jesus was using something with which they were familiar so as to help them understand something they didn't know about the kingdom. The seed, in this parable, represents the seed of the gospel of Jesus—the good news of Christ. The soil represents the hearts of the people who hear the message and what they do with it. As we take a closer look at the verses, I'll explain my thoughts.

The Hard Ground

Matthew 13:4 states, *"He scattered the seeds across the ground."* This represents the good news of Jesus going out, the kingdom of God being preached. Some seed fell beside a path and the birds came and ate it. As soon as the message was heard, the birds, which represent Satan, came and snatched the seed and ate it. Paths are usually hard ground. Some of us have allowed life to cause our hearts to become hard. The birds come and snatch the very thing we need.

Satan snatches the Word of God by telling us things such as, *"If God was a good and loving God, why did He allow us to be hurt the way we were?"* Or, *"If God was so good and loving, why does He allow bad things to happen?"* He will remind you of all the things in your life which cause you to have a hard heart in the first place. Some of our hearts are so very hard that the seed can't even penetrate it. It's because we believe the voices that feed us the lies.

The Rocky Ground

Matthew 13:5-6 reads, *"And some fell on rocky soil where there was little depth of earth; the plants sprung up quickly enough in the shallow soil; but the hot sun soon scorched them and they withered and died, for they had little root."* This is truly what I believe happened when I "got saved" in 2000. Yes, I heard the gospel message prior to 2000, but the soil of my heart was too hardened for the seed message to penetrate. I was excited about the seed. I was spending time with God and I had grown little roots. I didn't stay in that place long enough for my roots to go deep as referenced in Colossians 2:7-9. My relationship with God became a work system of, *"If I did the good things, God would take away all my problems; I just had to be good enough."* I tried to clean the outside when the inside was a mess. Like I've already said, I was a dressed up mess. There were several things wrong with my thinking:

1. My "works" were as filthy rags and self-righteous (Isaiah 64:6).
2. I was not saved by my works (Ephesians 2:8-9).
3. I foolishly thought God was supposed to make life all better for me (Galatians 6:7).

I didn't realize that it was my own way of thinking that had me in this mess. I wanted God to take my mess and bless it. And, when He didn't bless my mess, I blamed Him and turned my back on Him thinking I could do a better job managing my own life. I allowed the sun to come and scorch what little roots I had.

The Soil with Thorns

Matthew 13:7 states, *"Other seeds fell among thorns, and the thorns choked out the tender blades."* This one grew roots and it produced tender blades. The seed did take root but the plant it produced was weak. The thorns came and choked out the tender blades. This people group lost focus by taking their eyes off Jesus. They allowed the cares of this world to distract them. The loss of focus could have been due to lies, fear, relationships, junk they had allowed into or to remain in their thinking, etc. All of this has a part in the "choking out" which occurred. Remember, what we feed grows and what we starve dies.

The Good Soil

Matthew 13:8 goes on to say, *"But some fell on good soil and produced a crop that was 30, 60, and even 100 times as much as he had planted."* These people are not perfect by far, but they are determined, dedicated, committed, and anchored in Christ. They heard the gospel message and responded by allowing their roots to go deep. Do you remember Colossians 2:7 which reads, *"Let your roots grow down into Him, and let your lives be built on Him. Then your faith will grow strong in the truth you were taught, and you will overflow with thankfulness"*?

This group of people has their eyes focused on Jesus. Their lives are built on Christ and everything in their lives is surrendered to the lordship of Jesus. They learned how to relinquish the need to be in control. They allowed the Lord to direct their path through faith as noted in Proverbs 3:6. These folks daily spent time in God's presence longing to be, at all cost, as He is. They read His Word and take it at face value. They grew strong in the truth of God's Word. They grabbed hold to the promises of God. They became secure in who God says they are and went on to teach others. They were producing 30, 60, and 100-fold returns.

WHEN A SEED IS PLANTED, A HARVEST DOESN'T AUTOMATICALLY APPEAR.

Good ground was the soil of my heart the night I surrendered, the night I literally got choked out. No matter how hard my journey became, I pressed on. I kept my eyes focused on the Lord. The more I stayed in that place, the quicker I could see the birds and recognize the thorns. We must remember something very important about this parable. The Gospel seed was always the same; it was the soil—hearts of the people—that was different. When a seed is planted, a harvest doesn't automatically appear. It takes time to grow. It is the same in our spiritual lives once the seeds of God's Word are planted.

Once God's seed is planted in our hearts, it is up to us to make sure it receives what it needs to grow: water, sunlight, nutrients. Sometimes, weeds are inevitable and we can't always stop them from growing. We can, however, snatch them up by their roots as soon as we recognize them. I ask you, *"What is the soil of your heart?"* To know the soil of our heart, we must look at the fruit our life is producing.

Reflection Activity

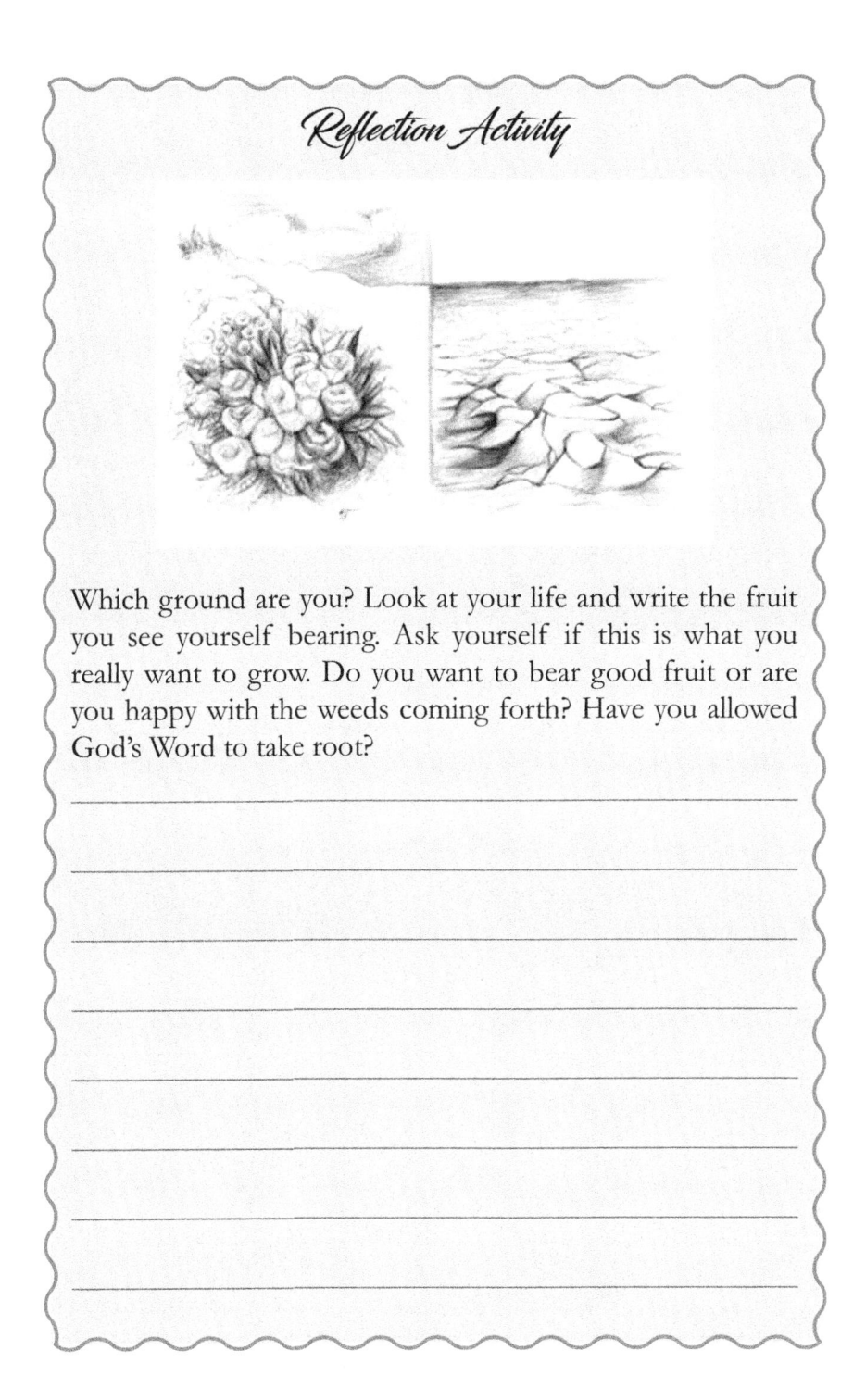

Which ground are you? Look at your life and write the fruit you see yourself bearing. Ask yourself if this is what you really want to grow. Do you want to bear good fruit or are you happy with the weeds coming forth? Have you allowed God's Word to take root?

CHAPTER TWENTY-EIGHT

The Fruit of God's Seed

"But the fruit of the Spirit is love, joy, peace, forbearance, kindness, goodness, faithfulness, gentleness and self-control (Galatians 5:22-23)."

"I will give you a new heart and put a new spirit in you; I will remove from you your heart of stone and give you a heart of flesh (Ezekiel 36:26)."

Ask and it will be given to you; seek and you will find; knock and the door will be opened to you. For everyone who asks receives; the one who seeks finds; and to the one who knocks, the door will be opened. Which of you, if your son asks for bread, will give him a stone? Or if he asks for a fish, will give him a snake? If you, then, though you are evil, know how to give good gifts to your children, how much more will your Father in heaven give good gifts to those who ask Him (Matthew 7:7-11)?

Abide in Me, and I in you. As the branch cannot bear fruit of itself, unless it abides in the vine, neither can you, unless you abide in Me. I am the vine, you are the branches. He who abides in Me, and I in him, bears much fruit; for without Me you can do nothing. If anyone does not abide in Me, he is cast out as a branch and is withered; and they gather them and throw them into the fire, and they are burned (John 15:4-6).

The fruit which comes from the seed of God's Word is found in Galatians. It will produce, but also is not limited to, forgiveness, healing, righteousness, grace, glory, compassion, holiness, hope, honesty, and integrity. No matter the condition of your heart, God can and will give you a new heart, but only if you want it. You must ask, seek, and knock. He is a good Father. His promises are for us to take hold. He has already done His part, now it is up to us to do ours. As we ask, seek, and knock, we also must abide.

Look at John 15 above. What does it mean to *abide*? The Greek word for abide is *menō* and means "to remain in, to tarry, to not depart from." When Jesus tells us to abide in Him, we are to remain in Him and not depart. I thought I was "abiding" when I was going to church, reading devotions, paying tithes, etc. I was doing these things out of duty—my due diligence. I wasn't doing them to know Him, but with the sole purpose of expecting something in return. I was doing these things out of manipulation. I was so used to manipulating people to get what I wanted that, naturally, I was doing the same with God. I was treating God as a vending machine. I would put in a few coins expecting what I wanted in return. As a side note, author Alexys V. Wolf speaks in some of her books about how most Christians attempt to use God as a vending machine, which is why we fail in our spiritual journey. In particular, one of her book sets, *Looking for God*, 3 volumes, seriously challenged and aided me in my journey with the Lord.

The word "abide" is close to the English word "abode" which means "a dwelling place or where we live." If we are *in* Christ, we are living *with* Christ. He is present with us in our home. He dwells where we dwell. During my marriage to the church guy, sure, we said Christ was welcomed in our , but the things we allowed into our home took precedence over Christ and His Holy Spirit (e.g. drinking, drugs, music, movies, novels). Ephesians 4:30 says, *"Do not grieve the Holy Spirit of God."* I was grieving the Holy Spirit and I didn't even know it.

Jesus Himself said in Matthew 7:16, *"You will know them by their fruit."* The absence of fruit is evidence that we are not abiding in Him. Looking back at my life, what I was producing was definitely not fruit. Everything in my life was rotten and foul. According to John 15:5, if we are truly abiding in Him, we will most certainly bear not just a little fruit, but much fruit. So when we say that we are a believer but we are bearing no fruit, then we are deceiving ourselves. I was deceived many years and didn't even know it.

A branch detached from the vine will wither and die. This is what my life felt like, withered and full of death. In order to abide, we must daily feed ourselves the Word of God, "our daily bread." There is no way we can abide in Christ without abiding in His Word. John 15:5b tells us, *"apart from Me you can do nothing."* I don't know about you but, as for me, this was a lesson I had to learn the hard way. Now that I do know, doing life any other way is no longer an option.

"Those who live in the shelter of the Most High will find rest in the shadow of the Almighty. This I declare about the Lord: He alone is my refuge, my place of safety; He is my God, and I trust Him," is written in Psalm 91:1-2. As you journey with me through the pages of this book, you can clearly see that the heart of the matter was the matter of *my* heart. Once I finally surrendered, I refused to give up. I kept on asking, I kept on seeking, and I kept on knocking. I wanted more of God than I did anything else. I received my new heart and this heart was burning for more, something deeper. I found myself delighting in the Lord and I could feel my desires changing. No longer was I concerned about the things of this

world. I wanted to experience the fullness of who Christ was living inside me.

No longer did I see spending time with God as a *duty*. It became a *delight*. My thought process changed from "*I have to*," to "*I get to.*" I get to spend time with God, the very One for whom my soul longs and needs. He is always available to me—no missed calls, no appointments. He is always available. My prayers went from praying about what I needed from God, to praying, "*God what do you want from me?*" To sum up my experience, Paul, who wrote this passage in Galatians 2:19-21, explains it very clearly, "*For when I tried to keep the law, it condemned me. So I died to the law—I stopped trying to meet all its requirements—so that I might live for God. My old self has been crucified with Christ. It is no longer I who live, but Christ lives in me. So I live in this earthly body by trusting in the Son of God, who loved me and gave Himself for me. I do not treat the grace of God as meaningless. For if keeping the law could make us right with God, then there was no need for Christ to die.*"

Reflection Activity

Personal Challenge

Anything we do for thirty days becomes a habit. I challenge you to commit to reading and meditating on the Scriptures in this chapter for the next 30 days. Keep a journal. Write your thoughts and feelings as you do. Watch how your life will begin to transform. I spent so many years not understanding, but now my heart and passion are helping others understand. Getting saved is instant, yet transformation takes a lifetime. Getting saved and getting into the transformation process simply means we are now under new management.

I want to paint a simple picture so as to help us understand what it looks like. My simple explanation does nothing compared to the deep truths found in God's Word. All I am doing is putting a little bit of paint on the canvas, per se. Getting saved is us marrying Jesus. Baptism is the wedding ceremony to show the world we have married Jesus. Then, we spend the rest of our days on earth spending time with and allowing our Husband to love, guide, teach, and protect us.

I often ask people who say they have a relationship with Jesus, *"If you spent as much time with your spouse as you do with Jesus, how well would that relationship work?"* I can't stress enough that being a Christian is so much more than following rules, going to church, praying, tithing, and doing good things. It's about becoming one with the person of Jesus. When you get to know Him, it becomes a delight to spend time with Him.

The more time we spend with Jesus, the more we won't want to do the things which displease Him. His love changes us. Seldom do we take the time required to learn of Him and how He feels about us because we are so caught up in the distractions of this world. We are too busy with our gods that we make up the excuse of not having enough time. Truth is, we make time for the things which are important to us. Some examples of our idols are social media, cell phones, television, and relationships including spouses and children.

I have often heard people say they weren't ready to get saved or they get saved and they say they are not ready to get baptized. Most people feel like they need to get themselves together first or they don't want to give up the sin in their lives they enjoy. Something important to think about—if we could change on our own, we wouldn't have a need for a Savior in the first place. We must not fall for the lies the enemy feeds us. God is inviting us into a love relationship with Him. He is not asking us to prepare ourselves first; He is saying, *"Come as you are and allow My love to change you."* Yes, He says to come as you are, but His intention is not for us to stay as we are.

His job is to change us. Our job is to abide in Him. Jesus is saying to each one of us, *"Give Me your heart the way that you have given it to others. I want to give you a new one in return for the old broken and hard one."* Jesus wants all of us. He wants our heart, mind, soul, and strength. What He gives us in return can't be compared to the things of this world. Have you given Jesus your heart? If not, ask yourself, *"Why? What is holding me back?"* I pray you don't allow fear, doubt, and disbelief to stop you. Are you ready to bear good fruit?

As self-examination, spend the next few days or weeks reading the Scriptures in this chapter. Ask yourself, *"Have I made someone or something my god or idol?"* Pray for God to show you any area of your life which makes Him jealous. Then, pray and ask the Lord to remove those things. When He shows you, be willing to surrender them. He will help you.

Questions for Self-Examination

Are there things in your life you have built and then asked the Lord to bless (Psalm 127:1)?

_____

_____

_____

Look at Matthew 13:1-9. What's your interpretation? Write it.

_____

_____

_____

What would you say is the soil of your heart?

_____

_____

_____

The hard ground?

_____

_____

_____

The rocky ground?

_____

_____

_____

The soil with thorns?

_____

_____

_____

The good soil?

_____

_____

_____

Do you see yourself as having deep roots (Colossians 2:7)?

What type of fruit does your life produce (Galatians 5:22-23)?

CHAPTER TWENTY-NINE

Who Told You That?

*"False words are not only evil in themselves,
but they infect the soul with evil."*
~ Socrates

We've all made mistakes in the past leaving us feeling unworthy of God's love and affection. The truth is, God loves us so much that, no matter how yesterday or today look, we can always start fresh beginning now. We must look past our faults and failures and see ourselves as God sees us.

When I was younger, my older brother used to pick on me for watching Sesame Street. He said I was retarded and slow and that the show was for dummies. Every time I would watch that show, I would watch in fear he was going to catch me. I would quickly turn the channel when I would hear him coming. Watching my favorite program made me feel ashamed and insecure all because of his slanderous words.

The favorite word my ex-fiancé—the one who choked me—was "Dumbo." He would call that when he didn't agree with something I said or did, or if he was frustrated with me. That was the nicer of the names he used. Dumbo was the one which had the most negative impact. It would take me all the way back to childhood and I would remember the slow classes I was in. I would hear the taunts of the other students calling me slow, stupid, or retarded. I would hear my brother's words as if I were a child again sitting in front of the TV. *"You're so stupid,"* would ring in my ears as if it were a loud fire alarm I couldn't turn off.

Remember, death and life are in the power of the tongue as noted in Proverbs 18:21. Words spoken and believed by us affect our lives on every level. All my life, I walked around wearing labels which became my identity. *"You're not smart enough, you're not good enough, you're fat, you're stupid, and you're slow."* I wore so many labels as though that's exactly who I was. Words are like seeds and, when they begin to grow, they become our belief. What we believe about ourselves shapes and directs our life. Our own thoughts become our fiercest strongholds. Our life will always move in the direction of our strongest thoughts. If our thoughts are wrong, it leads to wrong actions. We go through life making decisions based on the lies we have accepted as truth. Because I believed the negative words spoken over my life, my actions began to reflect that.

As in most of our lives, the labels I wore were placed on me by people who said they loved me—people who said they cared about me. It was from people who were supposed to protect me. It was family members, friends, lovers, husbands. *"You're too fat. Your hair is too short. You're stupid. You'll never amount to anything. You're no good."* The list is endless. In shame, I wore the labels as though they were mine. I wore them so long they became a part of me, they defined me, and they became my identity. My labels were who I was.

I don't want to paint a picture as if every day of my life someone was saying and doing mean things to me. Growing up, I am sure plenty of people spoke words of esteem, encouragement, and acceptance, but all the negative ones are the ones that stuck. There was a childhood saying I often heard, *"What you say to me bounces off of me and sticks to you.*" I must have been covered in glue because the negative never bounced off me!

It's interesting how our minds tend to remember all the negative stuff and we so easily forget all the positive things, especially the words spoken to, over, or about us. It reminds me of the most powerful statement I have ever read, *"Tell a woman she's beautiful and she'll believe it for a second. Tell her she's ugly and she'll believe it for a lifetime."* As long as the enemy can keep us focused on the negative and the hurt, it becomes our truth, our belief system. When we allow the labels to define us, it quickly becomes our identity.

The enemy's plans are to keep us in bondage to the things we wrongfully believe about ourselves. He wants to do all he can to keep us from knowing the real truth about who God says we are. As long as the devil can keep us from the truth, he can keep us from becoming what God always intended us to become. We know words are powerful. We must not believe the lie that says words don't hurt us, because they absolutely do hurt us. Knowing who we are in Christ will set us free from those words and the outcome they have over us. The power of the words already spoken to, about, and over us, along with the hurt they have caused, can and will be broken as we dig into the truth about our true identity.

Digging Deeper

Genesis 3:11 finds God asking Adam, *"Who told you that you were naked? Have you eaten from the tree whose fruit I commanded you not to eat?"* Today, God is asking us, *"Who told you that? Have you been listening to the lies of the enemy? Who is the father of lies as stated in John 8:44?"* Have you ever felt ashamed like you just weren't good enough, not worthy enough? Have you felt like, no matter how hard you try, it is never enough? Do you ever look in the mirror and hate what you see? Do you ever wish you could be like someone else?

Let's get honest with ourselves. As we do, we must ask the Lord to reveal the lies with which we have come into agreement. On a scale of one to ten, with one being at the very worst and ten the very best, is it hard for you to find anything good to say about yourself? Five is being just okay, not bad but not good either. Ten is being God-confident, you know God has created you and you are an original masterpiece made by the master artist Himself.

Reflection Activity

How do you see yourself on the one-to-ten scale?

1   2   3   4   5   6   7   8   9   10

Why do you see yourself that way, good or bad? Explain:

_____
_____
_____
_____
_____
_____
_____

What are the negative labels you wear?

Who told you a lie that became your truth?

What specifically did they say about you?

How did their statement(s) make you feel?

How have these labels affected your life?

Prayer: *Father, I pray that every lie ever spoken to or about me be broken. I ask that You replace every lie with the truth of Your Word. Remove every label and put upon my heart and mind the robe of righteousness so that I may see myself through Your eyes from this day forward. Cause me to rise up so that I will become the person who not only walks in Your truth, but sets others free because of Your truth. Let chains of low self-esteem, self-hatred, and envy be broken from me in the name of Jesus.*

The chains are broken but, in order for us to walk in the freedom and liberty, we must see ourselves as God sees us. Who we are is found in His Word, so we must set time aside daily to meet with Him, to read and to soak in His presence as He strengthens us by His love for us.

Loving Ourselves in the Grace of God

To love who we are in the grace of God is very different from loving ourselves in a fleshly and selfish way. We must not secretly wish we were someone else as if God made a mistake. What message are we sending God by not accepting ourselves in the beauty in which He has created us? As we get our eyes off of others–which is envy—and failures—despising ourselves—and set our vision on His grace, then we will love who and how God made us. God was very intentional about creating us all differently. That's why each one of us has our own unique set of fingerprints unlike anyone else's in this world.

Think of God as a master artist. Every one of us is a beautifully hand-crafted painting, an original design prized by our master painter. He has invested His love, time, and resources into each person and continues to do so. He sent Jesus to purchase us so that we would all find our place in His Kingdom—a place where all His beautiful creation will be displayed. The master artist brags on you, sings over you, and you are the apple of His eye. You were created by Him with love, purpose, and intention and you are made perfectly in His image. That's how He sees us according to Ephesians 2:10.

CHAPTER THIRTY

Label's Lie vs. God's Truth

The Label's Lie: I am stupid.

God's Truth:

1. I have been made in the image of God (Genesis 1:27).
2. I have the mind of Christ (1 Corinthians 2:16).
3. I can do all things through Christ who strengthens me (Philippians 4:13).

No matter how many times the devil tells me I am stupid, whether through other people or in my thoughts, I have to become anchored in the truth about who *God* says I am, not who *man* says I am. II Corinthians 5:17 (KJV) reads, *"Therefore if any man be in Christ, he is a new creature: old things are passed away; behold all things are become new."* The key word in this verse is *become*, meaning, "begin to be." *Become* is a process; we are learning and growing in God if we are staying connected to Him.

For us to become anchored in truth, let's look at what truth is. As Christians, we believe that every word in the Bible is true. From this truth, we build our lives. It becomes our very foundation for which we live. In John 14:6, Jesus said, *"I am the way, and the truth, and the life. No one comes to the Father except through Me."* II Timothy 3:16 states, *"All Scripture is inspired by God and it is useful to teach us what is true."* Jesus is the Word as written in John 1:1, 14. Knowing that the Bible is truth, hiding God's Word in our heart helps us to be secure in listening to the voice of truth vs. the voice of lies. Colossians 3:16 instructs, *"Let the word of God dwell in you richly."*

"Lead me in your truth and teach me, for You are the God of my salvation; for You I wait all the daylong (Psalm 25:5)."

"Teach me your way, O Lord, that I may walk in Your truth; unite my heart to fear Your name (Psalm 86:11)."

"Sanctify them in the truth; Your word is truth (John 17:17)."

"Because of the truth that abides in us and will be with us forever (II John 1:2)."

"And you will know the truth, and the truth will set you free (John 8:32)."

Let's look, once again, at II Corinthians 5:17. We "become" by continuing to grow and learn who we are in Christ. For us to be able to live the life God intended and to fulfill our destiny, we have to be secure. We do so by allowing our roots to go down deeply into the truth of God's view of us, how He sees us and feels about us. The more we read God's holy Word, the more we will expose the lies and come into agreement with God about our identity, worth, and value. The more we do this, the more our behavior will begin to reflect our God-given identity.

Please note that our identity doesn't depend on things we do or have done. Our identity is strictly based on who God is, who

He has created us to be, and His love for us. It becomes our choice to come into agreement about what God says. My self-esteem was so low. I was growing in Christ, but my self-esteem had not yet been built up in Christ. I would read Romans 8:28 which states, *"We know that all things work together for good to them that love God, to them who are the called according to His purpose."* I would read this and say to myself that I wasn't one of the ones *"called according to His purpose."* Because of my low self-esteem, my guilt, insecurities, and shame, I believed I wasn't worthy enough. I didn't understand, at the time, that we are all called according to His purpose. When He created us, we were called, but we must make a personal choice to believe and follow Him. If not, by default, we come into agreement with the enemy and his lies. Remember, God has a plan for your life just as well as the enemy has a plan. Which plan gets fulfilled is solely up to us. When we agree with the lies, the plans of the enemy are being fulfilled. When we agree with and follow Christ, our destiny in Christ is being fulfilled. We are *all* called, whether or not we are chosen is left up to us to decide. Will we follow Christ and be anchored in His truth or will we continue to live a painful destructive life of lies?

Lies versus Truth

Lie: Nobody loves me.
Truth: I am loved. (1 John 3:3)

Lie: I have been rejected.
Truth: I am accepted. (Ephesians 1:6)

Lie: God hates you.
Truth: God loves you (the whole world). (John 3:16)

Lie: You're not a friend to God.
Truth: I am Jesus' friend. (John 15:15)

Lie: God doesn't listen to you nor does He want to have anything to do with you.
Truth: I am united with God and one spirit with Him. (1 Corinthians 6:17)

Lie: God does not live in you.
Truth: I am a temple of God. His Spirit and his life lives in me. (1 Corinthians 6:19)

Lie: God sees you as a no-good sinner.
Truth: I am a saint. (Ephesians 1:1)

Lie: God doesn't forgive you.
Truth: I am redeemed and forgiven. (Colossians 1:14)

Lie: You are hopeless and broken.
Truth: I am complete in Jesus Christ. (Colossians 2:10)

Lie: God condemns you, look at all the mistakes you make and the wrong you do.
Truth: I am free from condemnation. (Romans 8:1)

Lie: You haven't changed.
Truth: I am a new creation because I am in Christ. (2 Corinthians 5:17)

Lie: God doesn't choose people like you, much less love people like you.
Truth: I am chosen of God, holy, and dearly loved. (Colossians 3:12)

Lie: You have nothing and you will never be anything.
Truth: I am established, anointed, and sealed by God. (2 Corinthians 1:21)

Lie: Fear controls me.
Truth: I do not have a spirit of fear, but of love, power, and a sound mind. (2 Timothy 1:7)

Lie: God doesn't move through someone like you.
Truth: I am God's co-worker. (2 Corinthians 6:1)

Lie: God's unconcerned with you and your problems.
Truth: I have direct access to God (Ephesians 2:18).

Lie: You will never produce anything good.
Truth: I am chosen to bear fruit (John 15:16).

Lie: You can't hear the voice of God and you are alone.
Truth: I can always know the presence of God because He never leaves me (Hebrews 13:5).

Lie: God's not with you but He expects you to be perfect.
Truth: God works in me to help me do the things He wants me to do (Philippians 2:13).

Lie: I am Dumb.
Truth: I can ask God for wisdom and He will give me what I need (James 1:5).

Reflection Activity

What are some of the lies you believed?

1. _____
2. _____
3. _____
4. _____
5. _____
6. _____
7. _____
8. _____
9. _____
10. _____

Now ask God to replace the lies with His truth. Write the truth opposite of each lie you listed:

1. _____

2. _____

3. _____

4. _____

5. _____

6. _____

7. _____

8. _____

9. _____

10. _____

Whenever we give our lives to Christ, we receive the gift of eternal life (Romans 6:23). We become a joint heir with Jesus (Romans 8:17). All our past mistakes are washed away. I encourage you to write the Scriptures which have helped you the most and read them daily. God's Word is full of hidden treasures. As you find Scripture that speaks to your heart, include them in your prayers. When the enemy starts to accuse, condemn, and taunt you, speak God's Word to Him. Let Him know you will no longer believe the lies. Let Him know, with boldness, you have decided to stand on the truth about who God says you are. As you have been on this journey of replacing the lies with truth, I want you to look at that scale again. How do you see yourself on the scale from 1-10? Is it difficult for you to find anything good to say about yourself?

Hopefully, you see yourself as a ten. If not, I hope that number has at least gotten higher than it was when you first started this chapter. I encourage you to keep climbing. Keep striving to see yourself in the fullness of Christ. Keep filling your heart with truth until you do see yourself as a ten.

When I was in agreement with the lying labels, I was lost, broken, bitter, angry, depressed, confused, disobedient, an addict, unworthy, defeated, unloved, rejected, insecure, miserable, a liar, and a cheater. My identity began to change as I filled my heart with God's truth. As I did so, God filled my heart with His amazing love. Today, I see myself as a new woman. I am a woman who has been adopted, a citizen of heaven, a child of the King, a woman who has been redeemed, forgiven, of great worth, accepted, free, valuable, whole and healed, unique, a masterpiece, the apple of my Father's eye, and, above all, I am loved with an everlasting love.

Reflection Activity

Who are you according to God's Word?

1. _____
2. _____
3. _____
4. _____
5. _____
6. _____
7. _____
8. _____
9. _____
10. _____

Every time thoughts and feelings arise which are not truth, you must use the Word of God as your anchor by letting the enemy know he can no longer cause you to feel as if you're drowning or drifting. You have become anchored in God's truth.

Prayer: *Lord, cause Your Word to fill every part of who I am. Flood me with Your truth. Let Your Word become my anchor and hope for my soul. In Jesus' name, Amen.*

CHAPTER THIRTY-ONE

A Sinful Woman

"I have wiped out your transgressions like a thick cloud and your sins like a heavy mist. Return to Me, for I have redeemed you (Isaiah 44:22)."

I can say, without guilt and shame, I used to be a sinful woman. My sins were many. I can say that without the guilt and shame because Jesus has forgiven me of all sins. I am a different person than I was then. Regardless, no matter how much Jesus has transformed me, there are those who will always see me as that sinful woman. They will always see me for who I used to be and not for who I have become. When they see me, they still see my past. I can say, with God-confidence, that I am okay with their opinions of me. My identity in Christ is secure. I know who I am.

There was, adversely, a time when I wasn't okay with it. I spent a lot of time trying to prove to others I had changed. I almost got stuck in people-pleasing. It wasn't until I let go of the need to prove myself to others and became focused on pleasing my Savior that things began to change in that area. I had to learn to just be me and, in time, freedom and security became mine. A butterfly doesn't worry about trying to prove it's a butterfly—it just is. The former life as a caterpillar is forever gone once transformed. I got free from what others think or say about me. My heart now wants to please the Lord above all else.

While I kept my eyes on Jesus, I became secure in knowing I was being changed from the inside out, that I was no longer the sinful woman they saw. I began to see myself as God saw me. Although my sins were many, I was forgiven. This was truth to which I had to daily anchor my soul. We must not allow the opinions of others to keep us from getting to Jesus and we must stop allowing the opinions of others to keep us in a place of bondage when God has set us free.

I want to share one of my favorite stories in Scripture of a woman who, I feel, I can most relate. The story is about two very different people. What's most interesting about this story as it relates to my life is that I have been both characters.

"When one of the Pharisees invited Jesus to have dinner with him, he went to the Pharisee's house and reclined at the table. A woman in that town who lived a sinful life learned that Jesus was eating at the Pharisee's house, so she came there with an alabaster jar of perfume. As she stood behind him at his feet weeping, she began to wet his feet with her tears. Then she wiped them with her hair, kissed them and poured perfume on them. When the Pharisee who had invited him saw this, he said to himself, "If this man were a prophet, he would know who is touching him and what kind of woman she is—that she is a sinner." Jesus answered him, "Simon, I have something to tell you." "Tell me, teacher," he said. "Two people owed money to a certain moneylender. One owed him five hundred denarii, and the other fifty. Neither of them had the money to pay him back, so he forgave the debts of both. Now which of them will love him more?" Simon replied, "I suppose the one who had the bigger debt forgiven." "You have judged correctly," Jesus said. Then he turned toward the woman and said to Simon, "Do you see this woman? I came into your house. You did not give me any water for my feet, but she wet my feet with her tears and wiped them with her hair. You did not give me a kiss, but this woman, from the time I entered, has not stopped kissing my feet. You did not put oil on my head, but she has poured perfume on my feet. Therefore, I tell you, her many sins have been forgiven—as her great love has shown. But whoever has been forgiven little loves little." Then Jesus said to her, "Your sins are forgiven." The other guests began to say among themselves, "Who is this who even forgives sins?" Jesus said to the woman, "Your faith has saved you; go in peace (Luke 7:36-50).

Journey with me through this story, experience it with me. We are often taught to read and memorize Scripture, but we aren't taught how to experience it. God has given us an imagination so as to connect with Him on a deeper level. What do I mean by "experience the Scripture"? Let's journey back in time. Visualize the people in their sandals and robes, smell the food on the table. Imagine what the atmosphere was like. What was the people's demeanor? Culturally speaking, was their disposition accepted or frowned upon? Go into the story. Now, let's experience this story together. Starting with verse 36, *"When one of the Pharisees invited Jesus to have dinner with him, He went to the Pharisee's house and reclined at the table."*

A Pharisee was a teacher of the law and they would pride themselves in the knowledge concerning the Scriptures. They loved to point out fault in others; they were "holier than thou," judgmental, and self-righteous. They were considered to be prideful and arrogant. What's interesting about this story is that a Pharisee invited Jesus to have dinner with him, yet Pharisees usually took issue with Jesus. They had a problem with His ministry and teachings.

A Sinful Woman

We should ask ourselves, "*What was the motive of this Pharisee named Simon? Was it to ask questions so as to find fault, or to accuse Him of not following the Law?*" Simon wasn't alone with Jesus at this dinner, no. He had all his other "high and mighty" Pharisaic friends there as well. Pharisees didn't hang around common men. They considered themselves too good for that. I'm sure Simon's friends wanted to witness the mockery and ask their own fault-finding questions. Jesus, knowing good and well the motives of each one of their hearts, was not offended. He accepted the invitation and welcomed any opportunity to teach and extend grace. It's important to know, women were not allowed in such a place, especially with men of such high stature. It was part of the culture of biblical times.

Side note: Reclining at the table? Back then, the tables were very low to the ground. You would sit on a cushion, use one arm to prop yourself, the other one to eat, and your legs would be stretched to the side behind you. Can you see it? If you're like I, it's hard to imagine. I had to Google pictures!

Continuing in verse 37, a woman in that town who lived a sinful life learned Jesus was eating at the Pharisee's house, so she went there with an alabaster jar of perfume. Depending on what version of the Bible you are reading, the description may be a little different. Some say she was a woman of the night, a prostitute, an unclean woman, an immoral woman, a notorious sinner. Let's just say she has many labels attached to her. She was looked down on and talked about. Needless to say, she was not one with whom you would be associated.

Back to this dinner, no woman was welcomed and especially not a woman of her reputation. What did she hear about Jesus? Was it the miracles of healing leapers, opening blind eyes, or raising people from the dead? Whatever she heard, she made a very strong decision— one which would require her to go against all odds; one which demanded an attitude of, "*I don't care what people will think of me.*"

I'm sure her heart was pounding, her palms were sweaty, and hands were shaking as she grabbed her alabaster box of very expensive perfume. It may have been the only thing she had of any worth. It was to be an offering to the One she knew could set her free from her shame, guilt, low self-esteem, and lifestyle of sin. There was a knowing inside of her that said, *"This is my chance, no matter the ridicule and judgment. I'm not going to let anything stop me."* It sounds to me like she got sick and tired of being sick and tired. She was desperate for something different. Surely there was more to life than the way she was living.

As she got closer to the house, think about what her thoughts may have been. I can only imagine fear trying to overtake her. No matter her thoughts, her faith overrode her fear. As she made her way through the house, I can presume she looked tentatively on the faces of the "holier than thou" men. The atmosphere quickly shifted, the whispers, the accusations. In disgust, they watched her every move. It didn't matter to her. She had one agenda, she was purpose-driven, and destiny was calling her forward despite her past trying to hold her back. She was focused, determined and broken.

The way she is described makes me think about the way people must have treated her. Thinking about the Pharisees, I'm sure they had a tendency to make others feel inferior to them no matter who they were. I can only assume it was worse for her. Have you ever been around someone who makes you feel uncomfortable? Just being in their presence made you feel horrible about yourself, like you were beneath them—like you are stupid and worthless. I'm sure she must have felt this way often.

If, in fact, she was a prostitute, she may have felt useless unless she was providing a sexual service. Or maybe she was a woman who was involved with married men. Whatever her lifestyle and whatever she felt about herself began to fade the moment she came into the presence of Jesus. It was as though it was just Him and her and nothing else in the world mattered. She began to experience everything for which she had ever longed. The tears, themselves, told the story of her heart.

Moving to verse 38, *"As she stood behind Him at His feet weeping, she began to wet His feet with her tears. Then she wiped them with her hair, kissed them and poured perfume on them."* She wasn't standing long before she fell to her knees. She had found her place of safety, a place of acceptance and worth. Gratitude filled her heart as she knew who she had become up until that moment, a worthless sinful woman. The labels she wore were an accurate description of her behavior but, at Jesus' feet, she knew she was being changed from the inside out. She was being transformed into something different.

I believe that, with every one of her tears, she was being delivered from the desire to want to go back to her life of sin and set free from the shame and guilt of a lifestyle of her sin. The night I was choked, with each one of my tears, I was the same as she while lying on my living room floor. I laid there knowing Jesus was my only hope.

Each tear brought deliverance, healing, and restoration. With each tear, her inner-man began to rise up. A sleeping lion was being awakened. A new strength, determination, and hope flooded her very being. She wasn't oblivious to the fact she was an immoral woman, but she knew she had found the One who would change the course of her destiny. She was being made new.

She let down her hair and wiped the tears and the dust from her Savior's feet. In pure gratitude, she kissed His feet over and over again. She couldn't stop. She was pouring out her very life along with the most expensive perfume she had. It was an offering of pure love and devotion. No ulterior motive, only authentic love, devotion, and gratitude.

Verse 39 reads, *"When the Pharisee who had invited Him saw this, he said to himself, 'If this man was a prophet, He would know who is touching Him and what kind of woman she is—that she is a sinner.'"* Here we go with the accusations. *"If He were,"* indicates Simon never believed

Jesus was who He said He was. And the sinful woman, how dare He let her touch Him! Jesus, knowing, the intention of man, wasn't offended. He used it as an opportunity to do what He does best—teach and extend grace.

Verses 40-42, *"Jesus answered him, 'Simon, I have something to tell you.' 'Tell me, teacher,' he said. 'Two people owed money to a certain moneylender. One owed him five hundred denarii, and the other fifty. Neither of them had the money to pay him back, so he forgave the debts of both. Now which of them will love him more?'"* Jesus makes it very clear and drives His point home. Any time money is involved, we pay close attention. I can't help but hear the sarcasm in Simon's voice when he replies, *"Tell me teacher."*

Verse 43 goes on, *"Simon replied, 'I suppose the one who had the bigger debt forgiven.' 'You have judged correctly,' Jesus said.'"* Instead of humbling himself, he responds in pride, *"I suppose."* I'm sure it took everything in him to answer the question. Verse 44 states, *"Then He turned toward the woman and said to Simon, 'Do you see this woman? I came into your house and you did not give me any water for my feet, but she wet my feet with her tears and wiped them with her hair.'"* In those days, it was customary to wash your feet as you entered into someone's house. Simon didn't offer Jesus the common courtesy of water when He entered his house. This supports my statement about why Simon had even invited Jesus in the first place. Jesus was calm, cool and not the least offended as He pointed out the issue of Simon's heart. Verse 45 reads, *"You did not give me a kiss, but this woman, from the time I entered, has not stopped kissing my feet."*

Again, it was common to greet your guests with a kiss. I wonder if Simon's friends had arrived before Jesus or after Jesus. Were they greeted with a kiss and water to wash their feet? Have you ever invited someone to something, but you really didn't want them there and your actions corresponded with your heart? Okay, so maybe I'm the only one. Hey, no secrets here. I was a woman of many sins—I'm sure not proud of it, but I thank God I've been redeemed and transformed.

I told you I could relate to both characters. I was a sinful woman, but I was also very much like Simon who was very prideful and judgmental. I would look down on other people who couldn't keep themselves together. Because I was what you would call a "functional" addict, I always made it look as though I had it all together. I was well-dressed, had a good house, stable job, nice car, etc. I would look down on those who couldn't keep a job, no place to stay, poorly dressed, etc. It's sad, but true. Also, in my pride, I couldn't stand to be corrected, even when someone was right in what they were saying.

Verses 46-47 continues, "You did not put oil on My head, but she has poured perfume on My feet. Therefore, I tell you, her many sins have been forgiven—as her great love has shown. But whoever has been forgiven little loves little." Jesus let everyone know He knew all about her sins. In fact, He said himself, "They were many." Her heart of repentance revealed how great her love was and He validated her value and worth in front of all of them. He let them know she was forgiven. Verse 48 says, *"Then Jesus said to her, 'Your sins are forgiven.'"*

HER IDENTITY WAS RESTORED AND THE COURSE OF HER DESTINY REDIRECTED.

Jesus then turns to this sinful woman—the one by whom He was deeply moved and for whom He had great compassion; the one whom He made sure she heard His words which were spoken to a room full of self-righteous, arrogant, religious leaders. And I believe He said it with power and authority in His voice, *"You are forgiven."* Not only was she forgiven, but also her life had completely changed because of this one encounter with this man, Jesus. Her identity was restored and the course of her destiny redirected.

Verse 49 goes on, *"The other guests began to say among themselves, 'Who is this who even forgives sins?'"* All the news which had spread about Jesus and they still had to ask who He was? I'm sure they probably had seen some miracles firsthand. Did they not hear what this woman had heard about Jesus that compelled her to go against the grain in the first place? Did they hear but not listen? I know, in my own life, I had heard many times, but I just didn't listen. It wasn't until I became so broken and scared by life that I finally decided to listen.

In verse 50 we witness, *"Jesus said to the woman, 'Your faith has saved you; go in peace.'"* Her faith in Jesus saved her. We hear so much about faith, but faith must have a substance. I have faith in a chair when I sit in it that it can hold my weight, but my faith in that chair can't save me. My faith must be in a Savior who took the penalty of my many sins and paid a price I never could. Simon and this sinful woman were both sinners. One saw the need for a Savior and the other one didn't. Romans 6:23 teaches us that the wages of sin is death. It's just like us going to work all week expecting our wages to be paid to us on payday.

Reflection Activity

How does this make you feel? What does this bring to mind? Can you see yourself in the sinful woman? Can you see yourself in Simon? What do you see about your own life? What would you like to see change?

_____
_____
_____
_____
_____
_____
_____
_____
_____

CHAPTER THIRTY-TWO

We Are All Sinners

"You will keep him in perfect peace, whose mind is stayed on You, because he trusts in You (Isaiah 26:3).*"*

According to Romans 3:23, we have all sinned and come short of God's glory. No matter how closely we come to following God's law, we all come up short. If we could do it on our own, we would not have needed Jesus' perfect sacrifice to take our place. What's our place? Death—the Bible tells us the wages of sin is death. It should have been me on that cross—I was the guilty one. But, through Jesus, God made a way for us to escape our rightful punishment of death and offers us a free gift of salvation. For us to receive this free gift, we must repent of our sin nature and follow Jesus.

"Repent" simply means to turn away from a lifestyle of sin and pursue the principles and priority of Jesus. We have to make God the Lord and Savior over our lives through faith. And, once we turn from our lifestyle of sin and make Jesus our personal Lord—giving Him full access and control of our life—and Savior—rescuer from sin and the grave—we can rejoice that our names are written in the Lamb's Book of Life. By doing so, we now have the gift of eternal life, a new identity, a new inheritance, and, most importantly, we become children of God. We are adopted into a new family. For those of us who put our trust and faith in Jesus when we die, we will spend eternity with the Trinity—God the Father, God the Son, and God the Holy Spirit. This is the good news about which we often hear believers talk!

Think about the sinful woman observed in chapter 31. Now, let us look at verse 50 which states, *"Your faith has saved you; go in peace."* Go in peace? How in the world was she to go in peace? Didn't Jesus know that, as soon as she left that place, the enemy would start throwing fiery darts at her mind? Didn't Jesus know that, in the days and weeks to follow, the enemy would flood her mind with accusations and taunts about who people said she was? Didn't He realize the enemy would whisper that what she had just experienced with Jesus wasn't real, that she wasn't really forgiven?

It's unclear as to her profession, but she's referred to as a sinful woman. For illustration purposes, let's say she was a prostitute. Once home, she couldn't just put a "closed" sign in the window. What was she going to tell the men when they came seeking her to fulfill a service to which they were accustomed. Maybe she wasn't a prostitute, maybe she was involved in an adulterous affair? How was she going to explain to her lover what just happened to her? How was she going to explain she could no longer see him? But Jesus tells her to "go in peace?" How was she to "go in peace" when all the odds were again her? It's true. She had just encountered a Jesus-transformation. But how was she going to handle it when the men (or man) came knocking on her door? And what about the people in the town? To them she was still looked down on and ridiculed. Even those who witnessed what had just happened would continue to see her for who she used to be—a sinful woman.

For her to not only go in peace but to stay in peace, she would have had to be so locked in and focused on the Lord of the encounter that nothing else mattered. She would have had to saturate herself in the person of Jesus, the man who made her whole, accepted her just the way she was, loved her despite her many sins, the man that forgive her, and who spoke identity into her very soul with mere words. She was going to have to use this one encounter as an anchor to keep her from being tossed to and fro. She was going to have to draw strength from that experience so as to say, "*No*" to everything to which she was accustomed saying, "*Yes*." As simple as this may sound, it requires so much on our part.

The biggest battle is in our minds. We must make our thoughts align with the truth. The truth was, she was forgiven and she had a life-changing encounter with Jesus. It was going to require effort so as to keep that encounter fresh in her heart and mind. This was going to be critical in the days, weeks, months, and years to follow. One simple encounter with Jesus can change the course of our lives forever just like this woman's life was forever altered. It can transform your life and countless others if we open our hearts and allow Jesus full access. She did not merely stumble upon this encounter with Jesus. She was intentional about seeking Jesus just like I was. It's interesting that some Bible scholars believe this was the same woman who was caught in the act of adultery. That story is found in John 8:1-11 which reads as follows:

> ...but Jesus went to the Mount of Olives. At dawn he appeared again in the temple courts, where all the people gathered around Him, and He sat down to teach them. The teachers of the law and the Pharisees brought in a woman caught in adultery. They made her stand before the group and said to Jesus, "Teacher, this woman was caught in the act of adultery. In the Law Moses commanded us to stone such women. Now what do you say?" They were using this question as a trap, in order to have a basis for accusing Him. But Jesus bent down and started to

write on the ground with His finger. When they kept on questioning Him, He straightened up and said to them, "Let any one of you who is without sin be the first to throw a stone at her." Again He stooped down and wrote on the ground. At this, those who heard began to go away one at a time, the older ones first, until only Jesus was left, with the woman still standing there. Jesus straightened up and asked her, "Woman, where are they? Has no one condemned you?" "No one, sir," she said. "Then neither do I condemn you," Jesus declared. "Go now and leave your life of sin."

For sake of argument, let's assume the scholars are right. I believe this would explain her boldness busting into a house full of Pharisees trying to get to Jesus. Perhaps this was the same group of men who stood before Jesus and accused her when Jesus, with His finger, began to write something in the dust. One by one, they all started high-tailing it out of there. Looking at John 8:3, can you imagine this woman standing there shaking, embarrassed, humiliated, and terrified? She was guilty. She knew her fate and she was going to be stoned to death. Guilt and shame consumed her with the thoughts of who she had become. Her need to be loved and accepted had led her to this place. If only she could do it all over again, she would do it differently. Jesus asked her in verse 10, *"Where are your accusers?"* They had all disappeared. Then, Jesus says to her in verse 11, *"I don't condemn you either, go and sin no more."*

Can you imagine the shock, relief, and astonishment she must have experienced? The words *"go and sin no more"* became a constant reminder of the gratefulness she possessed, which was rooted in the grace and compassion she was shown. If these two women referenced in the Scriptures were, in fact, one and the same, she probably had previously ended the adulterous affairs for which they were going to stone her. Most likely, she was so shaken at her near-death experience that it was easy to stop her sinful lifestyle. She had escaped death and was told to *"go and sin no more."* Talk about being scared straight!

Unfortunately, I had several adulterous affairs in my second marriage. In the first few years of marriage, I was totally committed and completely faithful. As the years went by, I started feeling justified in my affairs because of how I was being treated and cheated. As I stated before, I blamed my husband for my poor choices leading to each one of my affairs. If he wouldn't have cheated, if he would have loved me, if he would have met my needs emotionally and spiritually, I wouldn't have been looking outside the marriage in the first place. I had unrealistic expectations. What I needed never could have come from a natural man because only a supernatural encounter with the man named Jesus would suffice. I was going to a dry well expecting to get water, so to speak.

I didn't wake up one morning thinking, *"Hey, I'm going to have an affair."* After years of feeling lonely, unappreciated, unwanted, and trying to do everything I could to make the marriage work, I got tired. I began allowing thoughts of my current unhappiness to plant seeds which, eventually, took root. As those seeds took root, they quickly produced a harvest of weeds and thorns over which I had no control.

The first affair was unintentional. The more we start to compromise in small things, the easier it is to settle for the big compromises. *"It's the little foxes that spoil the vine,"* reads Song of Solomon 2:15. One day, while grocery shopping, I ran into Heather. It had been a few years since we saw each other. We talked for a while catching up on our current life events. In our conversion, she told me about an old childhood boyfriend of mine that she had recently run into. I thought to myself that it would be so awesome to just talk to him, just to see how he was doing.

My motives were pure. My mistake was entertaining that thought. Being married, I had absolutely no business checking on, talking to, or thinking about another man no matter how bad I thought my marriage was. Days went by and I couldn't stop thinking about wanting to check on him. Finally, I did some research and was able to get his number. We spoke on the phone a few times. The conversation was good, strictly friendly. I shared with him that I was a Christian now and how I had changed my life and was going to church.

I was so lost, but I thought I had been found. Remember, I thought going to church made me a Christian. Looking back, it breaks my heart to even think I considered myself as a Christian, much less telling others I was when my life was so out of control. If you were to examine the fruit in my life, it was far from the "Christian life." Remember what Jesus said in Matthew chapter 7—you will know them by their fruit.

Reflection Activity

SIN

What does this bring to mind in your personal life? Have you been referring to yourself as a "Christian" when all you're doing is going through the motions? Though we did this exercise earlier, now that you've read more, examine the fruit of your life. Have you experienced God on such a level that nothing will deter you from your Jesus-destiny?

_____

_____

_____

_____

_____

_____

_____

CHAPTER THIRTY-THREE

Only God Can Judge Me?

*"Do not judge by appearances,
but judge with the right judgment* (John 7:24).*"*

"*Only God can judge me,*" was my mentality for so many years—I even got it tattooed on my leg. How else will we know what type of fruit a person has if we're not judging them? My "*only God can judge me*" thinking came from my lifestyle of rebellion. I didn't want to be corrected so, when someone called me out on my lifestyle of sin, I quickly became defensive and used it as an escape to continue in my sin.

"*Only God can judge me*" is a lie from the enemy. This can be a really touchy subject for some people. If you feel this way, as I once did, please, before you start throwing stones at me, research and read Scripture about this matter. Ask God to reveal the whole truth about us judging others. And, if I'm wrong, then ask the Lord to show me. I want to make sure we are clear that condemning and judging are not the same. The enemy wants us to believe that, if we judge someone, we are condemning them. We are never to condemn anyone. The enemy will have us to think that, if a person corrects us in love as the Bible instructs, they are condemning us. This is a lie. Do not believe it.

This old friend and I went from talking on the phone a few times to, "*I just want to see him!*" We agreed to meet one day after I got off of work and I remember thinking how good it was to see him again. He looked pretty much the same as he did when we were teenagers. I was proud of how well he was doing after all he had been through. When he began to question me about my life, as I answered, he was very attentive looking me in my eyes with a genuine care and he wasn't distracted by his phone or busy multitasking. He was very engaged. Our visit only lasted about an hour or so when I decided I needed to get home. I left there feeling like a schoolgirl again. I felt welcomed and accepted in his company.

I went home that evening struggling with my thoughts and emotions. I felt guilty and ashamed as though I had committed adultery. Of course, we did not have sex and nothing about our conversation was sexual. Surely, there was nothing wrong with just talking. My husband was apparently working late because he still wasn't home by the time I arrived. Although he owned his own business and work for him ended at dusk, often it would be way after dark before he made it in the house.

I would always hear excuses like he stopped by the store and got to talking and lost track of time, or he stopped by a friend's house to watch the game and fell asleep; it was always something. It never failed, though, as he would come home smelling like a brewery. I went upstairs and sat in what felt like a dark dungeon. I was left all alone to my thoughts and feelings. Not only did I feel guilty and ashamed, but I felt overwhelming sadness and depression. I hated my life. As the days went by, I found myself thinking of this man a lot. I desperately wanted to see him again, but I refused to give in to those thoughts.

I couldn't take it anymore. I felt like I was going crazy in my own mind. Remember, my husband and I, along with the kids, were going to church together every week, yet our lifestyle hadn't changed very much. I wanted help and I felt as though

I needed to talk to someone who could advise me spiritually. I made an appointment with a trusted minister for counseling. We met and I was totally transparent as I explained all that was going on. From getting this guy's number, to going to see him, to my overwhelming thoughts of wanting to be with him, etc. Shamefully, I shared about having thoughts and dreams of being intimate with this man who was not my husband. I shared it all with this minister. I didn't want to do what my thoughts were telling me to do. I wanted my marriage to work, I wanted my husband to love me, I wanted my husband to want me, I wanted my husband to actually sit down undistracted and be attentive to my needs. I wanted to know he cared. I wanted to know he was listening. I wanted a way out of this hole I felt I was in. I was reaching out to the only person I knew could help me, someone who would be able to give me sound biblical advice and direction.

After laying it all out, what proceeded out of this minister's mouth shocked me. Instead of giving me biblical advice and guidance, he gave me his fleshy option. He even shared with me how he himself was attracted to me and how I deserved so much better. I couldn't believe it but, deep down, I welcomed the flattery. I couldn't believe a man of his stature would ever find me attractive. I was secretly enjoying the flirtatious conversation. It made me feel wanted and needed. It made me feel attractive, something I hadn't felt in a really long time. Emotionally, I was all over the place when I left that meeting. In the days which followed, I began to develop a newfound confidence that maybe I did deserve better.

Later that week, my old friend called just to check on me. He wanted to know how my day was. He shared how he couldn't stop thinking about me after I left that day. He asked if I could come see him. It led directly into an affair which lasted over a year. In the beginning, I had an internal warning. I would have crazy thoughts of crashing my car leaving his house. I knew the Lord was prompting me to stop this sinful behavior. I continued to ignore and suppress the inner voice of the Holy Spirit. Eventually, I no longer heard the voice of warning. I stopped going to church. Because I felt like I was a hypocrite, there was no need to go to a place where I knew I was pretending. Besides, going to church never changed my marriage. What was the point anyway? I was sick of hearing messages like *"fake it 'til you make it."* I had done enough faking it.

I started drinking more frequently and going out again. My attitude was that I could play that game way better than my husband. I was very cocky and prideful after months of seeing this guy and I hadn't been caught. Actually, I wasn't caught because my husband was so caught up in his own extramarital affairs, not because I was so good at it. On a few occasions, I even came home with passion marks on my neck and he didn't even notice. I prided myself on coming up with lies which were actually believable. I enjoyed the rush. It gave me a high and became exciting to me. I felt powerful and in control.

Eventually, I got bored and I needed a new fix. With each new man, I raised the stakes and took new risks. The more I got away with, the bolder I became. I would feel like I wasn't the one in control anymore, something more powerful was at work inside me. I never once got caught, unlike my husband, who was sloppy with covering his tracks. He couldn't tell a decent lie to save his life. From there, my life continued to spiral more and more out of control.

Sin will take you further than you want to go, keep you longer than you ever intended to stay, and cost you more than you are ever willing to pay. So, you see why the story of the adulterous woman with the alabaster box is so much like mine. I was that sinful and adulterous woman until, like her, I had an encounter with Jesus when I got sick and tired of allowing myself to be used and abused. I hated the woman I had become. That's when I made the decision to surrender everything, the sin and all the broken pieces of my messed-up life.

Unlike the woman in the story who anointed Jesus with an expensive perfume, I had nothing to give but a broken heart. He didn't mind, though, as He knew that, soon enough, I would have a new heart, one He would exchange for my broken one. As I gave up the brokenness, piece by piece, the more I became whole and healed in Christ. Years after my deliverance and living completely sold out to Christ, I sat on the floor during a worship service—something I don't usually do—closed my eyes and I remembered my life before Christ.

Tears streamed down my face as I reminisced on that life of bondage and pain. I was filled with gratitude and love toward God for having saved a woman such as myself. In that moment of worship, I thought about the story of the sinful woman. I began to imagine being her. I wept at Jesus' feet. I wiped the tears with my hair and I kissed His feet. I broke open my alabaster box and anointed His beautiful bronze feet. I had never experienced this type of intimacy in worship before. I was at the feet of my Savior, the one who had set me free and forgiven my many sins. In that sweet, sweet moment, it was just He and I and nothing in the world mattered anymore.

After that service, a beautiful young lady shared this with me. She said *"Jesus wants you to know you are like the woman with the alabaster box. Because you were forgiven much, you love much."* She continued to speak but I don't think I heard anything else. Only the Lord knew my thoughts as I sat on that floor that night. I was blown away. I still have to remind myself of that word when I get in a funk and feel like God is so far from me. Often, I have to remind myself that I don't live by my feelings any longer. I live by what I know. Experiences like these are what keep me anchored in His truth. As you read the story in Luke 7 about the sinful woman and the self-righteous Pharisee, where do you see yourself in the story?

Let me make a very important observation, one which I learned through my own experience of adultery. Adulterous affairs don't begin with sleeping together. They begin with inappropriate friendships. Friendships and emotional attachments with people of the opposite—or same sex if that is an area where you struggle—can spell danger for ourselves and for our marriage. We must protect ourselves and our marriage by avoiding private communications and intimate conversations with people outside our marriage. This goes for church folks and ministers as well.

I am not saying to not seek wise counsel—the Bible tells us to do that. I am saying to seek God first and He will direct you. Personally, I would suggest someone of the same gender or a husband and wife team. We must beware of co-workers with whom we may find ourselves spending way too much time where the conversations often lead to personal information being shared. Beware of those that give you compliments about the way you look. Any time we have to tell a lie, manipulate, cover up, or deceive others, it is a huge red flag. One good thing about telling the truth is that you don't have to remember the lie you told.

Allow God to build your esteem so that you're not flattered or moved by compliments. Often times, women are looking to be validated and approved by men. In this, compliments, whether given in pure motives or not, can cause us to become emotionally attached and wanting more. We fall in love easily. We are women who love hard and we give all of us. No matter the cost, we do it all in the name of love. Sadly, this is not love and it not a healthy behavior.

As you now know, I spent many years trying to find validation and sought love from men through relationships which were self-destructive. Relationships like these will never last and, when they end, they burn in heartache. They are self-destructive and very unhealthy physically, mentally, emotionally, and spiritually. Until we fully accept, love, and respect ourselves, we will continue to attract those relationships rooted in fear and insecurities. I can't say it enough that, in order to fully accept, love, and respect ourselves, we must know who we are in Christ. Our worth and value must be found in Jesus. Anything else is just temporal and vain.

Also, we must remember our God is a jealous God. No relationship will ever work when we put a person in the place of Him. At all cost, we must keep a healthy physical, social, and emotional distance between us and people of the opposite sex, especially when married. Affairs are not always sexual; most of them are emotional. Sexual or emotional, it's still an affair. Our emotions should be reserved first to Jesus and second to our spouse. The number one lie told concerning affairs is, "*It just happened.*" Factually, nothing "*just happens.*" This is why it is so very important for us to guard our hearts and protect what we allow access to our eyes and ears.

As you can see from sharing my story of adultery, it all started in my thoughts. Those thoughts eventually caused me to make small compromises that led to something so much greater than I could control. At the time, I didn't know how to take my thoughts captive and bring them into the obedience of Christ. I didn't know who I was. I was seeking validation and attention outside of Christ. *"You have heard that it was said, 'Do not commit adultery.' But I tell you that anyone who looks at a woman lustfully has already committed adultery with her in his heart,"* is found in Matthew 5:27-28. Scripture tells us that, if we even look at another person in a lustful way, we have committed adultery already. I'm sure we are all aware of the look of lustful desire, one that often leads to flirting and inappropriate conversations or fantasies. In order to have a healthy and trustworthy marriage, it is crucial to protect what we allow in and out. Integrity, honesty, and faithfulness must be worn like the physical clothes we wear. We must be intentional about putting them on just like we do when we get dressed.

I hope I am effectively drilling this point. Until I was secure in who God had created me to be, I was unable to walk in integrity, honesty, and faithfulness. Knowing who I was in Christ was the key to being able to live life to the fullest. It continues to open doors I never could imagine.

Reflection Activity

Who can you most relate to in the story of the sinful woman?
_____
_____

What are the important lessons Jesus is teaching through this story?
_____
_____
_____
_____
_____

How can you apply that in your own life?

_____

_____

_____

_____

Jesus told the lady in John 8:11 to *"go and sin no more."* Is there a current sin in your life about which Jesus is tugging on your heart? If so, what is it?

_____

_____

_____

_____

What are the steps needed in order for you to break free from the power of that sin in your life? It could be deleting some numbers, that favorite TV show, that adulterous affair, a relationship, etc.

_____

_____

_____

_____

_____

_____

CHAPTER THIRTY-FOUR

Dealing with Adultery

"But a man who commits adultery has no sense; whoever does so destroys himself (Proverbs 6:32).*"*

Are you a victim of an affair? I understand your hurt, disappointment, fears, insecurities, anger, and depression. I understand your pain and I support you. The pain I have experienced from men who were supposed to be faithful left me in a state which cannot be clearly explained by mere words. Indescribable emotional and physical pain had me longing for death. I have been there, I get it. I speak life into you. It was not your fault and you are not to blame. You are not the issue. You didn't make them do it. It really has nothing to do with you.

The issue is in the person who committed the unfaithful act. There is a root cause with which has never been addressed, I promise. There is nothing you can do to change that person. Your love, looks, or faithfulness will never be enough. You must release yourself from the bondage of that hurt and the idea of thinking you can change them. Please understand, it's not about you. Oh, sure, you may verbally be accused of being the problem but, I assure you, you are not. You may not be helping the situation by arguing, bickering, and accusing, but you're not the cause of the situation. I assure you, there's a deeper issue. It's a heart issue. Something is lacking and there is a pain and void which only Jesus can heal in that person. Jesus is the only one who can do it, not you. A person who has an affair does not understand or know who they truly are in Christ, if they are actually in Christ.

Speaking from a woman's perspective, as women, we so desperately want the "*why*" question answered. I believe a person doesn't understand the root of their actions until they seek the Lord to show them. Take me, for instance. If you would have asked me why everything happened as it did, I would have blamed it on my husband. But, the truth was, I was so full of baggage I didn't know who I was. I hadn't dealt with all the deeply rooted soul issues. I want to share with you something that happen during the relationship with my ex fiancé, the one who choked me.

Through this, I was able to find compassion even in my own pain of being cheated. At one point in our relationship, he reached out to get help. He started the process of getting inner healing by getting to the root of the problem. During his time seeking the Lord, he felt like God showed him why it was so hard for him to be committed to one woman. Through his fears and tears, he shared he had been molested by his uncle when he was a little boy. He grew up with hatred and anger in his heart. He said he often questioned his sexuality. He felt controlled by this need to prove to himself he was not gay. In his feeble attempt, he became a womanizer and slept with many women. It then became an addiction for him.

There is always a root to everything. It's just a matter of getting to it. Most of us are not willing to put in the work required for true healing. Sadly, he didn't stay at the feet of Jesus so as to allow complete healing and transformation. As a side note, I believe this was one of the reasons which kept me so tied to him. I felt obligated to help him. I felt sorry for him and, whenever he would hurt me, I would remember what he had been through and used it as an excuse to tolerate his behavior. I desperately wanted to help him while ignoring my own pain.

Never expect a man or woman to be faithful to you if he or she isn't first faithful to Christ. So, my beloved friend, I say to you, you are no longer a victim but a survivor. Are you in a marriage right now where infidelity is something you're facing? I beg you, as hard as it will be to push past all the distractions, take a seat in the loving arms of your heavenly Father. Take your eyes off what's going on around you and press into Jesus. Don't allow your emotions to control you.

Our emotions are only indicators, not dictators. Yes, it hurts. Yes, we want answers. We want to be investigators—we want to control what's happening. Stop it, stop it, stop it! Stop running behind, stop going through phones, pocketbooks, and wallets, stop scanning social media, stop going through private messages, stop checking emails, stop checking phone logs. My mother used to always say, "*If you look for something, you will find it.*"

I would do all the above and, sure enough, I would find it. Text messages from other females, condoms in his truck, hidden porn in the house. You name it, I would find it and it controlled my life. I couldn't focus or function. There were times I would have to leave work because I was controlled by the emotions attached to what I was going through. I literally thought I was losing my mind, that I was crazy. This was exactly what the enemy wanted. He wanted my mind. He knew that, if he could control my thoughts, he could highly influence my actions.

This thing which controls us has us on a road of destruction. Please understand that, although your husband or wife may be the one having the affair, the enemy wants to destroy *you*. I cannot tell you how many times anger and depression fueled my thoughts to the point I felt like I wasn't in control of my actions. Thoughts from murder to suicide flooded my mind daily. You must stop. Peace can only be found when we keep our minds on Jesus. It will never be found by keeping our minds on what's being done to us. I reiterate that hurt people, hurt people.

Release yourself from the dysfunctional cycle. Take your eyes off your spouse and the pain. Stop the arguing, questioning, and demanding. Learn to keep your mouth shut and your emotions in check. Stop with the *"he said, she said"* conversations. Stay off social media, turn your phone off if you have to, and stop entertaining the drama and foolishness. Stop worrying about the other woman or man.

God wants to meet with you, help you, heal you, restore you, and He wants to make you whole and complete in Him. Seek Him for the very thing you need. Let go and let God. The process is not easy but, I promise you, it will be worth it. In Christ, you are strong, you will make it, and you will rise up and overcome. I believe in you. I know it may feel like you are alone and you have been forsaken, but your Abba Father wants you to know you are not alone and you are not forsaken. Don't allow what a man or woman has done to you to blind you from the truth. No matter your past or your current situation, here is some truth I leave with you as you press into God. As you read these Scriptures, insert your name, read them out loud, and meditate on them daily.

Reflection Activity

"_____, be strong and courageous. _____, do not be afraid or terrified because of them, for the Lord your God goes with you; He will never leave you nor forsake you (Deuteronomy 31:6)."

"The Lord is near to me,_____, the brokenhearted, and saves the crushed in spirit (Psalm 34:18)."

Are you the one who has committed or is committing adultery? If so, ask yourself what's missing from your life. Ask the Lord to show you why you participate in this sinful behavior? Do you look at men and/or women and have lustful desires? Maybe the issue is lust. What I know to be true is that, whatever it is, when you get transparent before the Lord and seek Him for healing, He will do just that. Get in and stay in the process. No matter how many times you may fall, stay in the process. Greater awaits you, freedom awaits you, forgiveness and restoration await you. Rise up and walk in it.

Here's a great place to start. Confess to the Lord your sins and He will be faithful and just to forgive you. Seek godly counsel from someone who is of the same gender. Ask the Lord for a Christian brother or sister who will be an accountability partner, someone who will be willing to pray for and with you. Forgive yourself for the damage and hurt you have caused, whether known or unknown. Pray for and earnestly ask the Father to heal the broken hearts of those involved such as spouse and/or children. Just like in story of the adulterous woman, Jesus said, "*I don't accuse you either,*" meaning, you are forgiven. Go and sin no more.

"*If I, _____, confess my sins, He is faithful and just and will forgive me my sins and purify me from all unrighteousness* (I John 1:9).*"*

Prayer: *Lord, I pray that Your Word comes alive in my beloved friend's life. May You heal and help them though this pain of infidelity. Let them feel Your closeness, fill their hearts with hope, and confidence. Cause Your joy to be their strength. Help them keep their mind stayed on You. Cause Your peace to settle the issues which try to overtake them. May the peace of God that surpasses all human understanding became a reality, day and night. In Jesus' name, Amen.*

CHAPTER THIRTY-FIVE
Fit for the Master's Use

"Therefore, if anyone cleanses himself from what is dishonorable, he will be a vessel for honorable use, set apart as holy, useful to the Master of the house, ready for every good work. So flee youthful passions and pursue righteousness, faith, love, and peace, along with those who call on the Lord from a pure heart (II Timothy 2:21-22).*"*

My life revolved around me and my pursuit of happiness. God is more concerned with our holiness than He is with our happiness. What I have found on my journey of holiness is something far greater than happiness. It is contentment. I am content with God using me and my past life of sin to bring Him Glory, to be fit for the Master's use. *"Being fit"* means to be cleansed from our life of sin. We become a person striving to live a holy life, loving Jesus, and obeying His commandments. By no means does it mean we are perfect people or without sin. Let's let Scripture define what being fit for the Master's use actually means from God's perspective.

The word "holy" used to scare me, as I was anything but holy. Being holy made me think of a nun living a boring life full of religious acts. Holiness simply means to be set apart, unique, devoted to God, distinct, and different from the world around us. I spent much of my life being devoted to men, drugs, and running the streets. I spent much of my life being devoted to all the wrong things.

Letting all that go wasn't an easy process. Most of what made it so hard was my jacked up thinking about living for Christ. I had it so wrong. A life set apart and fully committed to Christ is anything but boring. Oh, yeah sure, we have days of being bored, but that's not what I'm talking about. Living a life devoted with our whole hearts produces the abundant life Jesus died for us to have. I never knew living a holy life would produce something for which my heart had always longed. I never knew how to have a life other than the dysfunctional mess I was in, although I wanted something different.

Prior to living a life completely devoted to Christ, I was addicted to drama and gossip. I was involved with everybody else's life or I had them involved in mine. Have you ever heard the phrase *"misery loves company"*? Well, that was my life, miserable and full of company. This was all part of the enemy's plan for my life—to keep me full of drama, busy, and distracted. In my drama-filled life, I didn't have time to focus on the real issue, which was me.

My focus was hanging out at the club with the girls or going away for the weekend. If you're anything like I was, whenever life stresses us out, we feel like we need to hang out with friends, get a drink, get away, go on vacation somewhere, or move to a different city or state. The problem with all of the above was that, everywhere I went, there I was. Since I was the issue, wherever I went, my issues followed me. I was trying to escape things going on around me when the real issue was what was going on inside me.

I was burned out and tired. The more distracted I was with the drama, the further it took me away from discovering the real issue, which was me and my need for a Savior and internal healing. I came to a point where I had to remove myself, as difficult as it was, from the people, places, and things I was used to. I was determined and it was a fight, but the biggest battle was internal—the fear of being alone, the insecurities of being separated from the life I knew.

The biggest battle you will ever have to fight is within yourself. I was my own worst enemy and I was my own hold-up. Once I was delivered from all the addictions, I got to the root of the problem. I got past the self-hatred and then learned to forgive. It was a complete transformation. Life was completely different. I began to look, talk, dress, hear, and see differently. I truly was a new person. God wants to transform us into holiness, into His image. Transformation is a lifetime process, not a one-time event.

The definition of transformation is *"a thorough or dramatic change in form or appearance."* Its synonyms are "change, alteration, mutation, metamorphosis, transfiguration, transmutation, revolution, overhaul; remodeling, reshaping, redoing, reconstruction, rebuilding, reorganization, rearrangement, reworking, renewal, revamp, remaking, remake; informal transmogrification, morphing."

Holy living isn't a bunch of rules to follow, no. It's all about an intimate relationship with Jesus. It's about learning to be confident in His loving and trustworthy character, all of which eventually create a beautiful life of contentment. When we learn intimacy with God, we gladly refrain from anything He restricts or withholds from us. We must always remember that when He withholds something from us, it is always for our good.

> "For the Lord God is a sun and shield; the Lord will give grace and glory; no good thing will He withhold from those who walk uprightly. O Lord of hosts, blessed is the man who trusts in You (Psalm 84:11-12)."

For they that are after the flesh do mind the things of the flesh; but they that are after the Spirit the things of the Spirit. For to be carnally minded is death; but to be spiritually minded is life and peace (Romans 8: 5-7).

"So all of us who have had that veil removed can see and reflect the glory of the Lord. And the Lord—who is the Spirit—makes us more and more like Him as we are changed into his glorious image (2 Corinthians 3:18)."

Psalm 84 is one of my favorite Scriptures. I often find myself camped out in these two verses when I feel disappointed or let down because something didn't go as planned or didn't go my way. Living holy isn't always easy because it goes against the grain of our innate sin nature. We are born selfish and grow up wanting to fulfill our fleshy desires. Galatians 5:16 instructs us to walk in the Spirit, and we shall not fulfill the lusts of the flesh.

Living a carnal life or, in other words, living a life after our fleshy desires, brings death—not necessarily a physical death but spiritual. Contrarily, living a spiritually holy life brings abundant life and peace. In order for us to live holy, we have to make a daily decision to walk after the Spirit. Every day I have been given air in my lungs, I am either helping build God's kingdom, Jami's kingdom, or the kingdom of darkness.

This means that, daily, I must choose to build God's kingdom. I have to choose to sacrifice my wants, pleasures, conveniences, comforts, frustrations, and fleshly desires. Many misquote what God's Word is saying, *"He will give us the desires of our hearts."* We often quote that Scripture, yet totally miss the first part which states, *"delight yourself in the Lord..."* The more we delight ourselves in the Lord, the more our desires change. As we delight ourselves in the Lord, we become one with His heart and we begin to desire things of the Spirit. We begin to see and understand the kingdom of God and His righteousness (Matthew 6:33).

God desires for us to bear good fruit. This is part of the holy transformation. God has appointed you to go and produce lasting fruit (John 15:16). We have been chosen by God and appointed to go and produce lasting, eternal fruit. The words *"go and produce"* require action. For instance, a farmer doesn't just hope for a crop—he has to plant, tend, and harvest the crop.

The point I am trying to make is we have a part to play. Holy transformation doesn't just happen, we must co-labor with the Lord. Into what are we being transformed? We are being transformed into the image of our heavenly Father. Why? It is so we will reflect God's glory and become ambassadors of Christ and ministers of reconciliation. We are Christ's ambassadors and God is making His appeal through us. We speak for Christ when we plead, *"Come back to God..."* as found in 2 Corinthians 5:20.

When I think about all the years I spent calling myself a Christian, it breaks my heart when I think of how I led people away from the Lord instead of to Him. The example I was to my husband and my kids was anything but reflecting God, much less his glory. A house without a foundation is sure to crumble. That is what happened to me—I didn't have a foundation. I came to Christ and started putting up walls and windows without a foundation. Personally, this is what I see among so many "Christians" today; they are without a firm foundation. This is why we have so much disorder, confusion, and chaos amongst believers.

Church Hurt

Let's talk about the church hurt. So many have left their faith in Christ because of what we call "church hurt." Church is supposed to be a safe and secure place where we can come to learn and grow in the image of God. Unfortunately, a lot of times, we have people—leaders included—who have no true foundation. They are still full of baggage and it causes disorder, confusion, and chaos. And the enemy is just sitting back laughing.

Hurt people, hurt people; never forget this. Whether we are laymen or leaders, if we don't get cleaned on the inside, the cycle will continue. Most of us who attend church get busy doing church functions, programs, choir, ushering, teaching, and more, but never get busy seeking Jesus for our healing. Going to church is not the same thing as going to Jesus.

I am not saying we should stay away from church but, what I am saying is, going to a building we call church is not the same thing as going to Jesus and allowing Him to heal us so that we can become the Church. We tend to go to a building with other broken and hurting people and, unfortunately, we place our hope, faith, and trust in man—the equally broken people. Then, when we get hurt, we blame God and say this "Christian" thing doesn't work.

Let's visualize the building we call church. Look at it as a hospital. All of us are sick and we need a hospital. In a hospital, you have different floors which treat different types of sicknesses. Some need short-term care and some long-term. The goal is to get you well so that you can help others become well (2 Corinthians 1:3-4). In order for us to become healed and whole, we must seek the physician—Jesus. We must take our focus off the other sick folks. Although it is easy to relate to people with our same sickness, when we get caught up in commiserating with them, we never get what we need. We attract what we are so, when we are sick, we attract other sick folk, usually the ones who indulge in the same sins. For instance, when I started going to church, I found the group of people who were like me. Instead of pursuing the Lord, we would get caught up in gossip, complaining, and being offended about the things we didn't like about the church. This is wrong focus.

It is the same with the leaders, teachers, ushers, deacons, and church staff. See them as the doctors, nurses, physical therapists, and other staff. It could be that they are sick themselves and cause you more pain and sickness. If, however, we take our eyes off them and focus on Jesus, He can use the "hospital" as a place of healing and recovery. I was so blessed to have been in an amazing church during the baby stages of my transformation. I often describe *Life Living Ministries* as my incubator.

It was a place I received unconditional love, guidance, and everything else I needed to grow into a mature Christian. Don't get it twisted, though. I easily could have gotten caught up like I did before. No matter where we go, no matter how great a church is, if our eyes are not fixed on Jesus, they will be fixed on something else. I can say from my personal experience, the foundation at *Life Living* was firm; it was built on Jesus and they are all for cleaning the junk built on the inside. That makes a huge difference in one's journey toward true freedom. From the pastor on down, they made it easy for me to be transparent about my struggles and sin without condemning me. With love and compassion, they would encourage me with Scripture and point me to Jesus as the one on whom I needed to focus. I am forever grateful for the leadership and members at *Life Living* for taking me in and nurturing me back to life.

Reflection Activity

Have you experienced a dramatic change in your life through God? Would you like to experience a dramatic God-transformation? If so, in what areas?

_____

_____

_____

_____

_____

_____

_____

_____

So, my sweet friend, where do you see yourself in your pursuit to becoming holy? Do you see yourself as being fit for the Master's use?

CHAPTER THIRTY-SIX

Reflection of God

"Don't copy the behavior and customs of this world, but let God transform you into a new person by changing the way you think. Then you will learn to know God's will for you, which is good and pleasing and perfect (Romans 12:2)."

"But we are citizens of heaven, where the Lord Jesus Christ lives. And we are eagerly waiting for Him to return as our Savior (Philippians 3:20)."

Be like children who obey. Do not desire to sin like you used to when you did not know any better. Be holy in every part of your life. Be like the Holy One Who chose you. The Holy Writings say, 'You must be holy, for I am holy (I Peter 1:14-16).'

"So set yourselves apart to be holy, for I am the Lord your God (Leviticus 20:7)."

We Christians are to reflect God's image, His character. We spend too much time being distracted and busy that we never take the time to know His character. We live in the leftovers of someone else's experience or what we have been taught by men. God wants to feed us directly from His table; He doesn't just want us eating other people's scraps or living out of someone else's experience. We will never know God's character until we know His Word and we will never know His Word until we spend intimate time in His presence while reading our Bible, fasting, and praying. "Bible" can translate into:

Basic
Instructions
Before
Leaving
Earth.

We talked about this Scripture in another chapter, but I wanted to highlight the importance of renewing our minds. By default, we model after this world until we learn a different way. Our part in co-laboring with the Lord is to fill our minds with His Word and, in doing so, He transforms us into His image. Then, we can rightly represent His character, thusly causing us to walk in holiness, our true purpose.

Change the way you think and it will change your life. Living holy means living in the light of what God's Word says and not according to the ways of this world. We are kingdom citizens. We must focus our minds on things eternal. Earth is not our home. As we eagerly wait for the Lord's return, in our waiting, we have work to do. The most important work is staying at Jesus' feet giving Him our full devotion and keeping the first commandment first—this is the most important. The time we spend with God is more important than the things we do for God. Life flows from this place. God is looking for those who will partner with Him in living holy and bringing His kingdom to earth (Matthew 6:10).

God is very passionate about us becoming holy. In Leviticus 19:2, the words God spoke to Israel still apply to us today, *"Give the following instructions to the entire community of Israel. You must be holy because I, the Lord your God, am holy."* When reading Leviticus 19, it's easy to think of holiness as a list of dos and don'ts. Remember my story? I spent years trying to follow a bunch of rules without real relationship. True holiness happens when our heart becomes one with His. Our hearts will only become one with His as we spend intimate time with Him.

I reiterate that this is a process, not a one-time event. And this doesn't happen when we only spend a few hours a week attending church services. God's holiness changes us from the inside out. The more Jesus you put in, the more junk comes out. God knows we are all sinners and we can't be holy on our own. When we try to be holy apart from Him, it only produces self-righteousness (Isaiah 64:6). If we allow God's Word to sink deeply into our hearts and minds, we will see a true transformation. God himself helps us as we yield to Him giving Him total control of our lives.

As we draw closer to the Lord, we will hear the voice of the enemy say things like, *"Don't be all holy, holy"* or *"don't be so heavenly minded that you're no earthly good."* I was guilty of this kind of thinking. I didn't know God or His Word the way I do now. God Himself is calling us to holiness, so why wouldn't we strive for what He commands of us? The truth is, we cannot rightly relate to God and wrongly relate to others. The closer we get to God, the better we can love ourselves and our neighbors in the way He intended. Jesus was all about relationships. He was intentional about spending time with, loving, healing, and teaching people. If being holy would cause us to not be able to relate to people, why would God require it of us?

In my ignorance, I have made the statement, *"I'm not trying to be all holy."* This was before I understood what holiness meant. *Acting* holy and *being* holy are two totally different things. *Acting* is when we don't understand and we are not connected to the

Father's heart. It is just a list of rules we try to follow. *Being holy* becomes who we are as we draw close to the Father in our devotion and prayer. Being holy happens when we become one with the Father; it's not something we have to *try* to accomplish. It is what we become. We can't act holy to our friends and family but ignore the personal convictions of sin. God's conviction comes so that we *become* instead of *act*. Let's let Scripture help us see the heart of God.

> "Because of the weakness of your human nature, I am using the illustration of slavery to help you understand all this. Previously, you let yourselves be slaves to impurity and lawlessness, which led ever deeper into sin. Now you must give yourselves to be slaves to righteous living so that you will become holy (Romans 6:19)."

> "Therefore, since we have these promises, dear friends, let us purify ourselves from everything that contaminates body and spirit, perfecting holiness out of reverence for God (2 Corinthians 7:1)."

> "And do not bring sorrow to God's Holy Spirit by the way you live. Remember, He has identified you as His own, guaranteeing that you will be saved on the day of redemption (Ephesians 4:30)."

> "Do not be misled: Bad company corrupts good character (I Corinthians 15:33)."

> "Those who cleanse themselves from the latter will be instruments for special purposes, made holy, useful to the Master and prepared to do any good work (II Timothy 2:21)."

As co-laborers, we have to do our part. The beautiful thing is that we never have to do it alone. Just as I had given myself as a slave to impurity and wickedness, I must now give myself to being a slave to righteousness. This leads to holiness. I had to purify myself from everything that contaminated my body and spirit.

We have become desensitized to the things which contaminate us, from food to TV and everything in between. We have let the world desensitize our reverence of the Lord and, whether we know it or not, it affects every aspect of our lives. So many of us are grieving the Holy Spirit by what we watch, the music we hear, the conversations we have, and the people we hang out with, whether family or friends. Each one of us has to make a daily decision to live for Christ or live to satisfy our own agenda. What kingdom are you building?

We cannot continue to hang around the same old people, do the same old things, go to the same old places, and watch the same old things and expect change. We must ask ourselves, "*Is what I'm doing taking me further from God or does it cause me to become closer to God?*" We must learn to yield to the promptings of the Holy Spirit. The more we obey, the easier it becomes and the more we become like Jesus. The more Jesus you put in, the more the junk comes out. It is God's desire that we all become fit for the Master's use.

Let's put it an analogy. God is the baker and we are the eggs. Let's say the baker wants to make a cake. First, he would choose what type of cake he desires and then select special ingredients needed for that cake. The goal is to make something beautiful and delicious for others to enjoy and, in return, the baker gets the glory. The interesting thing about the different ingredients is that they don't compete with each other; they work together in unity. The eggs don't compete with the sugar, the sugar doesn't compete with the flour, etc. All the ingredients blend together in unity. The baker doesn't give instructions to the eggs, they simply conform to what the baker is doing. It is only when the egg is broken and poured out that the baker can use the eggs for his purpose. This represents our lives. The baker wants to use each one of us. The eggs must become willing to be used, broken, and poured out. A broken and poured out life is a surrendered life. Nothing hidden, nothing left.

What's interesting about making a cake is, once all the ingredients blend together, they are put in an oven to bake. They go in one way and come out something completely different. The eggs, just like all the other ingredients, can never go back to being what they once were. Standing alone, they can't do a whole lot but, together, they create something far greater. Although the ingredients don't understand all the mixing and stirring, the baker knew he always had a greater purpose in mind. The ingredients had to allow the baker to use them. All of us together are Christ's body and each one of us is a part of that body (1 Corinthians 12:27). We must stop competing and comparing ourselves to others. We must stop being jealous and coveting what others have. If we would take our eyes off others and keep them on Jesus, He will show each one of us His plan and purpose as individuals within the whole of the body.

Competing and Comparing

I used to find myself doing all the above with my best friend, Heather. I was jealous of her personality as she is always bubbly and friendly, and she can walk up to anyone and start a conversation. Me, I am more laidback and shy. I wished I could be more like her. She has the most beautiful worship and I was always comparing myself with, "*Why can't I worship like that?*" God has created me to worship differently than her and it is okay. I had to learn that.

Today, I can say that, without competing or comparing myself to anyone, I love who God has created me to be. We all have a unique way and we need to spend time cultivating that instead of trying to be like someone else or wishing we were someone else. Jealousy is another one of the enemy's tricks. Jealousy is a murdering spirit.

Reflection Activity

Do you believe you are a reflection of God?

_____
_____
_____
_____
_____
_____
_____
_____

Why or why not?

_____

_____

_____

_____

_____

_____

What are the things you can do to co-labor with the Lord so as to draw closer to Him?

_____

_____

_____

_____

_____

_____

_____

_____

What are some things the Lord has personally spoken to you about in this chapter?

What Scripture stood out to you the most?

What is the Lord personally saying to you?

Prayer: *Lord, I thank You that we don't have to change on our own. The closer we get to You, the more we will look, be, and sound like You. Help us to stay focused on staying close to You as the enemy tries to do what he can to keep us distracted. I ask You to give us the wisdom to see clearly and to respond accordingly. Give us a desire to want to live a life holy and poured out, yielded to You and Your will. Not our will but Yours be done in and through us. In Jesus' name I pray, Amen.*

CHAPTER THIRTY-SEVEN

Diamond in the Rough

"Charm is deceptive, and beauty is fleeting; but a woman who fears the Lord is to be praised (Proverbs 31:30)."

Throughout my process of becoming the woman God created me to be, my desire to have a husband and family never changed. Oftentimes, I would find myself consumed with thoughts of trying to look for a husband or trying to figure out who my husband was. I had to continually redirect those thoughts and let it go. God's Word would remind me that it was not my place to find someone.

Proverbs 18:22 says, "He who finds a wife finds a good thing. . ." I needed to focus on being a wife before worrying about having a husband. Also, when I thought about wanting a husband, fear from all my past mistakes would well up inside. I was fearful of making a wrong choice. I was fearful of becoming codependent again. Remember, I had already experienced two failed marriages, I was on the verge of getting married a third time, not to mention the countless broken relationships in between. I didn't trust me. I was the reason for all the mess from which I needed deliverance.

Although I had a desire to be married, my desire to have the husband God had chosen for me was greater than just wanting to be married. I valued my relationship with God more than anything and I didn't want to lose that. One night, I was talking with the Lord. It was pretty much a one-sided conversation because I never heard Him say anything. I told God, again, of my desire to be married, that I was afraid of being married again to the wrong man, and I needed a codeword. I needed a specific word that he—my God-ordained husband—would say to me so that I would know it was him.

Of course, this conversation was taking place in my head. I dare not say it out loud, for I knew the enemy would use this codeword to send someone to deceive me. I thought to myself that I dare not write my codeword down because I didn't know if the enemy could read. I had to laugh at myself, but I was serious. I was no longer listening to secular music, but I immediately thought of one of my favorite songs. The words described what I had been through in my past and what I wanted from my husband. Here are the lyrics to "Diamond in the Rough" by Anthony Hamilton:

Better Babe
Looking at you, I can tell, you've had hard times in your life
Now it's time for me, to make everything right
I wanna shower you, with lovely thangs, help you smile again,
I wanna get to know you, make it right, so you can breathe again

You're my diamond in the rough girl
And I'm here to make it better
You're my diamond in the rough girl
And we gone shine in love together

*I see the scars from the broken heart; life's got you down
And the bags under your eyes have the smiles inside, that's
tearing you apart (weeellllll)
Girl you looking at change, I'm a man who prays and I'm
strong in faith (strong in faith)
God musta had a plan, placed you in my hand, let me lead
the way.*

*You're my diamond in the rough girl
And I'm here to make it better
You're my diamond in the rough girl...
(end)*

"*Diamond in the rough*" became my codeword. Now, let's talk music for a minute. As I shared with you before, music controlled so much of my thoughts, feelings, emotions, decisions, and actions. I could listen to certain types of music and get a high feeling, a high much like when I snorted cocaine. Certain types of music would make me feel powerful and in control.

For instance, Beyoncé came out with her hit song "Irreplaceable." Knowing all the dirt my then-husband was doing, listening to this song gave me a sense of entitlement to be unfaithful. It gave me this high, a confidence, a cockiness. I had a "*please don't get it twisted, he'll be here in a minute*" attitude. These were the lyrics of the hook to the song. When I would sing it, it was as though the song became who I was, it was a part of me, it came alive, and it activated and elevated my emotions and thoughts which led my actions.

Even today, I'm sure some of you can relate. I can hear a certain song and it will literally take me to a particular place in time. It has the power to bring up memories, both good and bad. For example, when I hear a certain song that's associated with a person, place, or thing of my past, I experience the memories of it. When I hear a certain song, it will take me back to a club, house, or hotel. I can see the person with whom I was having sex or the group of friends with me at the time.

Just like when hearing Vanity 6's "Nasty Girls," I go back to my room as a child. I experience me dressed up in inappropriate clothes pretending to be a dancer in a club. "Purple Rain" by Prince makes me think of Jazmine's dad as it was his favorite song. The day he died, I sat in my apartment crying my eyes out while I had that song on repeat. Now, anytime I hear that song, it immediately makes me sad because it is associated with Joe's death.

This is one of many reasons I had to completely stop listening to secular music. As much as I enjoyed it, I knew it had a huge impact on my memories, emotions, and decision-making. I'm not saying all secular music is bad. I'm saying that, for me, I had to be mindful of what I was listening to because of the influence it had on me. Take, for instance, the lyrics from the song "Diamond in the Rough." With me being a single woman who desired to be married, it awakened thoughts and emotions that did not need to be awakened. I chose not to listen to it because it would lead to impure thoughts and impure thoughts almost always lead to impure actions.

I had made a covenant with God and my own heart. I made a vow to stop breaking my own heart. This song would have had me fantasizing about having someone in my life who would buy me nice things and make me smile again. No thank you! I meant what I said when I asked God to keep me hidden until He was ready for me to be found. This song would have had me on a manhunt. I already had to redirect my thoughts without the influence of music.

I MADE A VOW TO STOP BREAKING MY OWN HEART.

I told the Lord I did not want to be attracted to another man emotionally, physically, spiritually, or sexually until it was the husband for whom He had designed me. I say all that to say, I had to do my part in keeping the covenant. The type of music I liked would have kept me from doing my part. It would have caused me to be distracted, to say the least. If I would have allowed myself to listen to such music, I would have been focused on every man I was attracted to instead of cultivating my relationship with the Lord. I would have been looking, yet again, for a man to be my savior instead of keeping my eyes on the Savior.

So, as for me, if the music wasn't talking about God, I had to close my ears. It was the only way I knew I was going to be able to stay focused. It wasn't just music, I had to be very mindful of what I watched on TV, conversations in which I was involved, and the places I went. Remember, for the first time ever, I was celibate, including masturbation. I wasn't trying to wake that demon. I wanted to keep my mind and heart pure.

Along with my codeword, I had a list of what I wanted my husband to look and act like. My first request (don't laugh), I wanted a white husband. Let me explain. I am white. Ever since middle school, I had an attraction for males outside my race. In school, I would get picked on and called names because of it. I had family and friends who were against it. It brought much shame and condemnation from others.

I was often told I was too good for that, as if people of other races were beneath me. I was called names and looked down on. People would say I was trying to "be black." They would say I had a "black" haircut. They would say I tried to dress "black." The one I hated the most was being told I sounded black. For the longest time, I tried to change the way my voice sounds. Through years of trying, I finally gave up and, through learning who I was in Christ, I began to embrace my individual personality.

Both my husbands and fiancé were all African American. Both my biological daughters are biracial. I have had women who are

African American be very disrespectful to me at various times in my life just because I was with an African American. I have always felt like people have pre-judged me without knowing me. I was sick and tired of the labels, the shame, and condemnation that came along with being with someone outside my race.

I wanted a white husband. Not only did I want a white one, but I wanted a white husband with lots of tattoos. I also wanted him to have a radical testimony about how God changed his life. I wanted him to have a similar experience like my own with abuse, drugs, and alcohol. My thought process was, if he had a similar testimony and God radically saved him and changed his life, then he would understand me and where I came from. He would be able to relate to me. Most importantly, I wanted a man that loved God with all his heart, and one who would love his family as Christ loves the church (Ephesians 5:25).

I wanted a husband who would pray with and for me; I wanted a man to love my children as if they were his own. I wanted a man I could trust and depend on. I wanted a servant-leader. As I wrote out this list, I felt God telling me I needed to focus on becoming the very thing I wanted. Become the change you want to see. I was far from being wife material, as you have been reading. I had a whole lot of junk, baggage, mess, and issues. Whatever you want to call it, I was full of it and getting cleaned was my first priority.

I needed to stay focused. With my list and my codeword safely tucked away, I was determined to keep my eyes on Jesus. I refused to let my mind be consumed with wanting a husband. I needed and wanted Jesus more than my desire to be married.

Reflection Activity

What are your personal thoughts about music?
_____
_____
_____

Do you think music affects our thoughts, behavior, and/or emotions?
_____
_____
_____
_____
_____
_____

What are some other thoughts or emotions that come to you as you read this chapter?

Personal challenge:

For the next 30 days, do not listen to any secular music. At the end of 30 days, evaluate your thoughts and feelings. Write your thoughts here.

CHAPTER THIRTY-EIGHT

Sinclair

"The integrity of the upright guides them, but the crookedness of the treacherous destroys them (Proverbs 11:3)."

Right before God delivered me from my drug and alcohol addiction, as I told you, God sent Heather back into my life. We were both living for the Lord and totally committed to our walk with Him. Heather and I began spending a lot of time together. We became inseparable. During this time, God also restored a relationship with a friend of ours named Kevin. He spent a lot of time with us as well. All three of us were helping each other walk and grow closer to the Lord.

People would call us the three amigos. I thank God for each one of our friendships. We would encourage and build each other in the Lord. We would hold each other accountable and correct one another in love. During this time, I was still trying to break free from the dysfunctional relationship I was in. God used both of those friendships to help me stay focused. Once God delivered me, they helped me stay free. They were my go-to help when my emotions told me I wanted to go back. They became my voice of reason on more than one occasion. They helped keep me strong when I felt I was too weak to keep going.

Anything kingdom, Heather, Kevin, and myself were there. From Christian concerts to church programs and conferences, it seemed like every church event held in Columbia, South Carolina or in the surrounding area, we were there. One of our favorites was Fabulous Friday's hosted by Gail Kyles with Clean Night Entertainment. I never knew you could be saved and still have so much fun. Every quarter, they had a night of all clean Christian entertainment from poetry, singing, live bands, comedy, dance, and so on. We always had an amazing time in the Lord going to Fabulous Friday's and other events hosted by Gail. For more information, please check them out online at http://www.CleanNight.com.

If we weren't at a church event, we were at my house in our pj's eating popcorn and watching preaching. One weekend, Heather and I attended a Girl's of Power Women's Conference. During this conference, I met two young men who were there to minister in Christian rap. In their introduction, they were announced as part of Dunamis Records. This brought back memories of when my ex-husband and I were going to church together with the kids. My ex-husband and I had met the founder of Dunamis Records through the church we were attending.

I remembered the first time we heard his music. It had a secular beat, but the words were about Christ. The kids and I played the CDs so much until we couldn't even play them anymore from all the scratches. After the conference, I introduced myself to one of the guys. His name was Sinclair. In our conversation, I told him about me having met the founder of Dunamis many years prior; that the CDs helped our family tremendously. I then asked Sinclair if he had his own CDs we could purchase. He told me he didn't have any with him at the time, so we exchanged numbers with the intention of getting some.

Once again, I loved music. Back then, rap music was my music of choice. Tupac was my all-time favorite, although I was no longer listening to it. Being able to get my hands on some new Christian rap was exciting for me. Sinclair and I talked a few times over the phone. In the very first conversation, he let me know he was engaged. I shared with him I was currently in a relationship, but I felt like the Lord was not pleased. I told him I was trying to break free, but it was hard. He encouraged me to seek God and to put Him before everything else.

There was something very different about Sinclair, something supernatural. I remember being in awe of his character and his commitment to his fiancé; how he would lift her up with his words. The men I was used to dealing with would acknowledge having a girlfriend, fiancé, or wife but still trying to hit on other women. He was different. Never did he say anything out of line. Never did he say anything to make me think he was trying to flirt with me. I knew God was showing me, through Sinclair, there were real godly men that were for real.

The few times we did talk, he would always ask how he could pray for me. The phone call would always end by him praying for me, my situation, and my kids. It was genuine and heartfelt. I was blown away that this man was not trying to hit on me, but he genuinely cared about my soul. It was something I had never experienced before. Again, I knew God was teaching me something very powerful in my conversations with Sinclair. It was something so different. I didn't even know what a man of integrity was, but I was being shown firsthand. God was showing me that all men were not the same.

One night, in our conversation, he shared this quote with me which was, *"A woman should be so lost in Christ that a man should have to seek Christ to find her."* I had never heard anything like that in my life. I was rocked and something leaped inside of me. I made him repeat it a few times so I could write it down. I was careful to make sure I got every word right. I remember feeling a paradigm shift inside me. *This* was what I wanted. I began to cry out to the Lord, *"I want to be so lost in You, Lord."* This became my heart's cry.

It wouldn't be until about a year later before I saw or talked to Sinclair again.

My heart, mind, and focus were on this *"being lost in Christ"* thing. Shortly after that, Heather and I were asked to join *Positive Image Consulting*, aka PIC. Every first Saturday of the month, the founder, Valerie Lane, would host an empowerment hour. Heather, myself, and a few other motivational speakers would use this hour to share a specific topic. We would each share our journey and/or perspective. Then, we would open up the floor for questions and answers.

I absolutely hated speaking in public, but I fought past the fear and did it anyway. I was told, even if I had to do it afraid, do it anyway. So, that's what I did, though I still don't like public speaking. The fear is so real that it takes my body through some serious changes I can't control. I feel as though I am going to pass out, throw up, and have diarrhea all at the same time. I also had to fight past the fear of feeling unqualified. I wasn't healed yet. I still had so much junk in me.

Looking back now, I see how God used this season in my life to bring healing in my own life as I helped others. I was always transparent about my journey. One topic we explored was *"loving yourself from the inside out."* I remember asking the Lord, *"How in the world am I going to share when I have no clue how to love me?"* This is how my journey to loving me started. I had to pray, read, and research so as to be able to speak about it.

Heather and I did that for the next twelve months with PIC. It was an amazing experience and I am so thankful for the personal and spiritual growth that came from it. During this time, I also started shadowing my mentors, Valerie and Daryl Lane, as they facilitated *Making Peace with Your Past*. They both began to pour into my life as they discipled me and taught me to how to lead my own *Making Peace* classes.

Heather started working at a church in West Columbia. The pastor had a heart for what we call "street ministry." Through a series of events, we felt like God was calling us to a particular neighborhood in which to minister. It just so happened that my girlfriend, Tasha, lived in this neighborhood. It was not by accident God was highlighting her, not just her neighborhood.

Tasha—mentioned earlier—and I met before I got pregnant with my oldest daughter. We used to work together and we quickly became close friends. We would hang out and party together on the weekends. Before I knew I was pregnant, I started having morning sickness. When I got to work in the morning, I would go straight to the bathroom where I would spend the next 30 minutes vomiting. She would always come in to check on me and bring me some crackers and something to drink.

She told me I was pregnant and I told her she was crazy. Turns out, she wasn't crazy. I was eighteen years old and pregnant. Knowing Tasha lived in this neighborhood and with some other signs and events, we felt like this was the neighborhood to which God was calling us. Me, Heather, and Pastor John—all being white—started meeting in this predominantly African American community every Thursday evening. We would walk the streets praying. We would stop people as they walked by and asked how we could pray with them. We would knock on doors asking the same question. Sometimes people were responsive, sometimes they weren't. Regardless of the responses, every Thursday, we were there faithfully walking the streets and praying with people.

While shopping one day, I ran into Sinclair. We chitchatted for a few minutes as we shared what the Lord was doing in our lives. He shared with me that he and some of his friends were preparing to do an outdoor Christian concert. I quickly told him Heather and I would be glad to help in any way possible. I told him about what we were doing in this neighborhood and asked if he and some of his friends could join us one Thursday. We exchanged numbers and, a few days later, we talked about the outdoor concert and what that vision looked like. One weekend,

I meet him and a few of his friends at the concert location so we could all do a prayer-walk on the grounds.

That night, one of the ladies spoke into my life about God sending a husband, but he wasn't going to look like what I wanted. What was that about? I tried really hard not to focus on it. I wanted so badly to know who it was. Was it someone I already knew? Was it someone I was going to meet in the near future? My thoughts were all over the place. I had been doing so well over the past year being single and celibate. I was okay in my singleness and I didn't want all those thoughts clouding my mind. I had to take those thoughts captive and make myself stay focused.

The following Thursday, Sinclair showed up to help with street ministry. We had such an awesome time that night. Sinclair walked the streets with us and prayed for folks. We saw God moving in ways we had not seen before. Every Thursday after that, Sinclair showed up faithfully. Tasha opened her home to have a community Bible study. Sinclair and I tag-teamed and facilitated the Bible study together. Heather and Pastor John spent that time walking, praying, and inviting people to the Bible study. During this time, Sinclair and I spent lots of time on the phone. We were talking about what we were going to teach the following Thursday and things about our personal lives. We shared our hopes and dreams with each other as well as our fears and struggles.

Our conversations were pure, transparent, and genuine. We became really good friends. I had been single for about a year and so had he. He told me that, right after he met me at the women's conference, he found out his fiancé was cheating on him and she no longer wanted to be with him. Again, I had prayed for a white husband, so he wasn't necessarily on my radar. As the weeks passed, the more time we spent together, Heather had started dating someone. I had more time on my hands than I was used to. I found myself texting Sinclair just to say *"Hi."* He was such an amazing man of God.

I began to ask myself, "*Could he be the one?*" I fought these feelings when they would come up. I would pray and ask God to keep me focused and at His feet. I knew my past tendencies were to get lost in a man. I still wanted, with everything in me, to be lost in Christ. There were times when Heather wasn't available and I would feel lonely. My thoughts were to text Sinclair. Instead of giving into those thoughts, I would turn to the Lord. *"God, I'm feeling lonely and I find myself wanting affection from Sinclair, but I submit those thoughts and feelings to You,"* I would pray. I knew I needed the Lord to fill the place in me that wanted attention. I needed God to meet my deepest needs of being wanted, needed, accepted, and valued. I reminded the Lord—more like I was reminding myself—of the commitment I had made with my heart and Him. I didn't want to be physically, emotionally, spiritually, or sexually attracted to another man unless it was my husband for whom He had designed me.

I was scared because I was starting to have an attraction toward Sinclair. The emotions I was feeling scared me. I never again wanted to go back to being codependent. I needed the Lord to know that, despite my feelings I was having for this man, I wanted them removed. I cared more about my relationship with the Lord than I did about my friendship with Sinclair. I reminded myself, "*Control your emotions or your emotions will control you.*"

Reflection Activity

How do you view God? Have you, in your relationship with God, found yourself temped to stray?

CHAPTER THIRTY-NINE

The Codeword

"Commit your ways to the Lord, trust in Him and He will act (Psalm 37:5)."

A few weeks went by. We continued to do Bible study together and we even started working out a few nights a week. One night, we were on the phone and he was talking about the mistakes he had made with his first wife—how he was so religious it caused him to be legalistic. He told me that, instead of loving his wife the way God intended, he was *"beating her in the head"* with the Bible, per se. He shared that he had been prideful and arrogant. Although she had an affair which caused the divorce, he said he could have been a much better husband and felt the blame was his.

He began to explain why, as the man, he was to blame. He explained that, as men, they are to lead by example; they are to spiritually cover their wives and love them the way Christ instructs them. He said men are to be servant-leaders, not dictators asserting spiritual authority so as to have things done their way. Furthermore, men are in control of the spiritual atmosphere of their homes which is why it's just as important for a man to be lost in Christ as it is for a woman. Geesh . . . he so gets it! In that moment, I thought to myself, "*He is going make an amazing husband for someone one day.*"

His next words were, "*My ex-wife is just like you, a diamond in the rough.*" Excuse me, but WHATTTTT?! Oh my, he just said the codeword! He just said the codeword! I have no clue what he said after that. I laid the phone down and ran through my apartment. I picked up the phone and he was still talking. I ran again. I could not believe he just said the codeword! I kept saying, "*God, he just said the codeword,*" as if it was a surprise to Him. I came back to the phone out of breath and he was still talking. I have no clue what the rest of the conversion was about or how it ended.

I was so excited, I don't think I slept that night! I was confused because he had never shown any type of interest in me at all. In fact, we were just having a general conversation when he said the codeword. It wasn't like he said it trying to ask me out. At one point in our friendship, I even tried to hook him up with one of my girlfriends. Clearly, he wasn't interested in me, but I knew he was a special man of God. I tried to set him up with a friend I thought would complement him. He wasn't interested in her either.

I saw Sinclair as a man of integrity and honesty, a man of great value. He was a treasure-chest full of hidden treasures from the Lord. Someone was going to be one blessed woman to have him as a husband. He actually said the codeword, though. I was the woman who was blessed. I was so in awe of God and how He had set up this whole thing. It was such an overwhelming peace, assurance, and calmness that came over me. God was telling me I was ready, that I didn't have to be afraid. I wasn't going to be codependent anymore. This time, I was going to be a co-laborer to bring God's glory through this marriage. I felt so honored to have been given such an amazing man.

"*Hold up Lord,*" I said to God, "*Sinclair doesn't even like me like that.*" Never had he shown any type of interest in me at all. I had to be patient and keep this to myself. I got myself together and acted like I always had. Sinclair and I continued to talk, workout, and do Bible study together. One day, after leaving the gym, I got a text from Sinclair that said, *"I think I miss you?"* That was it, *"I think I miss you,"* and immediately I was full of excitement. I could hardly contain it. I think I sent back a smiley face or something. I was so excited and caught up in being amazed at God that I couldn't even really respond to the text.

God and I were having a moment. I think it was the next day when he called and asked if he could come by the house—he needed to talk to me. He sat down on the couch and said, *"I think God is telling me you're my wife."* I busted out laughing and he was looking at me as though I was crazy. Then I said, *"Boy I knew, I was just waiting on you to know!"* I shared all about my codeword and the whole saying it in my head so the enemy couldn't use it. Then, I shared with him how, weeks earlier, he had said the codeword. And check this out, Sinclair had never heard the song "Diamond in the Rough." Sinclair sat on my couch like a deer in headlights. He said me and God had set him up.

I was like, *"So, when are we getting married?"* In my mind, there was no need to date, we already knew each other. It was so beautiful getting to know each other over the past year because it was not put on. We were both transparent in who we were, unlike people who build a relationship with motives of dating. Often times, we try to impress the other person or we suppress who we really are in these situations. We put our best foot forward, in a manner of speaking. Mine and Sinclair's friendship was built on something much different.

Our friendship was built on kingdom principles and motives. We became friends while advancing the kingdom of God together. This was our only motive. Obviously, this was all God and nothing of us. It felt amazing to know it was not me who had orchestrated this union. I didn't try to force anything or make it happen like I would do in my past relationships. Deep down, I knew this marriage was so much bigger than Sinclair and I. God was going to use this marriage for a greater purpose. It's funny because Sinclair had a list too—a list of what his wife would look like and possess the qualities he desired. Sinclair had never even dated anyone outside of his race, so marrying someone of a different race was definitely not on his list. Furthermore, he did not want to marry someone with kids.

To recap, I wanted a white man from the streets and lots of tattoos. God gave me a black man, no street, all church, and no tattoos. No children either. Cn I get a "what, what"? No baby-mama-drama. Praise the Lord! That was December 2012. We were married August 3, 2013. After a few months and a lot of praying, we finally settled on a date. I picked August because eight stands for new beginnings. I picked the third day because, for me, it represented the Trinity—God the Father, God the Son, God the Holy Spirit. It also represented the three-cord strand that would not easily be broken.

Sinclair was leaning more toward August of 2014 so he could save more money. I felt like God had us covered. My heart was set on August 2013. I shared with Sinclair my desire to get married on the beach and he was cool with that, but he still wanted to wait until 2014. We both knew we didn't want to do Myrtle Beach, South Carolina, so we started looking for beaches around Columbia, South Carolina. In my Google search, I found Tybee Island, Georgia.

I had never even heard of this place. It wasn't that far so, one weekend, Sinclair and I planned a day trip with Jazmine, Jada, our friend Kevin, and his daughter. It was very clean, quiet, and family oriented. I found the perfect spot on the beach where I wanted to have our wedding. I was getting excited, but Sinclair was still unsure because of his finances. He was still adamant about wanting to wait another year. I asked God to give us clear direction, both of us wanted to be obedient and we wanted to do it God's way, not our own.

I told God that, if he wanted us to wait another year, I would, but I didn't want to. I'm going to be really honest that, by this time, I was physically and sexually attracted to Sinclair. Waiting a whole other year seemed impossible. I found it very difficult, once those emotions were awakened, to keep them under control. On Mother's Day, May 2013, we went to church with his mother. The message was entitled *"God is in control of your finances." "Alright Lord, I hear ya, but does Sinclair hear ya?"* I said to Him.

I gave Sinclair a little nudge in his side just to make sure he was getting this message. Later, during service, Sinclair asked me for a pen, but I didn't have one. He asked the lady beside him for one. This time, he nudged me in the side, shaking his head in disbelief. He handed me the pen. The pen had a beautiful picture of a lighthouse and, in bold letters, Tybee Island, Georgia. We both knew, in that moment, God was letting us know He's got this. That settled it.

August 3, 2013, we had the most beautiful unscripted wedding ever. We didn't really have a plan other than walking to the spot I had chosen during our visit. We didn't do the whole bridesmaid, rehearsals, or any of that. We wanted it simple and intimate. We had about 60 or so family members and friends drive to Georgia to share this day with us. It was absolutely the most amazing day ever. I felt like I was standing under an open heaven. I felt like God's favorite daughter as I stood on that beach with the sand in between my toes, the sun shining down on me, and the wind blowing ever so lightly.

The beach is my favorite place. It's my go-to place. I feel so close to God because it reminds me of His perfect and endless love. It reminds me of His beauty and majesty. Getting married on the beach was a childhood dream come true. I thank God He gave me the man of my prayers, not the man of my dreams. It reminds me of this passage of Scripture found in Isaiah 55:8-9 which reads, *"This plan of Mine is not what you would work out, neither are My thoughts the same as yours. For just as the heavens are higher than the earth, so are My ways higher than yours, and My thoughts than yours."* God's ways are so much better than mine.

I am so pleased to have the testimony that we waited until our wedding night. I never dreamed it was possible for someone like me—someone who had been with countless men, someone who prostituted herself, not for money, but to try and gain love and security. I had become a wife before my wedding day. God had truly made me into a new creature. I was no longer the woman of my past and my life had truly been cleaned and transformed.

II Corinthians 5:17 states, *"When someone becomes a Christian, he becomes a brand new person inside. He is not the same anymore. A new life has begun."* My life reminds me so much of the life of a butterfly. I spent years as a caterpillar crawling around in dirt and nastiness. When I surrendered my life to Jesus, when I got tired of doing life my way, that's when He placed me in the cocoon. Even though the cocoon was dark, lonely, and unfamiliar, God was preparing me for something so much greater. Life, as I had known it, was getting ready to change forever. Just when I thought life was over, I received a beautiful set of wings. Since then, God has been teaching me to fly. Important fact about a butterfly is that, once it becomes a butterfly, never can it return to being a caterpillar nor can it return to the cocoon. That part of its life is over and gone.

This relationship with my husband is something so different than anything I have ever experienced. Jesus loves me through my husband. My heart's cry and one of my biggest desires is for every man and woman to experience this kind of relationship. It's not driven by that lustful physical attraction, but by spiritual intimacy, an intimacy which can only be experienced, not explained. It's God's original intent for marriages. This thing started with a marriage with Adam and Eve and it ends with a marriage—Christ and His bride, the church, us. Hallelujah!

Christian marriages are to be examples to the world of what wholesome marriages look like—two imperfect people dying daily to their arrogance, pride, and selfishness so as to serve one another unconditionally. Selfishness and pride are part of each one of us, so we have to fight past what comes naturally and do what's best spiritually. We do our best to out-serve the other one in words, deeds, and actions. This isn't always easy. I should be my husband's number one supporter whether I feel like he deserves it or not. I should be lifting him up with my words instead of tearing him down. Again, this isn't always easy, but it's always worth it. Many of us don't live in whole marriages because we never take the time to allow God to heal our individual brokenness. We continue to put Band-Aids over bullet wounds, metaphorically speaking. We are too busy addressing behaviors and not addressing the root of the issue. Or, if you're like I was, everybody else was to blame. In my mind, their actions caused my reactions.

When we take our eyes off our spouses and stop worrying about what he or she is or isn't doing and put our whole focus on the Lord, we will begin to see marriages healed. I have learned, and I am still learning, God has to be the One to meet my deepest personal needs. My self-worth, value, acceptance, validation, and security come from above. I have to be anchored in who and whose I am.

Some days, I need my husband to tell me I am pretty and, when I don't get it from him, I have to know I am beautiful because I have been made in the image of Christ. There is nothing wrong with us wanting our husband or our wife to give us compliments, that's not what I am saying. What is wrong is, if we don't get it from them and we allow it to determine how we feel about or see ourselves, we will seek to get that attention from an outside source.

I hope you are not reading this and thinking I live in a perfect world with the perfect husband, job, children, and pet. I don't. My husband still gets on my nerves. As amazing as he is, he still hurts my feelings from time to time. My job still makes me want to say some unholy words at times, my children still don't take my advice, and my dog still poops on the floor. Life is far from perfect and, in fact, there is no such thing as a perfect life. There is, however, such a thing as perfect love and it's God's love. When we become anchored in this love, it changes our lives.

Always remember that love is the most powerful force on earth. Love is a choice. Every day I wake up, I must choose to love my husband, kids, job, coworkers, etc. How often have we heard of married couples that have divorced because they have fallen out of love? Love is not something we fall in and out of. This is the world's definition of love, it is conditional. At its core, it is selfishness. When we say we have *"fallen out of love,"* what it really means is our husband or wife isn't meeting our needs, so we are ready to move on and find someone else who we think will or can.

Many of us leave marriages so as to find someone else but, what we find is only a temporary fix. This is what we see with people who have been married multiple times. Being that I have three marriages under my belt, I feel significantly qualified to call a thing a thing. That for which we are searching can only be found in our Creator. Only He knows our innermost parts; no spouse, man, woman, drug, alcohol, or child can ever know our innermost parts and fulfill our deepest needs (Psalm 139). The kind of love He has toward us is not even comparable to what we do or don't receive from others. *"What manner of love knows even the numbers of hairs on our head,"* reads Luke 12:7. It's a love that died for me when I was yet a sinner (Romans 5:8). When I think about the love I want from my husband, the Lord reminds me to be the love I want to receive. I Corinthians 13:4-7 reads much differently when I replaced the word love with my name. Here it is with my name:

"Jami endures with patience and serenity, Jami is kind and thoughtful, she is not jealous or envious; Jami does not brag and she is not proud or arrogant. Jami is not rude; she is not self-seeking, she is not provoked nor overly

sensitive nor easily angered; she does not take into account a wrong endured. Jami does not rejoice at injustice, but rejoices with the truth when right and truth prevail. Jami bears all things regardless of what comes, she believes all things looking for the best in each one, she remains hopeful in all things remaining steadfast during difficult times, through Christ, Jami endures all things without weakening."

I don't know about you, but I have a lot of work to do. I didn't even get past Jami is patient and I see so much of my sinful selfish flesh. So, what I want from my husband, God always reminds me to be the very thing I want him to be. Every time I point out what he is or isn't doing, God reminds me of the three fingers pointing back at me. I want to close this chapter with this: marriage is a covenant, not a contract. Our relationship with the Lord is a covenant, not a contract. My prayer is that we become people who live in covenant in our relationship with God and our spouses.

Covenant versus Contract

Covenant: God's love dictates that I'll do my part even if you don't do yours.
Contract: The world's love says that if you do your part, then I'll do mine.

Covenant: Unconditional.
Contract: Conditional.

Covenant: Love is a choice.
Contract: Love is a feeling.

Covenant: Marriage is living a promise.
Contract: Marriage is just a piece of paper.

Covenant: Divorce is not an option.
Contract: Divorce is an option.

Covenant: Forever.
Contract: As long as it feels good or as long as it satisfies my needs.

Reflection Activity

Did my story stir anything inside you to make you desire the right marriage? If single, are you willing to wait for God's best? If married, are you willing to make the adjustments within yourself so as to be a reflection of Christ?

_____

_____

_____

_____

_____

_____

_____

CHAPTER FORTY

The First and Greatest

"If you love Me, keep My commands (John 14:15).*"*

God will always uphold His part of the covenant whether we do our part or not. It is imperative that we understand what this actually means. We must never use God's promise to uphold His covenant of grace as an excuse to stay in rebellion, compromise, disobedience, or sin.

I said I loved God, but it was merely lip service. The truth is, my heart was far from Him. I tried so hard to keep what I thought was God's commandments and, when I came up short, I would just give up or give in. Allow me to explain. Since I often found myself coming up short, I would just forget it and go ahead and indulge in whatever sin I was involved in at the time. For example, the "no sex before marriage" rule. Since I couldn't keep this commandment, I just ignored the fact I shouldn't be doing it and continued in my sin. I felt like I couldn't help it and I couldn't. Compromise becomes a lifestyle when you don't know your true worth and value. Remember, what we feed grows, what we starve dies. My flesh was the one in control. It wasn't until I got serious about giving God my whole heart that sin started to lose its grip on me.

I was trying to keep God's commandments in an attempt to earn salvation. The results were defeat, sorrow, and despair. Once I experienced the gift of salvation, it became a delight to walk the path of obedience to God's laws. I had it all twisted. First of all, I didn't even know what God's commandments were for myself. I got bits and pieces of "do this, don't do that" from other people. One is *"love your neighbor as yourself."* This is the second of the Ten Commandments, but what about the first commandment? I totally missed that one. I was busy being codependent thinking I was *"loving my neighbor"* like God's Word says. Funny how I was so busy trying to love my neighbor, yet I had no clue how to love me. I was deceiving my own self. What I was really trying to do is get my "neighbor" to love me. I thought I loved God. I thought saying it, praying to God, going to church, and paying tithes was "loving God."

It wasn't until I began to seek God with my whole heart that my eyes were opened to my own deception. Mark 12:30 says, *"Love the Lord your God with all your heart and with all your soul and with all your mind and with all your strength."* We can be obedient to someone without actually loving them. God wants our voluntary love. For example, my husband doesn't just want my obedience, he wants my love. Obedience, apart from love, is not really love—it's just a set of rules we follow. But, when we love, it becomes delightful. Love removes the pain from sacrifice.

God desires us to be people who are faithful to Him because we love Him, not just because it's a command. God gives us all a free will. He doesn't want programmed robots. It's the same with us. I want my husband to love me with his heart, not just his head. I don't want him to not cheat on me just because it's the right thing to do. I want him to be faithful because he loves me. Have you ever asked yourself, *"What does God want?"*

God's ultimate purpose for creation is to provide a family for Him, children who will love Him and be faithful to Him. Just like being fit for the Master's use, it doesn't mean we will be perfect or never make mistakes. It simply means we strive to live our lives devoted to loving Jesus, following His will, and keeping Him first in our hearts. We were created to be loved and to love.

For so long, I had a wrong view of God. Although I sang songs and read Scripture about Him being a loving Father, it was hard for me to really get that. Many people have a warped or completely incorrect view of God. Before we can fully walk in the first commandment, we must settle in our hearts who God really is and what His posture toward us is.

Reflection Activity

How do you view God?

_____
_____
_____
_____
_____
_____
_____
_____
_____

How do you think God views you?

Growing In Love

God is love. It's who He is. It's His nature, His character. Because we loosely throw around the word "love," we don't truly know what it means. I don't know about you, but I had plenty of people who said they loved me, yet they still left me. I had people say they loved me, but they abused me. I had people say they loved me, but were unfaithful to me, etc. I love pizza, I love the beach, I love purple. You get the point. We have become desensitized to the word "love" and its true depth of meaning.

The love God has toward us is *agape* love, it's unconditional and it serves regardless of circumstances. It's a covenant. This kind of love gives unselfishly. *Agape* love is always shown by what it does. God's love is displayed most clearly at the cross.

> "God, being rich in mercy, because of the great love with which He loved us, even when we were dead in our trespasses, made us alive together with Christ—by grace you have been saved (Ephesians 2:4–5)."

We did not deserve such a sacrifice, *"but God demonstrates His own love for us in this: while we were still sinners, Christ died for us,"* states Romans 5:8. God's agape love is unmerited, gracious, and constantly seeking the benefit of the ones He loves. The Bible says we are the undeserving recipients of His lavish, *agape* love (1 John 3:1). God's demonstration of agape love led to the sacrifice of His Son for those He loves. 1 Corinthians 13:4-8 teaches what love is. God is love, so let's read it replacing the word *love* with *God*:

> "God is patient, God is kind, God is not envious. God does not boast, He is not proud. God does not dishonor others, He is not self-seeking. God is not easily angered. God keeps no record of our wrongs. God does not

delight in evil but rejoices with the truth. God is our protection, we can trust God. God is our very hope, and He perseveres. God never fails."

When I was in the world, I used to hear people quote John 3:16 which states, *"For God so loved the world that He gave His one and only Son, that whoever believes in Him shall not perish but have eternal life."* It didn't mean anything to me. I was too busy looking for a person to love me, a person I could see and touch. You already know how that turned out for me. I had allowed this world and my personal experiences with people to keep me in a place of bondage. *"Love hurts"* was my mindset. When I began to seek God with all of me, my eyes and heart were opened to receive. 1 John 4:19 states, *"We love Him, because He first loved us."* The foundational truth which equips us to love God is to know and feel His affection for us. God loves us in a way that God loves God.

Jesus feels the same intensity of love for us that the Father feels for Him. This is the ultimate revelation of our worth. This truth gives us the right to stand before God with confidence as one of His favorites. John 15:9 reads, *"As the Father loved Me, I also have loved you; abide in My love."* Affection-based obedience is obedience which flows from experiencing Jesus' affection for us and giving it back to Him. It is the strongest, deepest, and most consistent obedience. Why? Because lovesick people will do anything for love.

Duty-based obedience is our commitment to obedience even if we do not feel God's presence. God's Word requires we obey God without feeling inspired to do so. A fear-based obedience is motivated by the fear of negative consequences. Scripture does have dos and don'ts such as do not commit adultery, steal, slander etc. We know that God will use His rod because He loves us too much to leave us compromised (Hebrews 12:5-11).

The reality is, we sin because our hearts are unsatisfied with God, because we have not yet received God's love for ourselves. Most of us spend our lives being stuck in boredom, passivity, disloyalty, and compromise, which leave us broken and discontent. The awesome thing about the command to love God is that God Himself will supernaturally help us. Jesus prays for us that the love the Father has for Him will also be in us (John 17:26).

I don't know about you, but the revelation of the Scripture rocked me. Jesus Himself prays for me. He prays for you. He wants us to receive and experience His love. Also, Romans 5:5 tells us that the love of God has been poured out in our hearts by the Holy Spirit who has been given to us. We have been given the Holy Spirit as a comforter and a teacher. Everything we need is found inside of us—we just have to learn how to tap in and live in that power. The same power that raised Jesus from the dead lives in us. That excites me!

Prayer: *Lord, I pray you would open our eyes and our hearts so that we may receive the fullness of Your love, that we may have power together with all the Lord's holy people so as to grasp how wide, how long and how deep Your love for each one of us is; the love that surpasses knowledge. Cause us to be filled to the measure of all the fullness of who You are living on the inside of us. In Jesus' name, Amen.*

(Read and meditate on Ephesians 3:18-20.)

CHAPTER FORTY-ONE

A Shift in Our Thinking

"See what great love the Father has lavished on us, that we should be called children of God (I John 3:1)."

Prayerfully, by now, your view of God has shifted. He is with us, for us, and He is not mad at or disappointed in us. He is not some arrogant, prideful, hard, or harsh judge waiting to send us to hell or punish us every time we sin. God loves you and He has so much greater for you. Let's not view His laws and commandments as stringent either. It's natural to see God's Word that way if we don't truly understand who He is. His laws and commandments are not just a bunch of rules and regulations for us to desperately try and keep. Instead, they are loving boundaries, which are intended to keep us safe and protected and every one of them is rooted in His deep love for us.

Here's a quick and simple example. Let's look at a parent-child relationship. We wouldn't allow our child to play in a busy street, nor would we hand over our car keys just because our seven-year-old wants to drive. As parents, we set healthy boundaries so as to keep our children safe and protected because we love them.

Although that child doesn't understand at the time, it's for their own good.

Let's say a child goes into the street to play anyway and they get hurt. The tendency is to turn around and blame the dad for not protecting them. On the flip side, say the child doesn't get hurt but gets fussed at or spanked for playing in the street. In this child's mind, they may feel like their dad doesn't love them anymore or that he is disappointed in them. This child is not able to comprehend, just yet, that everything the father does is based on his love for his child. Our Father in Heaven is the same, but on a much deeper level. When we begin loving God with the whole of us, then it changes us. It doesn't always change our situations or problems, but it will change our attitude and response.

Now, I want you to take a deep breath. Inhale the new and exhale the old. You got this. Life is changing for your good. Greater is coming, as noted in Isaiah 43:19 which says, *"For I am about to do something new. See, I have already begun. Do you not see it? I will make a pathway through the wilderness. I will create rivers in the dry wasteland."* Let's journey through the first commandment together. It's one thing to read or say Scripture out loud but, when we actively spend time to seek understanding and meditate on what we are learning, it opens up a whole new world for us. We are all growing, and growth doesn't happen overnight. It's a process. Now that we have received God's love for us and we are secure in the truth that He does, in fact, love and adore us, let's unpack what it means to love God with all our heart, soul, mind, and strength. Let's look at each one individually.

With all your heart: affections (emotions). We set our affections on anything we choose. We can determine some of our emotions by setting the heart. We change our mind and God changes our heart. Our emotions will follow whatever we set ourselves to pursue. We can set our heart to be filled with a zeal for God. This was one of my biggest issues. I had no idea how to control my emotions. It was definitely a process. I had to lead my emotions instead of allowing my emotions to lead me. Jesus says in Psalms 91:14, *"because you have set your love upon Me, I will deliver you."*

We can intentionally set our affections to love Jesus. This requires that we remove anything which demolishes our affections such as bitterness, lust, unforgiveness, and secular entertainment including music, movies, reality shows, and things of the like. This requires that we are focused on pursuing love for Jesus more than gaining things and influence. We set our heart to love Him by committing to walk in obedience even when it is costly and we don't want to. We set our heart on loving God by regularly asking for supernatural help to love Jesus. We must ask God to pour His love for Jesus into our heart and to direct the reins of our heart into His love. II Thessalonians 3:5 tells us, *"May the Lord lead your hearts into a full understanding and expression of the love of God and the patient endurance that comes from Christ."*

With all your soul: personality (speech). Our personality is expressed most dynamically in our speech. We must be determined to express our personality by speaking and acting in a way that enhances, not demolishes, love. The most common way we quench love is by grieving the Spirit by our words. When the Spirit is grieved, we do not receive from Him in the same measure (Ephesians 4:29-32). We must walk in love by purifying our speech (Ephesians 5:1-6). Our love can be diminished by the fire released by wrong speech, which affects our inner man (James 3:6-10). In Ephesians 4:29, we read, *"Do not let unwholesome [foul, profane, worthless, vulgar] words ever come out of your mouth, but only such speech as is good for building up others, according to the need and the occasion, so that it will be a blessing to those who hear [you speak]."* We must remember that our very words can bring life or death.

We see in Proverbs 18:21, *"The tongue can bring death or life; those who love to talk will reap the consequences."* Our speech is not just what we say to others, but what we say to ourselves. We are not defined by our failures or accomplishments. You and I must settle the issue that we are not despised by God, nor are we a hopeless hypocrite because of our weakness. We must live by our spiritual identity—what we look like to God—instead of our natural identity—what we look like to ourselves and others—by confessing, *"Jesus, I am Your beloved, Your favorite one—a disciple whom You love. I'm loved by God and I am a lover of God, therefore I am successful."* What we say to ourselves, good or bad, has tremendous impact on our lives. We must become mindful of our words.

With all your mind: meditation (thoughts). We must fill our minds with loving meditation on God's Word and resist putting anything in our minds which demolishes love for Jesus and quenches the Holy Spirit. To love with all our mind is our decision to take time to fill our mind with God's Word and to agree with biblical paradigms of God. We gain revelation of God's love by meditating on it from God's Word. We position ourselves to receive by staying seated before God and His Word.

Psalms 1:2 states, *"But they delight in the law of the Lord, meditating on it day and night."* Our thoughts must remain on Jesus day and night. There was a time when my thoughts remained on a boyfriend, husband, or my problems, or all three. We must be transformed from our old way of thinking (Romans 12:2). Don't copy the behavior and customs of this world, but let God transform you into a new person by changing the way you think. Then you will learn to know God's will for you personally, which is good and pleasing and perfect.

Keeping our thoughts and mind stayed on God and His Word is a daily task, but a delight at the same time. I don't know about you, but it's easy for me to keep my thoughts toward God as long as everything is peaceful and going well. Oh, but let something happen and it can take me to a different place in my mind really quickly. Some days, it is a battle to keep my eyes and thoughts fixed on Jesus. As long as I stay fixed on Jesus and His Word, I find peace and comfort no matter how many times during the day I have to shift my thoughts and make them line up according to what God says.

We must think about what we think about. We all want to know what God's will is for our life. The only way we will know God's will, which is good and pleasing and perfect, is when we allow God to transform our way of thinking by mediating continually on the Lord.

With all your strength: resources. Our resources are our time, money, talents, reputation, and influence. The normal use of our strength is to increase our personal comfort, wealth, and honor. God wants us to freely give our resources back—they all belong to Him—to Himself so as to use them for a greater purpose in the kingdom. What we invest in, whether it is time, money, or talents, He always returns back to us with a much greater return rate than we could ever imagine. Luke 6:38 reads, *"Give, and it will be given to you. You will have more than enough. It can be pushed down and shaken together and it will still run over as it is given to you. The way you give to others is the way you will receive in return."* The question is, *"Are we going to continue to trust and rely on this world's system or are we going to do it God's way according to His truth trusting and relying on Him?"*

It is deeply encouraging to me that, when we do our part (obedience and abiding), blessings and promises are always attached to them. Also, when we live devoted—abandoned for the Lord—our works will follow us to heaven. Every day we should have an awareness that we are storing up heavenly rewards and treasures. Our works will follow us to heaven.

Let's be clear, salvation and rewards are very different. Rewards are about our work for God. We are not saved by our good works; we are saved for good works. Salvation is about God's work for us. It's a free gift, to which we can contribute absolutely nothing (Ephesians 2:8-9; Titus 3:5). Salvation is dependent on God's faithfulness to His promises and mercy. Belief determines our eternal destination where we'll spend eternity. Behavior determines our eternal rewards, what we'll have in heaven. Rewards are conditional, dependent on our faithfulness (2 Timothy 2:12; Revelation 2:26-28; 3:21).

God is looking for those of us who will live completely devoted to His lordship. Many professing Christians say they believe in God, but they don't follow Him. In order for us to follow Him, we must read, believe, and obey His Word. When we set our hearts to live out the first commandment, it moves the heart of God. The Lord values our journey to grow in love. The extended reach of our hearts to love Him moves Him. Where do you see yourself in keeping the first commandment? No matter where we see ourselves, we all have room to grow in the knowledge of God's love. Relax, enjoy the journey, and celebrate how far you have come and stop looking at how far you need to go.

Reflection Activity

Under each heading, write how you believe you can or need to improve.

Heart:

Mind:

Soul:

Strength:

What are some practical steps needed to make sure you're reaching to love God with your heart, mind, soul and strength?

Heart:

Mind:

Soul:

Strength:

Mike Bickle has an amazing, in-depth, twelve session study online called "First Commandment." I actually have all 12 of the sessions downloaded to my phone and I listen to them often. Some of my writing in this chapter comes from his teaching. My life has been deeply impacted by this. I encourage you to go to www.MikeBickle.org and search for his teaching.

CHAPTER FORTY-TWO

Anchored in Truth

"Lead me by your truth and teach me, for you are the God who saves me. All day long I put my hope in you (Psalm 25:5).*"*

An anchor is used to keep something secure and stable. Wall anchors are used to keep something, like a frame, attached to the wall. It secures it without the weight of the picture tearing the sheetrock, thus causing the picture to eventually fall and cause damage to the wall. Ship anchors are used to prevent the vessel from drifting due to current, wind, and all kinds of storms.

Fun Fact: The largest recorded anchor used on a vessel is thirty-six tons. Can you imagine how huge that is? It makes me think of Jesus holding the whole earth in His hand. God's strength, power, and magnitude are virtually unimaginable. So many times, I can find myself feeling as though I am drifting and other times like I am drowning in this thing called life. Jesus has never promised us a perfect life once we become saved. The Bible tells us not to worry about tomorrow, for tomorrow will bring its own worries (Matthew 6:34). Although Jesus tells us that, here on earth, we will have many trials and sorrows, but He also does promise that, in Him, we can have peace no matter what we go through. Just like the wall or ship anchor, Jesus must become our anchor. If not, when life happens, we will find ourselves in deep trouble. What does making Jesus our anchor look like?

Application

We have to do more than read God's Word. We must apply it to everyday life. For example, from my life's journey, there are so many times I found myself drowning in a sea of negative emotions. Life can be draining. No matter how much I grow in my relationship with Christ, I have times when I feel empty, less than, or left out. I find myself wanting, fighting, and competing for someone's time, attention and/or affection, but the anchor to which I hold is this: the Holy Spirit lives inside me and He is my companion (1 Corinthians 3:16 and John 14:26).

My anchor, which is my security, is the fact that the Holy Spirit lives inside me as my Companion. He cares about everything concerning me. Never do I have to "wait my turn" or make an appointment to commune with Him. He is with me always. In fact, He is longing for me to pursue Him the way I'm trying to pursue others. Never do we have to be intimidated by other peoples' relationships and how close to God they may seem. The truth is, we are as close to God as we choose to be. We have to decide if we are going to keep our eyes focused on others or keep our eyes on our Comforter and Companion, the Holy Spirit.

I choose whether I'm close to or far from Him. It's all about my own choices in which I am seeking daily. My eyes must remain fixed. Have you ever heard the statement, *"Life is what you make it?"* I used to be so frustrated that I wanted a better life, but I didn't know how to attain it. I didn't know God's Word, much less how to apply it. Now that I do know, it is a privilege to share my journey so that it will help others.

Each one of us is in control of our own destiny. Some people may disagree with that but, had I continued down the road of dysfunction, I would have ended up in prison or dead. I had to get up, I had to wake up, and I had to make a choice. I had to stop the cycle of dysfunction by doing something different. In the beginning, it didn't seem to make any difference but, the more I continued to walk toward God and the things of God, the further I got from the dysfunction and destruction.

I had to choose to seek after truth until it became my anchor, my foundation. With each new truth found in God's Word, my eyes began to open to the lies and deception I had called truth. Once I was introduced to the real truth, the counterfeit was easy to detect. Once I stopped listening to the lies of the enemy, the clearer I could hear truth as I read the Word of God. The more I read, the more I believed. The more I believed, the more stable and secure I became.

I want to share something with you that I have found to be very powerful. That's learning the different meanings of God's varying names as they are found in the original Hebrew and Greek languages. When we understand the different meanings, it helps us better understand who He is. Knowing His character causes us to see Him for who He really is. Knowing who He is causes us to become anchored in His love for us. It helps us build trust and confidence in the way He cares about us and how He provides all our needs. The storms of life will happen, it's a guarantee. However, where that storm takes us will be determined by the weight of our anchor.

Elohim: The strong, Creator God
Verse: *In the beginning God (Elohim) created the heavens and the earth. The earth was formless and void, and darkness was over the surface of the deep, and the Spirit of God (Elohim) was moving over the surface of the waters* (Genesis 1:1-2).

El Emunah: The Faithful God
Verse: *Know therefore that the Lord your God is God; He is the faithful God (El Emunah), keeping His covenant of love to a thousand generations of those who love Him and keep His commandments* (Deuteronomy 7:9).

El Hayyay: God of My Life
Verse: *By day the Lord directs His love, at night His song is with me — a prayer to the God (El) of my life (Hayyay)* (Psalm 42:8).

Elohim Machase Lanu: God Our Refuge
Verse: *Trust in Him at all times, you people; pour out your hearts to Him, for God (Elohim) is our refuge (Machase Lanu)* (Psalm 62:8).

Elohei Mikkarov: God who is near
Verse: *Am I a God (Elohei) who is near (Mikkarov), declares the Lord, and not a God far off* (Jeremiah 23:23)?

Jehovah Jireh: The Lord will provide
Verse: *So Abraham called that place The Lord Will Provide (Jehovah Jireh). And to this day it is said, "On the mountain of the Lord it will be provided* (Genesis 22:14)."

Jehovah El Emeth: Lord God of Truth
Verse: *Into Your hand I commit my spirit; You have ransomed me, O Lord (Jehovah), God (El) of truth (Emeth)* (Psalm 31:5). God desires intimacy with us, I can assure you. God is present, accessible, and near to those who call on Him for deliverance (Psalm 107:13), forgiveness (Psalm 25:11) and guidance (Psalm 31:3).

Ehyehasher Ehyeh: the eternal, all-sufficient God
Verse: *God said to Moses, "I AM who I AM"; (Ehyehasher Ehyeh) and He said, "Thus you shall say to the sons of Israel, 'I AM has sent me to you* (Exodus 3:14).'"

Other names for God are:

1. YAHWEH (God)
2. YESHUA HAMASHIACH (The Anointed One)
3. El Shaddai (Lord God Almighty)
4. El Elyon (The Most High God)
5. Adonai (Lord, Master)
6. Jehovah Nissi (The Lord My Banner)
7. Jehovah-Raah (The Lord My Shepherd)
8. Jehovah Rapha (The Lord That Heals)
9. Jehovah Shammah (The Lord Is There)
10. Jehovah Tsidkenu (The Lord Our Righteousness)
11. Jehovah Mekoddishkem (The Lord Who Sanctifies You)
12. El Olam (The Everlasting God)
13. Elohim (God)
14. Qanna (Jealous)
15. Jehovah Shalom (The Lord Is Peace)
16. Jehovah Sabaoth (The Lord of Hosts)

God told Moses in Exodus 3:14 to tell the Israelites, "*I AM has sent me to you.*" God describes Himself as, "*I AM who I AM.*" He is the same yesterday, today, and forever more. He is still the Great "*I AM.*"

1. God is our refuge from the storm (Isaiah 25:4)
2. Our resting place (Jeremiah 50:6)
3. Strong tower (Proverbs 18:10)
4. Hiding place (Psalms 32:7)

5. Everlasting Father (Isaiah 9:6)
6. Restorer (Psalms 23:3)
7. Advocate (1 John 2:1)
8. Friend (John 15:15)
9. Deliverer (Psalm 70:5)
10. Redeemer (Isaiah 59:20)
11. Our strength (Psalm 43:2)
12. Spirit of Truth (John 16:13)
13. The Lord who provides (Genesis 22:14)
14. The Lord of peace (2 Thessalonians 3:16)
15. Living Water (John 4:10)
16. Our shield (Psalm 144:2)
17. He is the God of comfort (Romans 15:5)
18. He is our hope (Psalm 71:5)
19. He is healer (Exodus 15:26 and Psalms 103:3)
20. He is our counselor (Isaiah 9:6)
21. He is Our Husband (Isaiah 54:5)

Reflection Activity

Anchored In God's Truth

There are so many more treasures in Scripture about His names and their meanings. I strongly suggest doing an in-depth study of the names of God. It will take you so much deeper. This list doesn't even begin to scratch the surface. As you read the ones I listed, which names and meanings stand out the most?

_____

_____

_____

_____

_____

_____

_____

Why do they stand out?

God is saying I AM. What does that mean to you?

Ask yourself, "What do I need God to be for me in my current season?"

In what truth found in Scripture do you need to be anchored?

ow, describe how to apply the above Scripture(s) to your daily life.

Prayer: *Lord, give me the Scriptures I need to anchor me in whatever season I am in. Cause Your Word to come alive in me. Lord, help me to trust completely in You. Cause Your goodness to settle my heart. I declare You, and You alone, are my place of refuge. You are my Master, my Lord, You are my strong tower. You love me and You are faithful. You are the God of my life; You are the God of all significance. You are near to me no matter how I may feel. When the storms of life come, give me a heavenly perspective so that I may rightly see You. In times of trouble, help me to trust You even when I can't trace You. For I know You are God and God alone, You will never fall off Your throne. You are good, You are faithful, and You are in control. You are my God who has supplied all my needs before I need it and, Lord, I declare, You are the Lord of truth. My hope is in You. This hope is a strong and trustworthy anchor for my soul. In Jesus' name I decree, Amen.*

"The Lord is good, a strong refuge when trouble comes. He is close to those who trust in him (Nahum 1:7)."

CHAPTER FORTY-THREE

Marriage on a Mission

"Do two walk together unless they have agreed to do so (Amos 3:3)?"

"For My thoughts are not your thoughts, nor are your ways My ways, for as the heavens are higher than the earth, so are My ways higher than your ways, and My thoughts than your thoughts (Isaiah 55:8-9)."

Remember my list? God has such a sense of humor! I asked for a white man, lots of tattoos, from the street-life, redeemed and transformed. God gave me a black man, no tattoos, and church was all he knew. Of course, my husband had his own list as well. Neither one of us got what we asked, but we both agree we received better than we could have ever imagined. Again, God was saying to me that His thoughts are so much higher than ours. One thing I have learned in my journey is that He can be trusted and His plans for my life are far greater than anything I could ever come up with on my own.

I could not have picked a better husband. The best way to describe our marriage is this, *"Jesus loves me through my husband."* My past experiences with so many broken men give me a greater appreciation and respect for the man God has given me. Sinclair truly is a man who loves the Lord with all his heart and he is a servant-leader. When we became engaged, he sat all three of us—myself and my two biological daughters—down on the couch one evening. He presented both of them with a promise ring explaining that he was here to love them as his own and to love me.

Then, one at a time, he began to wash our feet. While doing so, he spoke into each one of our lives promising to love, protect, and serve us. I must admit, it was a little awkward for the girls, especially the feet washing, but he did a great job explaining what washing feet meant biblically and symbolically (John 13: 1-7). It was his way of humbling himself and showing what a servant-leader looks like in action, something we had never seen before and especially not in a man.

My husband was a gift from God and he is an amazing man, but let's not skew the picture I just painted. He was not a super saint who was perfect or that never had any issues. In the last chapter, I'll let him tell you his story. We are still two imperfect people trying to learn how to do life together God's way. It's not always easy. We still have disagreements, we get on each other's nerves, and we still have issues we need to work through. Although I can say, our disagreements are nothing like what I experienced in my past marriages and relationships. They are very different.

Marriage is work. It's all about sacrificing, compromising, and submission to one another in love. And, some days, it's not easy, but I can promise you it's always worth it. Remember, marriage is very important to God. It started with a marriage, Adam and Eve, and it ends with a marriage, Christ and His Bride. We both took time to rid ourselves of all the baggage. We were both healed and whole. We were both complete in our relationship with Christ and content in our singleness. We were both focused on Jesus. Never once did we get up from the place of sitting at our father's feet to look for each other or anyone else. God had honored both our requests of being lost in Him.

We knew God had joined us together for a far greater purpose than us just being husband and wife. We both work together toward a common goal and that goal is fulfilling God's agenda in the earth through us, both as individuals and our marriage. We don't always know what that looks like, but we do know God was and is very intentional with everything He does. This marriage was definitely intentional.

No matter how mad I may get at my husband at times, I can stand on the anchor of truth knowing God gave me His best which helps keep my heart from storing up any ill feeling, anger, or bitterness toward him. The following are two very simple but practical examples of how easily ill feelings, anger, or bitterness have attempted to creep in.

When we first got married, he would leave the showerhead pointed to the back wall. Therefore, when I would turn the shower on to allow the water to warm up, water would go all over the floor. For a few weeks, I would get so angry at him every time I would go to take a shower. He had no clue I was going through emotions over it. One day, I was in my feelings and the Lord said to me, *"You point the showerhead down before turning on the water, it's really simple. You are getting mad and allowing funk to enter your heart over something you have control over. If you want the showerhead to point in a different direction, you do it."*

I sat there speechless. Why had I allowed myself to get so mad and frustrated over something so simple. God was so right (which He is all the time). All I had to do was take one little extra step to point the showerhead down before turning on the water. I was getting upset about something over which I had complete control. You would have thought I just received some super deep revelation. To me, that's what it was. Sounds silly, but it's true. From that day forward, it never bothered me again. Although, not long after this super deep revelation, we moved into our first house together and I didn't have to worry about it anymore because we had a walk-in shower.

Unfortunately, I don't always get it the first time around. More times than not, God has to remind me or point out my pettiness. I often find myself needing a refresher course. I can be a little slow at catching on, but that's okay. We have a loving and patient Father who doesn't mind giving us reminders. About a year later, I started noticing I was holding onto frustration toward my husband once again. It was over the way he would replace the empty toilet paper. He always puts it on backwards. I know I am not in this struggle alone—some of you know exactly what I'm talking about! It literally frustrates the daylights out of me to have the paper coming from the back and not the front. Anyway, I would usually discover this horrible thing in the middle of the night while half asleep, while desperately trying to find the start of the roll, which is much easier when it is put on correctly. Each time it happened, I found myself getting more and more aggravated and angered at him. Again, he had no idea.

One day, in my frustration, God just politely reminded me of the showerhead and that this was something I could do myself without all the extra emotions. This time, He said, *"Taking the roll off and turning it around the way you like is no different than you having to get a new roll from under the sink and putting it on yourself. Look at it as him helping you. All you have to do is take it off and flip it around. He could have just left the empty roll; at least he was polite enough to change it in the first place."*

Conflict is when we don't get our way. It goes back to the simple question, *"Whose kingdom am I building? Mine or the Lord's?"* Who am I to get aggravated, mad, or upset over something I want him to do my way? Who am I? Our selfishness is so easily detected in marriage. This is why it requires so much work. Covenant says that I am required to do my part even if he doesn't. I don't know about you, but I tend to lean more toward *"I'll do mine if and when you do your part, even if it is silly and unrealistic."*

During conflicts, I have to ask myself if I am trying to prove I'm right or am I trying to improve the relationship? This usually helps me to refocus. As sad as it is to say, sometimes it doesn't and I follow after my selfish, fleshy ways, and nothing good ever comes of that. I usually end up having to repent and apologize to God and my husband. But, thank God, we have a loving Father who never gives up on us. He loves to correct and teach us. All I can say is that He sure has a way of running over my toes and sometimes I get completely run over. It's not always an easy journey but it's always worth it. Prayerfully, I have been able to set some of you free with my testimony of the showerhead and toilet paper. I know I'm not alone in this struggle.

Looking back at all the broken, abusive, and dysfunctional relationships, I can honestly say that, deep down, I knew I was not supposed to be in any of them. I chose to ignore all the warning signs and I chose to do things my way. I was caught up building the kingdom of *self* and that always leads to destruction. If we are brutally honest with ourselves, we know when we are in a relationship we shouldn't be. I knew the two previous men I had married were never supposed to be my husband. Nor was the last one I was planning on marrying. I knew, but tried so desperately to make it work.

This time it was the complete opposite. I knew with everything in me this was all God. So, no matter how many times my God-given husband may hurt my feelings or let me down, I know that, no matter how I feel, my husband loves me and God has blessed me with him. Also, I know Sinclair would never purposely hurt my feelings or let me down. Through our union, God teaches me that I need to surrender my emotions and feelings to God and that I need to forgive quickly. Before getting healed and whole, I would make it the burden of the person I was with to complete me. I was codependent upon them for my happiness, validation, emotional well-being, and worth.

There are times when I can feel myself depending on my husband, yet Holy Spirit reminds me I need to be completely dependent on Him and Him alone. If I don't stay close to Jesus, I can quickly find I have put an unrealistic expectation on my husband looking for him to meet a need only the Lord can. When I start feeling a certain way, I ask myself, *"Is what I'm feeling really about my husband or am I just being needy, insecure or just plain selfish?"* No matter what the issue is, the Lord is the one to whom I must turn. I must give my emotions over to Him so as to expose my selfishness, fill me, and heal me. Surrendering all of who I am to the lordship of Jesus is the only thing that can truly sustain me. Sitting at the feet of Jesus is my only means of survival.

Reflection Activity

Can you think of times in your marriage where the little things nearly ate you alive? Can you recognize the pettiness in these destructive patterns? Can you list areas where you know you can control something yet choose to be angry?

_____

_____

_____

_____

_____

_____

_____

_____

_____

CHAPTER FORTY-FOUR

Life Lessons

I want to leave you with some very important life lessons I learned during this beautiful journey. Although, as you have read, the journey wasn't always beautiful, but the further and further I got from the darkness, the more beautiful life became. It's as if I went from living in black and white to living in bright vibrant colors. No matter where you are in your journey, don't give up and don't give in. Keep taking baby-steps if you have to, but keep moving forward, my beloved. A beautiful life of color, freedom, and unspeakable joy awaits you.

Life Lessons

Obedience: We can choose our sin, but we can't choose our consequences.

I have noticed my eyesight and hearing has slowly been declining. The last few years, I have needed to use reading glasses when reading normal sized print. The words are a big blur without them. Recently, I had to up the strength. When conversing with others, I find myself having to ask people to repeat themselves because I can't hear them. Oftentimes, phone conversations are the worst because they sound muffled. I don't have selective hearing anymore—I really can't hear.

I remember when I was much younger, my mother would not only correct me, but she would warn me, *"Don't sit too close to the TV, it will mess up your eyes. Don't read in the dark, it will mess up your eyes. Don't have the TV so loud, it will mess up your hearing. Don't have the music so loud. Turn down those earphones. You're going to mess up your hearing."* And more of the same. Blah, blah, blah. . .I didn't listen. I continued to ignore her warnings and do what I wanted. Why? It was because there were no immediate affects. What I was doing was harmful to my hearing or my eyesight, yet I could not immediately detect it. Oh my, my, my. How I wish I would have listened to the wisdom of my mother!

One day, the Lord showed me this is what the sin in my life looks like. Just because I can't see or feel the immediate effect of the sin or poor choices in my life, I must not ignore the reality of the aftermath. Although I may "feel" like what I am doing is not hurtful or harmful, or it may even "look" like I have gotten away with a certain sin or behavior, the reality is, there is always a repercussion.

Although we may not feel or see the immediate repercussions of sin, it most certainly affects us and those connected to us. Remember, we can choose our sin, but we can't choose our consequences. This is where my relationship with my loving Father comes in. He knows best and He is full of wisdom. This is why it is imperative that I read and obey His Word. He cares about me. He is not just full of wisdom—He *is* wisdom.

His Word, the Bible, is full of loving boundaries which are used as safeguards so as to protect me, you, and all His children. If only we would read and obey. The Bible is not just a book of religious rules; it is a book written by a caring Father to help His children navigate through our earthly life until He returns. The choice is solely up to me. Will I continue in sin because I don't feel the immediate consequences, or will I listen to the instructions of my Creator?

Obedience leads me to the next lesson I learned—the Lord's wisdom. I heard a teaching by Andy Stanley entitled "Ask It." You can find it on YouTube or I'm sure it's on his website. When I heard it, it was like a light bulb was turned on. In this teaching, he introduces this one simple question that we can ask ourselves and it has the power to change the course of our lives. The question is, *"What is the wise thing for me to do?"*

It's one simple question, but it has such a powerful impact when applied. When I look back at all my mistakes, failures, brokenness, and financial struggles, I can't help but think how different things could have been if I would have known how to ask and apply this one question. Everything which was within my control, I had the power to change and I didn't even know it. I just went along with status quo, I followed the crowd, and I did it because everybody else was doing it. I did it because it felt good in the moment. I did it because it was pleasurable. I did it because I wanted to. I never thought about consequences or the aftermath. Never did I ask myself, *"Is this the wise thing for me to do?"* I didn't even know what wisdom was. Had I known, I would have been asking:

1. Is it wise to leave my daughter while I hang out and party all night?
2. Is it wise to leave with a man I just met?
3. Was it wise to think I was "in love"?
4. Was it wise to allow men into my life that had no job, no stability, no car, no leadership qualities, etc?

Instead of asking myself if it was wise, I allowed my feelings to dictate my decisions. Reading those questions now, they seem so silly. Of course those were not wise things to do but, when you don't know wisdom, you get sucked into the counterfeit wisdom of this world. Counterfeit wisdom says to just go with the flow, you only live once, follow your heart, do what makes you happy, and more nonsense. Never did I stop to think about the backlash.

Never did it dawn on me this was the reason my life kept going around and around in the same dysfunctional circle.

Before I knew it, my life was so far out of control that, at one point, I didn't have hope. I didn't see a way out. But, now that God has shown me the way out, I must share it with others. I give you what I now have and that is hope and a toolbox full of tools that, if used correctly, can begin to change the course of your life.

IS THIS A WISE THING FOR ME TO DO?

No matter your past, you can start right now by applying this question to every decision you make. No matter how big or small, remember, every choice we make has a consequence, whether good or bad; whether immediate or down the road.

Walk in wisdom and you will not live in regret. As Andy Stanley teaches, *"What may be wise for me may not be wise for you."* In every season, the wisest thing may change. For instance, is it wise to stay on my job or should I stay home and home-school my kids? The initial wisdom to take and keep the job may no longer apply. The job may have been great when someone was single or had young babies, but things change all the time. Again, I highly encourage you to listen to the "Ask It" sermon. I must warn you, it will change your life.

1. Never trade that which you profess you want most for that which you want in the moment.
2. Personal pleasures make a good slave but a poor master.

Growing In Faith

Borrowed faith has no value. What is faith? Hebrews 10:22 teaches us that faith is the leaning of the entire human personality on God and absolute trust and confidence in His power, wisdom, and goodness. Faith has nothing to do with feelings. Our feelings are constantly changing, but a life lived by faith in Christ completely depends on an unchanging God. Faith disregards feelings. A person of faith does not look at their situation. Rather, they look at the risen Christ as the one in whom they believe, trust, and depend. A person of faith lives knowing God is in control and He can be trusted no matter what we face.

Faith is like muscles. We are all born with a measure of muscles, but some of us develop them better than others. Bodybuilders, for example, exercise their muscles very regularly so as to make them grow bigger and stronger. Likewise, your measure of faith grows when you feed and use it. Each time you hear or read God's Word, you are feeding your faith. When you confess God's Word and expect good things to happen to you, you are using it. The more you use it, the more your faith grows and the stronger you become. A faith not tested is a faith not proven.

"The way of a fool is right in his own eyes, but a wise man listens to advice (Proverbs 12:15)."

Journaling

I have found journaling to be very helpful and, although I don't do it daily, I probably should. I mostly journal my so-called "God winks" or "God moments." Like the story I told you when the woman spoke to me that night after the worship—the one where she told me that God saw me as the woman with the alabaster box, which was exactly what I was imagining during worship. God-winks, God-encounters, whatever you want to call them, these are the times when I experience special moments I want or need to remember, so I journal them. With all the distractions, frustrations, disappointments, and just plain life, it is easy to forget the times God has spoken, delivered, provided, or even done something through us.

We have all had moments like this, although we may not have known it was God. We may have credited something or someone else. An example of one of my "God-winks" is when I was starting a new lifestyle change called "Trim Healthy Mama." In their recipe book, there was a recipe for a cake in a mug. I really wanted to try it, but we didn't have a single mug in our house. I went to bed praying for God to help me incorporate and stay committed to this new lifestyle of eating.

I told myself I would stop by the Dollar Tree and pick up a mug when time permitted. Well, the very next day, while at work, a lady I had just helped said she wanted to give me a small gift. She reached in her bag and pulled out a mug and handed it to me. I smiled so big as tears started falling from my eyes. I quickly got myself together and shared with her about my commitment I had made with this new way of eating and how I wanted to try this recipe, but I needed a mug. I shared with her that I had just prayed the night before for God to help me.

She was as blown away once I explained my excitement. To her, it was just a simple little mug. This lady, who didn't even know me, blessed me with this gift that meant so much to me. Yes, she blessed me, but God was the Mastermind behind it and she didn't know God was moving through her. She just wanted to do something nice. God set us both up. He set me up by blessing me with a mug and He set her up because He knew I was going to tell the story behind the tears over a simple mug, and He got all the glory.

Oh, how the enemy would love for me and you to forget these encounters but, if we started writing them down in a journal, he could not take them away. Journaling is such a great spiritual tool which helps build faith in the Lord as well as creating intimacy. I love to go back in my journal and read how God showed Himself mighty or small in my life. I especially appreciate it when I am faced with a new challenge or if I'm simply having a hard time believing or trusting, or just need encouragement. For whatever I am in need, I can read my journal and get full of His faithfulness, mercy, kindness, peace, love, and His everything. All the lessons are important and significant, but this one is most powerful when you need encouragement as King David did in 1 Samuel 30:6.

Seeking God Daily

You will never see true change until you change something you do daily. Life is full of demands, challenges, and distractions. Therefore, we must make time daily to spend with the Lord. We are as close to God as we choose to be. Let's not get caught up in the hustle and bustle of life. Learn to slow it down and seek God's kingdom and His righteousness so that everything else will be added. I encourage you to make Matthew 6:33 your life verse as I did. This verse is the very foundation on which I have built my life.

Don't fall into the trap which, at times, both myself and my husband have found ourselves. It's the trap of doing religious activities, going to church, participating in programs, ushering, singing in the choir, etc. and think it's the same as seeking the Lord. Oftentimes, we fall in love with doing the work of the Lord, instead of loving the Lord of the work. Intimacy never takes place during the work. It only happens during the quiet meditations of our heart, the sitting at His feet, and reading His Word so as to know Him. Intimacy happens when we turn off the noise and long after His presence so He may come and fill our hearts. Intimacy happens as we include Him in everything we do; by praying continually without ceasing. He and I are always communing with one another.

Think about a husband and wife. I can get so busy with wifely duties that I ignore or neglect the intimate part of our relationship. Not that it's done purposely, it happens, but I must be aware of the dangers it causes. I must set boundaries and safeguard the intimate part of our relationship at all costs. Without intimacy, we become nothing more than roommates. We suffer and everything connected to us suffers because of our lack of intimacy. The same is true with our relationship with God. At all costs, whether I feel like it or not, I must choose the wisest thing. Wisdom says to seek first the kingdom of God and His righteousness.

"The wise in heart accept commands, but a chattering fool comes to ruin (Proverbs 10:8)."

Let People Be Right

While out shopping one day, I overheard a conversation that has stuck with me ever since. As I headed to the checkout, the cashier was explaining to her co-worker about a gentleman she had just helped. She asked him to make sure he had the right amount of change because she thought she may had given him less than she owed him. His response was something like, *"You should learn to count."* When I heard it, automatically, in my flesh, I felt some kind of way! Immediately, negative thoughts of how I would have responded flooded my mind. Then, the co-worker responded with what he would have said. It was more along the lines of what I was thinking in my own head. Then I asked, *"What did you say???"* Her response blew me away. She said, *"I just agreed with him."* Then she said, *"My grandmother always taught me to let people be right."* I was immediately convicted by the Holy Spirit as I recalled my own negative thoughts of how I would have responded.

My conviction was this: How often do I get offended and/or angry because I want to be right. How dare you disrespect me or insult my intelligence?! Letting people "be right" goes against my very nature. That very nature will always be the one who responds until I relinquish "my" nature and ask the nature of God that lives in me to respond through me. So, I am learning to let people be right, and it's not always so easily done. It makes me think of Galatians 5:16-17, where Paul wrote about walking in the Spirit, *"I say then: Walk in the Spirit, and you shall not fulfill the lust of the flesh. For the flesh lusts against the Spirit, and the Spirit against the flesh; and these are contrary to one another, so that you do not do the things that you wish."*

I don't want you to finish this book thinking I have it all figured out, because I don't. I don't claim to know it all, I don't even claim that what I have taught you through my own personal understanding of Scripture is right. You may even disagree with some things I have said and that's okay. But, what I do claim is that my own personal experience with the Lord is not make-believe or just a bunch of coincidences. It is a true encounter with the true and living God.

It's not just what I read—it's what I have experienced. People may deny the very existence of Jesus, but one cannot deny the power of a transformed life. As my beautiful sister in the Lord, Brenda Dukes, always says, *"We are all learning and we are all growing."* We are all a constant work in progress. My prayer for you, my beloved, is that you would begin to celebrate you. Stop looking at how far you have to go and rejoice in how far you have come. I pray that you will begin to see in color. No matter where you are in your journey, greater awaits you.

There is hope. There is healing. There is freedom which awaits you. Continue to keep your eyes fixed on Jesus and use the tools I have given you to tear down the strongholds in your mind. You are still here. You are strong, no matter how weak you may feel. You matter, you are valuable, and you are worthy, despite your past. I support you and I believe in you. Stop looking back. Stop asking the *"why"* questions. Stop holding onto the things which cause you so much pain. Stop and reevaluate your life. You are the only one in control of your destiny. You are your own holdup. If you haven't already, I urge you to make Jesus the Lord of your life, surrender your all, and repent from your life of sin.

The journey won't always be easy but, I can promise you, it will always be worth it. As for me, the beautiful journey continues, my life is no longer my own. I owe it all to the One who has redeemed me and set me free. The Lord has called me to set others free. I fought for my freedom. Now I fight for yours. Remember: hurt people, hurt people but, free people, free people. Trust the process, my beloved. You do not have to live codependent upon anyone other than the Lord Jesus Christ. He is faithful to release the chains that bind you.

Reflection Activity

What wisdom have you gained from your life lessons? What wisdom would you like to gain from your experiences? Do you want to be free and healthy?

_____
_____
_____
_____
_____
_____
_____
_____
_____
_____
_____

CHAPTER FORTY-FIVE
Sinclair's Closing Words

It's funny how, from a human perspective, our plans and pursuits change over time. Initially, we map everything but, eventually, we make changes based on what we *think* is needed. From God's perspective, the completed book for our lives was already written in His mind before the foundation of the world. God, our creator, intimately knows us. God often reminds me that, while I was in Betty Salter's womb, He had carved a plan for me, not to harm me, but to prosper me. From the beginning, I was on a journey learning how to follow God's plan instead of my own.

I'm a well-rounded guy in my late forties and I feel I have, somewhat, gotten a grasp on life. But one thing I must admit, I still don't have a clue how or why God would etch out a purpose for insignificant old me before I was ever formed. When I share my story, I always tell people I was born on a church pew. I was raised in a very religious and pious home with an older sister. Both my grandmother and my father were pastors. My father was also a high school history teacher at Fairfield Central in Winnsboro, South Carolina. My mom was a very kind, loving firecracker for Jesus. Both sides of my parent's families were, and still are, devout God-fearing clans.

As a child, I was embarrassed of the church we had in our home. Right in the heart of our community, in a 20 by 20, two-car garage, was a little church. My friends never picked on me too much but, trying to fit in was very hard, especially being a preacher's and a school teacher's kid. In the mist of street wars, house parties, dope, and sex houses, stood a lighthouse. My orange trimmed house was a key location where God was working His love and grace through my family's sphere of influence. Needless to say, I didn't have a clue, nor did I care, about any of that. I just wanted to be normal. I wanted to fit in. It makes me tear up as I write how my father established a small city of refuge for the broken and lost.

Growing up, my friends nicknamed me "yum-yum, eat'm up." I was a chubby kid and would eat just about anything. Although this nickname didn't bother me, there's one name which stands out that I'll never forget. I was called a "walking conscience." It was a name I despised. I was given that name because the dark evil deeds which flooded people's hearts were countered by the anointing light God had placed on me. I was not aware of this anointing.

I wanted so badly to blend in. I wanted to do what everyone else my age was doing. Sure, my "friends" included me in backyard basketball games, Nintendo battles, football games in the street, walking to school together, etc. but, when the typical shams, mischief, and foolery began, those same friends abandoned me. I was reminded often that I was their walking conscience. I neither knew nor understood it at the time but, just my presence alone would make them feel guilty.

I didn't understand why I couldn't go to the sex houses or why I wasn't told about my best friend's grandfather allowing them to drink alcohol and smoke weed in his backyard. I didn't even know that one of my friends, who lived right next door, was selling dope. I found out only after his house got shot up one night over a bad dope deal. I was never even warned or given a heads up. Geez, he stayed right next door to me—true story.

Apparently, I reminded those around me of the Jesus-lovers which gathered on Sunday mornings in the small little house-church in the neighborhood. What they didn't know was that it was full of dysfunction. As I got older, the pressures of being a youngster became more intense and stifling. With me feeling like the odd-ball, I had more and more thoughts which quickly turned me into a deep hole of insecurity.

It was bad enough I was embarrassed by our house-church; it was even worse when my dad came to substitute for my sophomore history class. I was already feeling inadequate and embarrassed being *Sinclair* and now this. I was picked on for months because of my dad teaching our class. It wasn't until I became a man that I found out there were more kids who admired me because of a dad who was avidly involved in my life instead of a non-existent dad. My neighborhood friends felt the same way, though no one ever shared this with me until we were much older.

Even though I now walk in freedom due to my validation in Christ, I still, to this very day, battle with approval and being accepted. In my youth, with ensuing pressures, I convinced myself that, if I outperformed others, changed my clothing style, cursed, sold drugs, started fights, became loud and vulgar, and more of the like, *then* I would be fully included and accepted. Obviously, this was false thinking and, deep down, I knew that wasn't me at all. It was a lie from the enemy so as to lure me out of my covering shelter and my godly upbringing. Out of all the things I mentioned, at some point in my life, I tried them all, sans selling drugs.

Three different times, I was offered to sell dope but I couldn't bring myself to do it. Either I didn't have the guts to follow through or I was scared to death of my 5'5" firecracker of a mother that was bionic strong when it came to beating me down.

My father was a terror as well, but mothers are endowed with divine might when they chastise their kids!

The turning point of my young life was when my father, *Sinclair Salters, Sr.*, died. I was sixteen years old and in the 10th grade. It was only weeks after he substituted for my history class. I remember being mad at God, not because my dad had died, but because I desperately wanted to be someone else. The death of my father hadn't even sunk in when, on the night of his death, members from the church came to the house consoling and comforting the family. They filled it with much needed support. I remember being naïve and clueless. I didn't know how to respond or how I should feel. I recall walking down our stairway into a house full of visitors with the fake, depleted, and despairing look on my face with a poked out chest.

I remember feeling troubled that the leader of our tribe was gone but I wasn't crying. I didn't want people to think I was heartless, so I put on the pretense of despair. I was numb and I didn't know what I should feel. I had a million questions running through my head such as, "*Is my dad coming back? Am I supposed to be the man of the house? Why is my mom so hurt? Where's my sister? What is she saying or doing? What is she feeling?*" I never felt as vulnerable in our sheltered childhood home as I did that night and the days following.

Shortly after the funeral, my mother couldn't continue to live in the house without thinking about her husband. We began to move from place to place like vagabonds from apartments to family members, never really settling in one place very long. I began working at a grocery store to so-call "support the family." All the while, it was our mother who was sustaining my sister and me. My chest was still poked out and I was still lost.

The quintessential figure for a compassionate servant and providing leader was my dad and he was a great legacy builder. I must say, even though I didn't want to listen, he taught me a lot about family and education. He forced me to read every day:

newspapers, cereal boxes, Bibles, pamphlets. It didn't matter what it was; I was made to feed my mind by reading something. He was a great all-around father, so I had no excuse to feel mad at the world or at God. I couldn't even pretend that my dad had failed me by leaving me. I didn't have that excuse, although I wanted an excuse—one which would allow me to pursue a life of sin and rebellion. I wanted to find acceptance and validation by any and all.

The ways of God were imprinted on my brain by my parents. Sealed in my core was the handprint of God where Christ is King. His calling and leading in my life were infinitely stronger. I couldn't depart from it even when I wanted or tried to. After my dad died, I began to religiously hide from peers in school or any type of social events. I remember that, all through my junior and senior years, I would fabricate projects hiding in the library and media center just to avoid the cafeteria crowd or pep rallies. At the time, I lived just two blocks from our sports arena, but the thought of going to a basketball or football game horrified me.

Girls would try to get my attention, but I felt so ugly and bent emotionally that I would shy away from specific areas so as not to be noticed. No matter how many compliments I received, I never believed any of them. I even created a fake girlfriend claiming she went to another school just so I wouldn't get picked on about not having sex like the other boys or to deter girls from hitting on me. By this time, my insecurities and self-hate were so deeply embedded that I began to live like a hermit. 1995 was the year I graduated and I couldn't have been more ready to get out of there.

I had no desire or zeal to pursue higher learning nor did I have anyone to really push me toward it. One of my uncles convinced me to try a local tech college in pursuit of having my own HVAC—heating, ventilation and conditioning—business. I was longing for acceptance and guidance, so I took hold of his dream and made it mine. It was irrelevant that I didn't really want to do it. Just to please him, I said, "*Cool, I'll do it.*" I didn't stick to it because I always had that feeling of not fitting in. I was the youngest in my class. The guys were twenty to twenty-five years older than I. I'm pretty sure they were excited that a young black man had goals and aspiration but, in my mind, they thought the worst of me. See, I was the problem, not them. I felt less than. No matter who was around me, I always second-guessed myself. Somebody once told me, "*Stop caring about what others think of you, it's none of your business.*" At that, I dropped the class and began to pursue jobs.

Before completing high school, God sent me the Priester family, whom I considered as my second redemptive covering. The spiritual leader of the house was a pastor, his wife was a loving woman of God, and they had four children—one daughter and three sons, all older than me. Two of the sons were married and I found myself wanting to be like those guys. I would find myself at their house hours on end sitting at the feet of their spiritual leader, Pastor Priester. He took me under his wing teaching me sound biblical teaching over sensationalism. Line upon line, precept upon precept. Time in his presence had a profound impact on my life. He taught me to be a student of Scripture and how to hide God's holy Word in my heart that I may not sin against God.

Do you remember when I said God had mapped out a plan for our lives in eternity past? I began to feel God's heavenly weighted presence upon my life, and boy do I mean heavy! I couldn't figure it out, but God quickly transitioned me from entertaining the thoughts of doing being "big and bad" enough, to now having a male figure to which I could look up. God definitely used this family to help me during my dark moments of temptation. This family was a place of safety for me. It was a place where there were people I wanted to mimic. Being around godly counsel was a healthy place, yet it seemed unhealthy from the perspective of the broken place in my life.

I didn't know it then, but I was trying to earn their validation. Throughout the latter part of my teen years and into my twenties, I began to embrace my spiritual roots more seriously, though still half-heartily and for the wrong reasons. God was still using my reluctant heart through it all. For once, I felt like I belonged. I was somebody in someone else's world and I loved where I was—so long as I didn't have to be what I saw in my world. I wanted to stay under the shadow of man and not God.

Through a poor evaluation of me, God used all of it for His purpose, the good, bad, and ugly. I became zealous and hungry for God's Word. Instead of partying, clubbing, and chasing after girls, I would spend time reading the Bible. Even if I didn't understand a lot of what I was reading, I became intensely intrigued with how God dealt with fallen man all throughout existence. Instead of my interest in the Bible igniting an intimate relationship with Jesus, in my pursuit for knowledge, I became proud and arrogant with a false sense of humility.

I believed the church-world was my life, my end-all-be-all. I became comfortable hiding behind church activities. I became the golden boy of the church doing everything I could to impress people. Ushering, playing the drums, caring for the disabled, and more. God also had given me a gift of rapping and writing songs. I was living for the praises I would receive from people. It became a drug from me. I started losing weight and working out since I had to make sure I presented a polished me. Externally, I had it all together.

Still wanting to mimic Pastor Priester and his sons, I desired a wife. Still in my early twenties, I did something very foolish. I went into a marriage full of pride. I was arrogant and way too young. I made my marriage excruciatingly miserable because everything had to be by the book, rigid, and ascetic. Because of my insecurities, I became very cold and unlovable. I made my wife, and everyone around me, feel like, *"If you don't serve and love God the way I do, you aren't saved or accepted by God."* I didn't say those words but, through my passive aggressive demeanor, it was loud and crystal clear. She was not used to the church culture in which I was raised. Often times, I would make her feel like the third wheel or an outcast when being amongst church folks. She expressed this to me, yet I would always push it off on her citing, *"You're not praying or reading enough, it's just your emotions."* The truth was that I took more pride in wanting people to think I had it all together rather than actually making our marriage work.

Now remember, in my mind, as long as I was in the church serving, I was totally free from reality. I was in for a big fat reality check! I didn't see it coming but, after three years of marriage, the bottom fell out. Prior to this, I was feeling I had finally arrived in life. I was building my kingdom and I was in control. Marriage was under my control like I wanted. I had a decent job, served in church, and I had approval from those around me. I even felt like I knew the Bible better than God. I had too many *"I"s* in my internal conversation. Suddenly, my wife didn't follow my playbook and she left. I must tell you that, because I was so arrogant and prideful thinking that I had to build my little kingdom perfectly with everyone playing their part, I never saw divorce or rejection on my radar.

At the time, I was like, *"No. I'm the only one who can walk away."* My childishness became fully exposed and it was ugly. She left, expressing in so many words, *"If I have to earn or love God the way that you showed me, no thank you."* Not only did I reject her, but I made her feel as though she were rejected by God. She started drinking and partying and, eventually, she started cheating on me, which subsequently ended in our divorce. I was so embarrassed. I was still more concerned with what others thought rather than about the actual marriage ending. I never stopped to think about the role I played.

In the months which followed our divorce, I lost my home, was fired from two different jobs, and got hurt playing a recreational sport. It was all back to back. I was so hurt. I went from being a super religious jerk to a mega super religious hypocritical jerk. I began having sex with a woman who wasn't my wife with no intentions of making her such. I started hanging out at bars, even though I wasn't a drinker. It was all about coping. There I was, back at the same hiding place again while still in church, still ushering, still doing Christian rap, singing on the choir, and still Bible-thumping. I was rotting away on the inside. I was lost, once again, and I didn't get it.

But Jesus was still gracious, loving, and kind to me, delivering me through my mess. It was my rock bottom. I was very ashamed of the choices I was making and I knew I was wrong for using God's grace as a pass to break Him commandments. I remember the day when I broke down and prayed like I had never prayed before. I expressed to God that I was tired. I repented of my sin and then I began to tell God that, if I have to earn His approval, I was going to crash and burn. My way was based on a work-system. I told God I wanted to live for Him. I asked Him to humble me and make me new. In that moment, I encountered God in a real and core-shaking way. I learned that, though you can be surrounded by people in circles who truly love Jesus, anyone can mimic other people's spiritual walk, live by moral values, and still be totally out of the will of God and His blood covering. I was claiming to know the intimate Son of God in my heart yet, all the while, I had become infatuated with the historical figure named Jesus. All that time I had thought I was saved and I wasn't.

I repented and went back to Christianity 101: intimacy with Christ. It was a hard and sobering journey. No matter how embarrassing and awkward I felt in my new place of humility and transparency, I never felt so alive and liberated. For the first time ever, I was free to be broken in God's sight. God's opinion is the only one which truly matters and, for the first time, I was free to be me. You see, my whole journey of getting to this place was the condition of my heart. The heart of the matter was the matter of my heart.

I had to give Christ access to revisit that place in my heart where insecurities and rejection initially began for me. Having one purpose in mind—to heal and make me whole, God said, *"After I heal you, I'm going to allow your scars to remain. Your scars are to humble you so that, in the future, you'll be a testimony and witness of My power and grace."* I could truly feel God's love and compassion without the idea of needing to earn it.

In my late twenties, my music started to blossom. God connected me to some Christian brothers who started a Christian rap label named *Dunamis Records*. We began performing at Christian events, traveling to different states to minister in music, and doing community outreach. I started serving more in my local church. When the doors were open, I was there. If anyone needed my help, I would do what I could. Servitude to Christ was no longer coming from a place of earning people's approval or impressing others. It began coming from a place of servitude. I was doing it for an audience of One. For once in my life, I felt whole and I knew who I was. I was a validated child of God.

As time went on, our music label began to take off. People were investing in our vision to share the gospel of Christ to the world. We began to travel more and, to be honest, I felt like my flesh was getting a kick out of the whole music thing and God wasn't pleased. The whole time, Holy Spirit pressed upon my mind telling me I was out of His will using the gift He had given me.

I tried hard to drown out God's voice by convincing myself, *"Yes, Lord. This is Your will. It has to be. Look at all the doors opening for us. It's a great opportunity for me and You."* I ignored God over and over again and I found myself slowly drifting into a dry place, no longer feeling His peace, joy, or approval. I began to realize that being out of the will and the purpose of God is a lonely place on earth and it's dangerous. Although that didn't change His everlasting love and relationship with me, it did keep me from experiencing the fullness of who He was in my life. My fellowship and peace with God had been interrupted. I believe now, looking back, God was saying, *"I'm not going to badger you to fall back, Sinclair. I'll wait right here and, when you're done doing what you desire, we can pick up where we left off."*

I was relying on my disciplines so as to do morally and godly things, yet with no anointing power. As time went on, I began to feel empty and insecure again looking for anyone with a pulse to please and satisfy me. Around thirty, I began going through the whirlwind of courting again and making horrible decisions in the process. I started dating a young lady and, soon after, we were engaged.

I and one of my music partners were asked to come and minister at an upcoming women's conference. God really used us to speak life into those young girls. God's presence was undeniably there that evening. In the audience were two familiar faces that would show up and support any Christian youth event. I had never met them personally but, their reputation preceded them. They were known as the *Golden Girls*. They were on fire for God and loved to worship Him. Many artists knew that, when they showed up, God's glory went before them.

At the close of the conference, one of the young ladies approached me asking about *Dunamis Records*. She told me how much she enjoyed our music and asked if she could purchase a copy of my music. I wasn't prepared because, to be honest, no one usually asked for my music. I was used to hiding behind the guys in my group and pushing their music. My insecurities had definitely seeped into my music. I got her contact information and told her I would make sure I got her a copy as soon as I could. About a week later, I gave her a call to make arrangements to get my personal CD to her. We started talking about who God was in each other's life. I was truly blessed by our conversation. I don't remember if I ever got a CD to her or not, but I do remember one of our conversations vividly. I was inspired to encourage her by sharing a quote from Michelangelo, *"A woman should be so lost in*

Christ that it takes a man to seek Him to find her." She expressed her desire wanting that in her life. I was able to pray with her and we didn't speak again until about a year later.

I was still out of God's will and, not only was I ignoring God's voice about my music, I had fallen into sexual temptation with my fiancé. I soon found out she was cheating on me. Not only was I dealing with insecurities, but now I had to deal with the rejection from being cheated once again. I told myself, *"Self, you've been here before and you promised yourself you wouldn't go back."* At that moment, I knew I needed to be revived. I knew I needed to get back in right standing with Christ. Once again, I felt polished on the outside. I was going to church, talking church Christianese, but it wasn't genuine intimacy. I had allowed other things into my heart which took the place of Christ.

God's grace swiftly pulled me back in harmony and fellowship with Him. I repented and asked God's forgiveness. I told the Lord I wanted to be in His perfect will for my life. I asked Him to help me get out of the current commitments I had already made with my music group, family, and friends. Not long after that, our rap group began to have conflicting views as far as the direction the ministry needed to go. As our egos began to flare up, we started fighting and arguing more frequently. One day, I shared with the group what I was feeling, which was that God wanted us to do more boots on the ground and disciple-making. I told them I felt like God wanted us to become more involved with community outreach, not just performing music. I was so excited and I felt God's presence radiating through me as I spoke. I felt like this was the answer for us all yet, when I shared this with my brothers—with whom I am still connected and dearly love—it was gingerly shot down.

I expressed to the guys that I felt like we weren't practicing what we preach in our music. We were rapping about going out in the highways and byways but really, we were just going from one church event to another rocking out for the name of Christ, but not being His hands and feet. To their ears, it was noble and honorable. At that point, I knew God was pulling me into a different place. God's message was not for them, it was for me. Fearfully, I said to the Lord, "*I have never shared the gospel or evangelized ever in my life by myself. I'm not the leadership or outspoken type. I'm not smart or articulate enough.*" I gave God all the excuses. All of my life, I hid far behind people and I was okay hiding in someone else's shadow. Genesis 2:18 reads, "*The Lord God said, 'It is not good for the man to be alone. I will make a helper suitable for him.'*"

I reminded God of His Word, but humbly and carefully this time. I desired to be married. In the past, I had done the entire "wife-seeking formula" of which the church-mamas had instructed. Make a list of all the things you want your future wife to be, pray over it, put it under your pillow, and use it as a bookmark as you quote Scriptures over it for eighteen hours. It makes me tired just thinking about it! Geeezzzz.

They meant well, but this is a word to the wise: wait on the Father. He knows best. He knows you're lonely. He's the one that said it's not good for man to be alone. Occupy until the one comes. One day, I pulled out my list of things I wanted in my wife-to-be and started boo-hooing and pouting because I still wasn't married. God whispered in my ear, "*Stop that crying like a baby. I want you to throw that silly list away. Now, I want you to make another list. I want you to write and pray over what I want you to be for whomever I have hidden away for you until the appointed time.*"

I was like, "*Wow God, didn't see that coming!*" On that list, He told me to write, "*God, I want Sinclair to be loving, godly, kind, charming, patient, a listener, gentle, caring, concerned, physically attractive, healer, warm, funny, and servant-leader toward the wife You have for me.*" At that point, I never asked my Father again, "*Where's my wife?*" I only trusted as I continued doing the work of an evangelist. After that day, I was okay being single. I devoted my time and intimate worship to being the hands and feet of Jesus. There were times of doubt and loneliness but, in those times, God gently reminded me, *"Not yet."* He also reminded me of the Michelangelo quote. He said, *"The same goes for a man. A man should be so lost in Christ that it takes a woman to seek after Christ for her to see him."*

One day, while browsing in one of the local clothing stores, I ran into Jami. It had been about a year since the last time we had talked or seen each other. We talked for a few minutes catching up on all God had been doing in our individual lives. Before we parted ways, she mentioned to me about an urban community. A few of her friends were planning to reach them for Christ. I told her how crazy it was that God had been speaking to me about that very thing. God has a odd way of piecing things together with us not having a clue what's going on at that moment. I knew then we had some type of divine connection, partners in ministry, or something of the sort. We were both great networkers, so I was thinking that maybe God was connecting us in that fashion.

A relationship wasn't on my mind—a relationship would have been the last thing on my mind. I was so numb to the idea of courting that it never came across my radar screen that this precious woman could or would be my future wife. She shared with me a time and place for the evangelistic launch and I ended the conversation by telling her I would think about coming and joining with the team. For several days after running into her, I kept thinking about how wonderful it would be to live out loud by engaging the culture for the gospel of Christ.

I made up my mind that I was going to check out their meeting and see what it was all about. I didn't know what to expect. I was so nervous but, when I arrived, I was totally blindsided in a good and revelatory way. They were all white and I was the only black face. Don't get me wrong, I was so welcomed and I felt at home, but to see whites willing to go out and love on an all-black community was mind-blowing. Most of them were from different churches, but each one of them had the same agenda—to bring the hope of Christ to a broken and lost community. We had so much fun going out getting to know the people of that community. We moved in unity and transparency as we engaged with the unchurched. Some got saved, some were set free, and others received deliverance. We witnessed gang members and prostitutes coming to Jesus. We watched others grow spiritually in their relationship with Christ.

One of the ladies in the neighborhood opened her home to have Bible study. This beautiful young lady's name was Tasha. She and Jami used to party together before Jami surrendered her life to Christ. Jami and I tag-teamed and facilitated this Bible study while the rest of the team walked the streets praying and inviting others in the community to join the ongoing Bible study. We faithfully and consistently poured into this community for about a year. Race was never an issue at all for the fire starter team— what we called ourselves—and God used all of us together as tools in His toolbox for reconstruction and transformation.

During the weeks and months that passed, Jami and I were not only going out once a week to this community, we were also talking almost daily. Together, we would come up with topics to discuss in Bible study along with sharing our personal life's journey with each other. It was so refreshing to have a genuine friendship with a female with whom I had like passions and convictions. It was in our time of ministry that I realized I may have been longing for silver when gold was right under my nose the whole time.

Jami is extremely delightful to the eyes. She has an outward beauty to which almost any man would be attracted. I know it sounds crazy because men are visual creatures, but I truly believe that, during our friendship, God shielded my sight from her outward "art" because my heart was still in a purging process. If He had not, I would have gotten the wrong motivation from the beginning, lusting for her, wanting her body, and to use her as a bragging piece instead of seeing her true beauty and worth. The Bible says, *"The Lord beautifies the meek with salvation"* and *"a wise and prudent wife is from the Lord."* After much community outreach and many Christian events together, I began to single her out. I was becoming so captivated and mesmerized by her love and passion for Jesus.

She had something most Christians don't have and that was a solid grasp on what sound teaching is when it comes to the Word of God. She was a student of Scripture, a prayer warrior, and fully submitted to Jesus. I was totally blown away by her pursuit of living a holy life, something I'd never experienced in a woman her age. Please understand that I had been in so many relationships where the lack of these things caused conflict. I was used to women who had a form of godliness but denied its power. They attended church but lived a very carnal life. They had accepted Christ as Savior but rejected Him as Lord.

I'm not talking about the hang-ups we all have and will have until Christ comes back. I'm speaking of an unwillingness to be totally transformed to Christ's image. Jami was a diamond in the rough, indeed. As time passed and God's gold—the father's virtuous daughter—was still veiled from my eyes, it's important to remind you that we were both intently focused on a vertical relationship with God and at peace. Everything else had simply lost its appeal.

As individuals, we were both completely satisfied with Jesus and our singleness. Both our past relationships had taught us the importance of allowing God to have His way in our lives instead of trying to do things our own way. God has a much greater design for marriage than we will ever understand this side of eternity. It's so much more than just having a wife, more than being attracted to someone, more than sex and being compatible. Just to name a few, the purpose of marriage is about conforming us into the image of Christ. Marriage reveals the dark ugliness that's in our hearts such as pride and selfishness, which God wants to expose. Marriage is about dying to self, relinquishing our rights, and being a servant-leader. It's about making a choice to love unconditionally.

Above all else, I wanted God's ultimate calling and purpose for my life. As time passed, we were both still in a pure place in our friendship with no ulterior motives, but undeniable feelings started to grow toward each other. The appointed time came when the Father said, *"Okay, Sinclair, now you are ready for Me to remove the veil which shielded her physical beauty from you."* It came on a pleasant Friday evening totally unexpectedly. A team of us were planning a big gospel hip-hop outdoor community event. We had been talking and planning this for many months. This particular evening, a team of us were meeting at the event site to strategize and pray.

I am so serious when I say this but, when she walked in, it was as if I were seeing all of her physical beauty for the very first time. I even recall the outfit she wore. It was a long checkered skirt, black boots, and a turtleneck. In that moment, my Daddy had removed the veil from my eyes. Instantly, emotions I didn't realize I had began to run through my body. All of a sudden, the world was right with me. That night, my best friend, which was at that meeting, called me and said, *"Bro I think you...you. You need to..."* I said, *"Bruh, I already know!"*

I am, by far, one of the biggest procrastinators you will ever meet. My procrastination tends to fall under the pretense of "caution." It is so bad that I'm cautious of being cautious, if that makes any sense. Okay, maybe not, but you get the point. God was not going to allow my procrastination to get in the way of His divine plan. The following day, Saturday evening, I was lying in my bed and, all of a sudden, I felt like that well-known illusionist, David Copperfield. I felt God's heavy hand snatching me up with a strong grip and I began to levitate, as if cement enveloped me and moved me swiftly to the edge of the bed. I was compelled to put on my shoes and shirt and, in my mind, I kept saying, *"I've never encountered something so pressuring and so intense."*

I didn't remember picking up the phone and dialing, but I called Jami, said I thought we needed to talk, and that I was coming over. To all you men that are reading this, women will almost always know before you. I was saying to myself, *"Wait, I must be dreaming. Let me go back to sleep."* Then I heard the voice of Holy Spirit as if it were a bullhorn in my ear. He said, *"No, you are going and you're going now. You don't have a choice."* Immediately, I was at her doorstep. I know this sounds crazy, but I don't remember the drive over there. I don't even remember getting in my car. I was totally "under the influence" of the Holy Spirit and it felt amazing.

I rang the doorbell, eagerly awaiting her as I knew my purpose for being there. I entered and we both sat on the opposite ends of the couch, not an ounce of procrastination. I was so confident and sure of myself. I felt I had to get right to the point. I said, *"You, woman, me man and we marry."* No, just kidding! I did tell her that God, through Holy Spirit, told me that we were supposed to be together. She replied, *"Sinclair, that's exciting you've finally gotten the revelation, but He showed me already."* Then she shared her journey and the whole "codeword" thing, how I had said it one night during a conversation we were having. I sat there feeling like I had totally been set up by God and I was okay with it.

I have a strong belief about courting and not rushing into relationships. I feel as though people should take as much time as needed to truly know each other. I also strongly advise those who are considering getting married *not* to rush into marriage. Notwithstanding, when I tell you it was obvious God was fast-tracking us into a marriage covenant, that is an understatement. It was a unique plan from the Lord and not a knee-jerk decision based on physical attraction or emotion. God had a vested interest in this union. From the very beginning, we knew that this marriage was so much bigger than us.

We had both surrendered to God first, individually, while allowing healing and wholeness to take place in each one of our lives. My wife often says, *"Two broken people can't make a whole."* Both she and I, in our past, had tried to make broken people love and accept us only to realize we were broken as well. We had to come to the end of ourselves and surrender our wants and desires for a spouse, career, comfort, house, car, dreams, ministry, and so on. We had to choose to swap wills—our will for God's. Jesus said that he who loses his life for My sake and for the sake of the gospel shall find it. We had to learn how to let go of the control we thought we had in order for us to gain all God intended for us. The only way we were able to find it was through our intimate relationships with Jesus.

I didn't stay long after that announcement. The only thing I could say with a joyful heart was, *"I'm not sure what this is supposed to look like, but I trust God."* When I left, I remember laughing at God. I was in total awe of Him and how He totally blew up my plans on my list. He reminded me that His ways are so beyond mine and His thoughts are higher than mine as well.

Looking back, Jami and I both laugh about our list of what kind of mate we wanted. We often joke that both of our lists were comical to God and all of heaven. I'll bet the angels were saying to each other, *"These two knuckleheads have no clue how God's eternal agenda works when He gets involved in making two become one."* The lesson is that God knows us far better than we know ourselves and He is our Creator. He will not give us the blueprint or His plan of execution. It's up to us to seek God and allow His plans to unfold. We must place all our trust in Him instead of ourselves. In seeking God, we are to give Him our heart, soul, and mind. The God of heaven has already given us His best, His son—Jesus, so as to take away the penalty of our sins. To those who belong to Him, no good thing will he withhold. Oftentimes, we try to do things our own way and then get upset with Him when it doesn't go according to our plan.

As for me and Jami, God gave us way beyond what we wanted or needed. You see, the list we tried to make Him was based on what *we* wanted and needed. God being our Creator and knowing every detail of our being, He did what He specializes in doing.

He gave us abundantly above that for which we could ask. I'm still in disbelief how good to me God has been by giving me my precious Jami. I truly seek to make her happy always, putting her above all that I am. I humbly and excitedly submit to her well-being, no exception.

Our wedding day was August 3, 2013, at Tybee Island, Savannah, Georgia. A few weeks before our wedding, I remember sitting Jami down as I shared with her how scared I was about becoming a father. I was going from a single and selfish man to a full family man. Jazmine was seventeen and Jada was seven, both of whom lived with Jami. Jami also had an ongoing relationship with her ex-husband's children and two grandchildren. She told me, from the very beginning that, even though her stepchildren were grown, they were still her children.

I was scared, I needed a formula—the ABC steps on how to be a parent. She laughed and said, *"Sinclair, just be you, a follower of Jesus."* Then she said the most powerful words and it hit me right between the eyes. They were words which gripped me and soaked every fiber of my being. She said, *"God has made you a kinsman redeemer."* I grew up in church all my life so I was very familiar with the phrase in the story of Ruth and Boaz. However, when she said it, the Scripture began to come alive.

It was like fireworks going off in my head and heart. God was entrusting me to mimic what Christ, God the Son, did for God the Father. He redeemed His prodigal sons and daughters back to right standards. Jesus, our Savior, repaired the breach between God and man and now God was commissioning me to repair the breach for Jami and her children. By modeling heaven and expanding heaven here on earth, I'm showing them what the love of the heavenly Father looks like toward them. They were left damaged due to having so many broken men, men who were not following Christ, and men who had broken so many promises. They had no idea what a godly husband and father was like. They were like sheep without a shepherd. Jami assured me saying, *"They will follow and submit to you as you follow and submit to Christ, the Good Shepherd."*

Her words of encouragement and assurance awakened something deeply within me. I had a mini revival going on in my soul. It was the power of God showing Himself mightily through me and that was really scary. He planned every detail of it down to the microsecond before the foundation of the world. Years later, Jami and I are still enjoying each other as best friends and covenant partners who embrace doing life together. My desire is for my ceiling to be their floor. The vision for our home and marriage is the same as it's always been, even while Jami and I were friends. That goal is to bring heaven to earth by advancing the kingdom of God. We are to be boots on the ground reaching people and families by being the hands and feet of Jesus. We do this first in our home and then in our communities.

At the writing of this book, we are aspiring to be full-time missionaries in our hometown of Columbia, South Carolina, with emphasis on world missions as well. I am at peace with Jami. There's no pushing and pulling when it comes to building a godly legacy for family. Yes, we still have our ups and downs, disagreements and arguments, just like any marriage.

MARRIAGE TAKES CULTIVATING AND SPONTANEITY; YOU GET OUT WHAT YOU PUT IN.

Marriage takes work. I'm learning that, even though we are best friends and we both love Jesus, we can't put our marriage on autopilot. Marriage takes cultivating and spontaneity—you get out what you put in. If you invest in peace, you're going to reap peace. If you sow forgiveness, you're going to reap the same. If you sow anger, resentment, selfishness, harsh words, unforgiveness, lies, or any other sin, you're going to reap the same.

I have to remember to be the change I want to see. Change must start with me. I have to choose to put her affections and thoughts higher than my own. Love takes the pain out of sacrificially loving her. Honestly, it isn't always easy, some days and some seasons are harder than others. I act like a jerk sometimes, we get on each other's nerves, and we've been known to say things we don't mean out of frustration or anger. Nevertheless, what binds us together is so much stronger. Our marriage was built on a covenant between us and God. I'm committed to Jami forever. I need her, I choose to love the woman of my life, and I will honor her and our children and grandchildren with my whole being.

A dear friend once told me that the best way to win the affections of children is to love on their mama visibly and publicly. Exalting her melts children's hearts like nothing else. I feel them watching me closely, as well they should. I want them to trust me with their hearts and their deepest concerns. My journey is so humbling and moving that it's truly hard to put all the details in my writing. I feel as though I'm God's favorite because I don't deserve what He has given me in all areas of life. I'm not the smartest, the wisest, or the strongest, but I do know God loves me and I trust His plan for my life.

Sinclair, Sr. and Betty Salters are amazing Jesus-lovers who were deeply in tune with the heartbeat of heaven. I love them so much for what they did for me and my sister. Along with all the virtuous attributes of being compassionate, supportive, great providers, and good teachers, most importantly, they taught us how to chase after and fall in love with God. This is a much more productive path to an authentic relationship with Christ as opposed to simply going to church eight days a week. Yes, I said eight days a week because, growing up, that's what it felt like! I truly saw their heart, mind, and soul poured out as an offering to Jesus: their utmost for His highest. To this day, my mother and my sister live for Christ in a sweet and powerful way.

I must admit, I made light of my father modeling integrity, compassion, and hard work. Growing up, I was looking for validation from the world, but my dad validated me before I could do anything of merit. He was proud of me just because I was his son. There was one particular day that stood out to me the most, the day my father made me stand still as he looked me in my eyes. As our eyes locked, he told me he loved me and he was proud I was his son. It was only that one time, but that's all it took. It awakened something down in my soul. I tried to play it off but, even then, I knew something moved in me that day. It was a transfer of the fear and passion for God from one generation to the next. For the next thirty years, more or less, I had no idea how that one encounter would set the course of my ultimate destiny.

Once embarrassed, I am now eternally grateful for the way my parents reared me and my sister in the way of holiness. The Bible says that a righteous man or woman leaves an inheritance for their children and their children's children. They left me with a spiritual inheritance which will continue throughout the generations before and after me. There's so much more I could share, but I would have to write my own book. God is mind-blowing and everything else loses its appeal in comparison to Him. Marriage, in itself, isn't the end-all-be-all. Christ is.

My prayer is this, *"Lord, help me continue to be the man You want me to be for my wife, my children, and my grandchildren. In all that I do and say, I want to model Christ to them. Give me the grace and wisdom to teach them their identity in Christ and help them fulfill their God-given purpose on this earth. Let my life of obedience and intimately chasing after You be passed to them. In Jesus' name, I pray. Amen.*

Reflection Activity

How do you view God? How do you view yourself? How do you want to view God? How do you want to view yourself? What changes do you choose to make in your life? Are you willing to let yourself go and allow God to take over?

_____
_____
_____
_____
_____
_____
_____
_____
_____

Afterword

After writing this book, a friend sent me a link to session one of Tim Fletcher's talk on Complex Trauma. I spent the next few hours captivated by the information. I spent the next few days watching all the videos in the series and I have continued to follow and watch many more. Hearing the explanation of CPTSD, I felt as if a light bulb came on, much like when I discovered codependency. Putting a name to what I had experienced in childhood, which shaped my coping skills, was freeing. In fact, I wasn't crazy and I wasn't just being rebellious. I felt a sense of relief and gratitude for a moment and then I became angry. I was angry that I spent years in counseling never being properly diagnosed nor treated. Angry for being put on medication, angry for the added labels, angry for the years of tormenting thoughts that said *I* was the issue, and angry that I had carried this weight feeling "something must be wrong with *me*."

I cried as I thought about and processed this transformative information. As I was processing, I was reminded that this is a new field-study and the information I know *now* is not the information I knew *then*. I was then able to release the hurt and anger that surfaced. I went through a new process of forgiveness. I forgave those who counseled me, medicated me, locked me up in a padded room and said I was crazy, and, once again, I had to forgive myself. I had to remind myself that I had neither the knowledge nor the tools needed back then and, for that matter, neither did anyone else.

As I continue to learn more about CPTSD and its effects, I feel a burning desire to help others in this area. All of us, to some degree, have experienced Complex Trauma. Some will continue on with life as is, whereas others will delve deeper in their knowledge and understanding so as to gain freedom. I truly believe there is always a deeper level of healing that awaits us. It is a journey we will be on until Christ returns. I was once told, *"When the student is ready, the teacher will show up."*

Deeper Levels of Healing

I was listening to Tim Fletcher one day. He was talking about getting sick and how he was unable to connect with his kids during a certain season of his life. This caused Complex Trauma in the lives of his children. Immediately, I thought about my own mother, how she had gotten injured when I was little. Although I was too young to understand, I felt abandoned and rejected by her. My early memories of my mom are of her lying on the couch all day watching TV and reading novels. In my eyes, she could care less about me or what I was doing. Recently, this opened a door for my mom and me to have a very powerful conversation. I told her about Tim Fletcher and his ordeal with a sickness he had for a period of time and about the trauma it caused his children. I began to explain to her I felt like she just didn't care about me. I shared how I felt unwanted and unloved. My perception was that she cared more about her TV shows and love novels than me. *"She certainly didn't care about my wants or needs"* were the thoughts that continued to haunt me.

She then began telling me about her accident. Remember, as I said, I knew she had gotten hurt, but I did not know the seriousness or extent of her injury. I was only six years old when it occurred. She told me how she would be hospitalized for months at a time, one surgery after another. She said that, on the nights my stepdad was at work as a firefighter—he worked 24-hour shifts, my brother and I would have to help her use the bed pan, give her sponge baths, and even feed her. I remembered none of these things. She told me about all the surgeries and how being in the hospital weeks and months at a time was so hard for her. Through sobs, she told me about the time she was hospitalized during Thanksgiving, Christmas, and New Year's. She cried as she shared how guilty she felt for not being with us. As I listened, I felt such sadness and compassion. I couldn't even imagine how hard that must've been for her. I thought about how traumatic that was for *her*. Thoughts of her being in extreme physical pain as well as emotional and mental pain helped me to see things from a different perspective. I truly believe this experience not only brought us closer together but, for me, it definitely helped me experience a deeper level of healing, one for which I will be forever grateful. I strongly encourage you to look up *www.findingFreedom.ca* as well as watching Tim's teaching videos on YouTube.

Sharing My Journey

I think it's important for me to share this part of my journey with you so as to encourage you. I was invited to speak at a conference one weekend several years ago. Afterward, the minister asked me specifically if I had started writing my book or had I finished? Then he said a few other things to me that I vaguely remember. Before I left that day, a young lady approached me and handed me a copy of her book and said that whatever I needed, she would help me.

On my way home, I called my husband and he asked how the conference went. I began to share with him the details and then told him what the minister said in reference to me writing a book and about the young lady that gave me her book. At the time, a book was not on my radar, though I had felt for a few years I had a book title, *Confessions of an X-Codependent*, but that was it. Besides, there was no way *I* could write a book! So, as for a book title, I just left it alone and suppressed the idea. As I was sharing this with my husband, I kind of dumbed down the idea and said, *"Everybody has a book."* Sinclair immediately began to encourage me. Did he really believe I could write a book?? Fear was screaming in my ear so loudly, *"NO, YOU CAN'T!"* I began to express to him how there was no way I could write my story.

"I can't even type. I don't know basic writing skills such as knowing how to begin or end a paragraph and so forth. I dropped out of school in the 9th grade," I said to myself and Sinclair. Internally, fear began to overwhelm me. I felt as though I was going to have a panic attack as I expressed my thoughts. When I finished explaining how I could *not* do it, my husband simply said, *"You can do it! You know how to send text messages and you know how to take notes on your notes app,"* he said, *"so use that."*

Although fear was telling me I could *not* do it, the words from my husband helped me to override my fear and press into the idea of actually doing it. Although I was afraid and I kept asking, *"Well, what about this and what about that,"* I did it.

I started. The moment I started telling my story, the words flowed out of me like a river. Within two to three months, I had it all written. I did as my husband had said—I used my notes app, sometimes typing, other times I was speaking, especially when I didn't know how to spell a word—which was quite often, might I add. As I typed or spoke out a chapter, I would send it to my email and to the lady that offered her help. When I sent it to her, she was going through it and putting it in manuscript form—I didn't even know what that meant. Due to the busyness of her own life, after the first few chapters, she was unable to continue. So, I was left with a bunch of chapters sitting in an email.

After that, I had a few different people offer to help and, for whatever reason, they were unable to finish. This isn't about them or me shaming them for not helping. Rather, it is simply to share the struggle I experienced. I started having nightmares and flashbacks of traumatic events, something I had never had before when it came to my past. I felt defeated, helpless; thoughts of fear and a bunch of *"what if"* questions began to surface. I didn't know where all of this was coming from. Now, looking back, it was the enemy's way of trying to keep me from moving forward and actually publishing the pages contained in this book. About a year after I had completed the writing, I ran into a lady, different than the aforementioned author, whom I had the pleasure of meeting years earlier. At the time of our first meeting, she blessed me with one of her books she had written. At that particular moment, I wasn't able to purchase one, so she gave it to me and said she would rather me have the book than me pay for it! That book, *Looking for God*—now it's three volumes, helped me deeply grow spiritually as I learned so much through her words of grace and wisdom contained in those pages.

Fast forward a few years later as my friend, Heather, and I entered yet another conference, I saw her again. I remembered her book and how it had blessed me in such a tremendous way. I pulled out $20 and walked over to her and began telling her about how she had blessed me years ago by giving it to me and that I wanted to pay her. As the three of us sat and talked, Heather shared with her that I had written an autobiography and wasn't sure what steps I needed to take to complete it. Alexys immediately offered to help in any way she could and gave me her number. I was unsure as to whether or not I was supposed to call her. Up until that point, so many people had offered to help, and even started helping, but they were all unable to stick with it. I was afraid she was going to be the same. You know when someone offers to help but they really don't mean it, or they want to charge you a crazy amount of money, or they simply have ulterior motives? Needless to say, I was very skeptical and uncertain. Finally, after a few weeks and much debate, I decided to give her a call. She was so encouraging and assured me she wanted to help. She put in so much time, money, and energy into making the words I had written into a beautifully assembled manuscript. Her only motive was to see others blessed through the telling of my story! She is responsible for the birth of this baby and, as I've already stated, I am eternally grateful for her and her ministry.

Additionally, since my book was first released, she has now branched out as a publisher through *The Fiery Sword Global Ministries Publications*. For reasons I won't mention, I have shifted from my original publisher to *The Fiery Sword Publications*.

The other huge factor of fear was the picture I was painting and what that picture said about my parents. I was afraid people would see my parents as horrible or think I lived as though every day of my life was dark and hellish, but that was not the case. My parents did the best they could with the baggage they each carried. I no longer blame them. Rather, I take ownership over what shaped my belief-system and I extend grace and forgiveness for the things for which they were directly responsible.

There were many other challenges throughout the process, too many to go into detail. But I will tell you this, from the time I started until the time the book was finally printed was exactly three years! So, I want to encourage you, no matter what you feel you *can't* do, if it's God's will, you *can* and you *will*. Trust in Him and the process. Relax and enjoy the journey! Don't allow the roadblocks to deter you from your God-ordained destiny. Let the hurdles be nothing more than stepping stones.

Author Bio

Jami Salters and her husband, Sinclair, currently live in and are natives of Columbia, South Carolina. They are the founders of a 501c3 nonprofit outreach ministry called 4Runners4Christ. It is a discipleship ministry that helps people pursue the person and priorities of Jesus Christ. Their ministry is focused on reaching the inner cities of their hometown and beyond with hopes of bridging the gap between the two worlds of the church and the streets. Jami and Sinclair go where most are unwilling to go and do what most are unwilling to do.

Jami currently works in the banking industry and has done so for the past 20 years. It is her desire to pursue full-time missionary work alongside Sinclair who, through faithful supporters of 4Runners4Christ, is a full-time missionary. Her focus is being able to start *Finding Freedom* services in different locations in Columbia, South Carolina and elsewhere, and to open an outpatient treatment center that specializes in recovery education for addictions and Complex Trauma. Currently, Jami facilitates *Making Peace with Your Past* classes throughout the year and Sinclair holds Bible forums for men of all ages. Both are engaged in one-on-one discipleship along with other ministry tasks. They are faithful members of *Christian Life Church*, located at 2700 Bush River Rd., Columbia, South Carolina, 29210. If you're looking for a place of worship, the Salters extend a personal invitation.

If you are interested in partnering with the Salters in prayer and/or in becoming a financial supporter, please contact them. Jami and Sinclair are both available for speaking or training engagements. If you're interested in inviting them to your next event, you can reach them at:

Email: 4R4Christ@gmail.com
Address: 4Runners4Christ
P.O. Box 7492
Columbia, South Carolina 29202
Website: www.4Runners4Christ.com

"Since we are surrounded by so many examples [of faith], we must get rid of everything that slows us down, especially sin that distracts us. We must run the race that lies ahead of us and never give up (Hebrews 12:1, GOD'S WORD® Translation)."

BIBLIOGRAPHY

Alexys V. Wolf:
Looking for God, 3 volumes
Wielding the Sword of the Spirit

Joyce Meyer:
Battlefield of the Mind
Living Beyond Your Feelings
Beauty for Ashes

T.D. Jakes:
A Lady, Her Lover and Her Lord
Woman, Though Art Loosed!

Tim Sledge:
Making Peace with Your Past
Help for Adult Children of Dysfunctional Families

Melody Beattie:
Codependent No More
Beyond Codependency and Getting Better All the Time

Howard Marvin Halpern:
How to Break Your Addiction from a Person

Robin Norwood:
Women Who Love Too Much
When You Keep Wishing and Hoping He'll Change

Marvita Franklin:
He Makes All Things Beautiful

Heather Pounds Cook:
Behind the Bars: One Woman's Journey to True Freedom

Online Resources:

- http://www.findingfreedom.ca
- https://livingfree.org
- https://www.ihopkc.org
- https://mikebickle.org
- https://www.amazingfacts.org/bible-study/free-online-bible-school
- https://first5.org

Made in the USA
Columbia, SC
12 August 2024